I C E

STORIES OF SURVIVAL FROM
POLAR EXPLORATION

I C E

STORIES OF SURVIVAL FROM
POLAR EXPLORATION

EDITED BY CLINT WILLIS

MAINSTREAM
PUBLISHING

EDINBURGH AND LONDON

Adrenaline ™ and the Adrenaline™ logo are trademarks of
Balliett & Fitzgerald Inc. New York, NY

An Adrenaline Book™

First published in Great Britain in 2000 by
MAINSTREAM PUBLISHING COMPANY (EDINBURGH) LTD
7 Albany Street
Edinburgh EH1 3UG

ISBN 1 84018 315 2

First published in the United States by
Thunder's Mouth Press
841 Broadway, 4th Floor
New York, NY 10003

and

Balliett & Fitzgerald Inc.
66 West Broadway, Suite 602
New York, NY 10007

Series Editor: Clint Willis
Book design: Sue Canavan
Frontispiece photo: Courtesy of the Scott Polar Research Institute

Printed and bound in Great Britain by Butler and Tanner Ltd, Frome and London

For Abner Willis, whose heart is warm

c o n t e n t s

p h o t o g r a p h s

The literature of arctic exploration is frequently offered as a record of resolute will before the menacing fortifications of the landscape . . . It is better to contemplate the record of human longing to achieve something significant, to be free of some of the grim weight of life. That weight was ignorance, poverty of spirit, indolence, and the threat of anonymity and destruction. This harsh landscape became the focus of a desire to separate oneself from those things and to overcome them. In these arctic narratives, then, are the threads of dreams that serve us all.

Barry Lopez
Arctic Dreams

Introduction

Travelers in the polar regions find something there that no one else has found on earth: a strange, mysterious beauty that inspires many of them, makes them artists.

It is easy to say that something is beautiful; hard, though, to convince a skeptical world. Yet reading these travelers' work, I'm convinced: They found something beautiful, perfect in its way—at any rate, perfect for them. Some found death there; many found their versions of happiness.

But this is too vague. What did they find there, really? People are confused about this. The great Norwegian explorer Fridtjof Nansen (1861–1930) cited a Norseman of six centuries back, who in turn cited three motives for going to the Arctic, the only polar region then known: glory ("It is man's nature to go where there is the likelihood of great danger, and make himself famous thereby"), knowledge ("It is man's nature to wish to know and see those parts of which he has heard"), and profit ("Men seek after riches in every place where they learn that profit is to be had, even though there be great danger in it").

I'm not convinced that such motives explain the record of polar exploration. Here is a story about Nansen himself, who in 1888 led the first crossing of Greenland and in 1893 set out to reach the North Pole. His plan: Take into the Siberian ice a custom-built ship, the *Fram*, with 12 crew and supplies to last six years. Get stuck in the drifting ice, and then ride its drift to the Pole.

After 18 months and two winters in the ice pack, Nansen lost patience and left the *Fram*. He set out for the Pole with ship's stoker Frederick Hjalmar Johansen. Nansen left the remaining crew with the ship, believing that the ice eventually would carry them back to open water (it did).

The pair traveled north for three weeks by dogsled and kayak before giving up their attempt: A sea of jumbled ice made travel by either means impossible. With no hope of regaining their ship, the pair headed for civilization.

A third arctic winter overtook Nansen and his companion five months into their trek. Their dogs gone (eaten), their clothing and gear in tatters, the men used walrus bones to dig a ten-by-six-foot pit for a shelter. There they spent much of their time mending clothes (they resoled their boots with walrus skin), sleeping (Johansen snored) and sharing fantasies of food and clean linen.

Spring came, and the two men set off yet again. Their troubles were not over: Walrus herds attacked their kayaks; ice gave way beneath their feet and Nansen nearly drowned. Then something strange happened: Trudging alone across the seemingly endless ice, his weary companion lagging behind, Nansen encountered a man. The man was a young British lieutenant, out hunting, a member of another expedition. That expedition's leader, Frederick Jackson, witnessed the encounter through a telescope and came out from his camp to investigate.

It was in effect the end of Nansen's epic journey. After three years of appalling hardship and danger, he would see his home and his family (he'd left behind in Norway a young wife and a six-month-old daughter). He would enjoy the tangible fruits of his achievement: fame, money, reputation. He would share the knowledge he had acquired. He would once again enjoy home cooking, hot baths, domestic happiness.

It must have been an appealing prospect. Yet Nansen kept his distance—almost as though he'd prefer to keep walking alone across the barren ice.

John Maxtone-Graham writes of this "surreal" encounter in *Safe Return Doubtful*, his 1988 history of polar exploration:

> "I'm immensely glad to see you," ventured Jackson, as though in the anteroom of his club.
>
> "Thank you," replied Nansen, teeth glinting against his blackamoor face. The two men fell in step together.
>
> "Have you a ship here?" inquired the Britisher.
>
> "No, my ship is not here," countered Nansen. He noticed how pleasantly the Englishman smelled of perfume.
>
> "How many of you are there?" pursued Jackson.
>
> "I have only one companion, at the ice edge."
>
> Only then did the penny drop. "Aren't you Nansen?"
>
> "Yes, I am."
>
> "By Jove!" cried Jackson. "I am glad to see you."

Why wasn't Nansen glad to see him?

Governments and speculators who pay for polar trips usually do it for gain of some kind—political, financial, even scientific—and resourceful explorers exploit those desires. Early explorers such as John Davis, William Baffin and Henry Hudson sailed into the Arctic during the sixteenth and seventeenth centuries because their backers wanted a northwest passage to the riches of the East. Scott's backers financed his 1910 *Terra Nova* expedition to Antarctica in part because England's politicians wanted their countrymen to be first to reach the South Pole. Richard Byrd helped raise money for his 1928 solo winter sojourn in Antarctica by an appeal to science: He'd be taking plenty of weather observations.

And, in fact, explorers themselves often share such motives. Robert Peary hoped that getting to the North Pole first would make him rich and famous. Scott dearly wished to reach the South Pole ahead of Norwegian Roald Amundsen; having missed that goal by 21 days, he died regretting the heroes' welcome he and his men could have counted upon had they done so and survived to return home. (Here is Scott preparing to return from the Pole: "Well, we have turned our back now on the goal of our ambition and must face our 800 miles of solid dragging—and goodbye to most of the day-dreams!") Byrd cared about his weather observations; he routinely risked his life and sacrificed his comfort to make them.

But fame, money, even weather observations often seem little more than superb excuses for explorers to go where they hope to find something else entirely. They don't know what it is until they get there the first time; they may not know it's there until they arrive. But it is there, and it changes them.

What exactly is it?

Barry Lopez in *Arctic Dreams* hazards part of an answer: He observes that Peary and other explorers see their first trip north (or south) as a source of prestige, money or adulation. But that fades, writes Lopez,

> . . .tempered by a mounting sense of consternation and awe. It is as though the land slowly works its way into the man and by virtue of its character eclipses these motives. The land becomes large, alive like an animal; it humbles him in a way he cannot pronounce. It is not that the land is simply beautiful but that it is powerful. Its power derives from the tension between its obvious beauty and its capacity to take life. Its power flows into the mind from a realization of how darkness and light are bound together within it, and the feeling that this is the floor of creation.

Do they see God?

Whatever they find, explorers of the Arctic and the Antarctic are willing to suffer for it. Three men set out on a sledge journey. One falls into a crevasse with most of the party's supplies; the other two eat the dogs ("Had a good breakfast from Ginger's skull—ate brains, thyroid, and all"). Another starves to death; the last man, Douglas Mawson, continues to walk; the pads of his feet come off, leaving raw tissue to walk on. He binds the flesh back on, dons six pair of socks, and keeps walking.

During the winter before Scott's polar journey, three members of his

Terra Nova expedition set out from their base in the total blackness of Antarctic winter to obtain eggs of the emperor penguin. Weather and snow conditions are such that for weeks at a time the men, pulling three sledges (total weight: 757 pounds), travel only an average of one mile a day. It sometimes takes an hour to light a match. Their clothes are frozen solid, caked with ice; waking one day to a temperature of 55 degrees below zero (Fahrenheit), the three men are relieved to find it so blessedly warm. And remember, it is always dark.

Apsley Cherry-Garrard, at 26 the youngest of the three men, compares the party's pain during one particular day—the day they obtain the eggs—with that of an English officer in the Dardanelles, blinded and left for several days between the English and Turkish trenches. Both sides fired at the man as he groped to and from them. . . "Such extremity of suffering [writes Cherry-Garrard] cannot be measured: madness or death may give relief. But this I know: we on this journey were already beginning to think of death as a friend."

Here is an almost random selection from the journal of George W. DeLong, who in 1879 set out for the North Pole and with most of his men found starvation in Siberia. ". . . Lee begging to be left. Some little beach, and then long stretches of high bank. Ptarmigan tracks plentiful. At three halted, used up; crawled into a hole in the bank, collected wood and built fire. Alexy away in quest of game. Nothing for supper except a spoonful of glycerin. All hands weak and feeble, but cheerful. God help us."

Cheerful?

So, again, what do these people seek in those latitudes? Perhaps they seek the opportunity to behave well—to stay cheerful—in straits so dire. "I never heard an angry word," writes Cherry-Garrard of the emperor penguin outing, which lasted five weeks, and it is possible to believe him.

Both of Cherry-Garrard's companions, Henry "Birdie" Bowers and Bill Wilson, will die with Scott nine months later. Meanwhile, back at their Cape Evans hut with Scott and the others, the egg hunters sing, talk, smoke, take and pose for photographs, dodge killer whales, eat; they inhabit a temporary world whose bulwarks even at this distance are clear: friendship, competition, curiosity, self-respect—the things you learn in the company of people who are more engaged by the world than afraid of it.

Author and student of the Antarctic Charles Neider in 1973 tracks down Sir Charles Wright, age 86, the last survivor of Scott's final expedition. Neider quotes to Sir Charles a passage from Scott's journals:

> One of the greatest successes is Wright . . . Nothing ever seems to worry him, and I can't imagine that he ever complained of anything in his life.

Oh, says Sir Charles, Scott was wrong there: "I was complaining to myself."

Neider tries again: ". . . he had in mind your willingness and eagerness—"

Wright: "It was all very interesting, you see."

The thing is, most knowledge exists apart from science. During his solo winter in the Antarctic, Byrd—disoriented, suffering from depression and carbon monoxide poisoning—goes out in a blizzard to make one of his weather observations. The entrance to his underground cabin jams shut, trapping him outside: a death sentence.

Near panic, Byrd finds a shovel buried in the snow, and uses the tool to force an entry: "When I tumbled into the light and warmth of the room, I kept thinking, How wonderful, how perfectly wonderful."

Byrd came close to dying more than once that winter, and later wrote that those close calls were ". . . to the good. For that experience resolved proportions and relationships for me as nothing else could have done; and it is surprising, approaching the final enlightenment, how little one really has to know or feel sure about."

What did he know? If nothing else, he knew—had known for a moment at least—that the light and the warmth of his solitary room were, as he put it, perfectly wonderful. There's an antarctic discovery for you; there's knowledge.

And what of those polar explorers who did not escape death, however narrowly? Scott wrote a stack of letters near the end of his party's attempt to return from the Pole; by now, it was clear that he and his remaining companions were going to die in their tent; at least two of the five already were dead. This from his letter to his old friend Wilson's wife:

> . . . I should like you to know how splendid he was at the end—everlastingly cheerful and ready to sacrifice himself for others, never a word of blame to me for leading him into this mess . . . His eyes have the comfortable blue look of hope. . .

And here is from Scott's farewell letter to his own wife. He desires her to protect their young son:

> Above all, he must guard and you must guard him against indolence. Make him a strenuous man. I had to force myself into being strenuous, as you know—had always an inclination to be idle. . .
>
> What lots and lots I could tell you of this journey. How much better has it been than lounging in too great comfort at home. What tales you would have for the boy. But what a price to pay!

Was it worth it? We have the stories. But Scott and others paid for them. What was their recompense? No further answers are forthcoming.

—*Clint Willis*

from Mawson's Will
by Lennard Bickel

Douglas Mawson belongs to a triumvirate of polar heroes that also includes Robert Scott and Ernest Shackleton. During a 1912 expedition to the Antarctic, Mawson was traveling with two teammates when one man fell into a crevasse with most of the team's supplies. The remaining men's attempt to rejoin their expedition is one of the twentieth century's great survival epics. Lennard Bickel (born 1923) retold the story in his 1977 book.

The nights following Christmas were filled with the drudging toil of climbing out of the Ninnis Glacier. The struggle to reach the 3,000-feet high plateau of ice on the western side carved deeply into their reserves of strength, and on the third night they sorrowed at the loss of the last husky.

Ginger fell into a tangled heap with 15 miles still to go before they cleared the glacial fringe. Full of mingled pity and admiration, Mawson laid her on the sledge as she quivered with the last dregs of energy. He stroked her head and covered her with a bag, and as her glazed eyes watched him walk back to his sledging harness, Mawson remembered how this remarkable animal had run back to their previous camp through The Crater on the outward journey; she had now outstayed, outlasted by days, the biggest and strongest dogs of the team.

She rode the sledge as a passenger for three miles, and when they camped it was obvious she would never walk again. Now she had to serve a further purpose—as bone jelly, meat and liver. The rifle had been dumped to save weight; the spade was the only weapon, and Mertz could not face the task. Mawson was compelled to deal the death blow, breaking Ginger's neck. "A pitiful thing to finish off such a fine animal in such a way."

Mertz helped with the butchering, remembering as he did the long weeks at sea with Ninnis tending all these charges. Once the tent was up he felt exhausted, dizzy, and sick; silent, he went directly to his sleeping bag, there to record the day's events in a brief note—ending unknowingly with a paraphrase of the words of Captain Scott written that same year on the Ross Shelf:

"I am sorry, but I don't think I can write any more."

In the early morning the wind blew sheets of snow against the tent. Mawson ached for food, but first answered the constant nag on his mind—the weight of the sledge; the bones would be boiled down to marrow jelly, and then "the skeleton could be safely jettisoned." After simmering out the skimpy nutriment from Ginger's depleted marrow, one source of food was left which he could not ignore—Ginger's head.

It made a scene that burned into his memory. Two haggard, tattered men, crouched in the narrow tent, watching the skinned dog's head cooking.

When Ginger's head had boiled for 90 minutes, they lifted it with the two wooden spoons onto the lid of the cooker. Mawson ran a knife across the top of the skull for the demarcation line. They took turns in gnawing their different sides, biting away the jaw muscles, lips, swallowing the eyelids and gulping down the eyeballs. With the wooden spoons they scooped out the contents of the skull—and then split the tongue, the thyroid, the brain into two servings; only their fierce hunger made them grateful for this macabre feast, only the pangs of starvation made it possible for Mawson to write before sleeping: "Had a good breakfast from Ginger's skull—ate brains, thyroid, and all."

The devouring of Ginger left a new loneliness in both men. They missed her presence and were more aware of the weight of the sledge on their aching bodies. As well, her end came at the time when Mertz showed the first clear signs of decline. Mawson noted, almost suddenly, that his cheerful and noncomplaining sledging mate was morose, downcast, and depressed:

"Xavier is off color. We did a good 15 miles, halting at 9 a.m., but he turned in at once, all his things very wet on account of his lost water-proofs. This fine drift penetrates all our clothing and doesn't give us a chance to dry things. Our gear is deplorable!"

With so far to go to safety and so little food there was dark fore-boding in Mertz' dwindling health; yet Mawson would not allow his mind to preview disaster but fixed his attention on how to travel faster, go farther, lighten the sledge. In the center of this problem was the "wretched, makeshift tent." The crude structure was a tormenting waste of time. He wrote of his frustration: "Eight to 10 hours straight-out pulling is a great strain on two men which could be avoided if only we could pitch the tent halfway through and halt for a boil-up . . . but to halt in our poor condition in the open would be to freeze. There is no alternative to this slow, ceaseless, seemingly endless pulling—hour after hour."

Very soon Mawson would be grateful for such marches, for never again would they trudge such distances together. Dragged down by his dreadful illness, Mertz sought the fatal alternative to the endless slogging; to lie in his sleeping bag and wait for ideal weather. On the evening of the first day of the year, he was already committed to this policy of inaction. With his cold-bitten hands he wrote in his diary:

"January 1, New Year; 5 p.m. Only made five miles before having to camp and am now back in my sleeping bag. The light is terrible, the sky clouded. We could not get far in such weather. It is best to wait for sunshine. I cannot eat of the dogs any longer. Yesterday the flesh made me feel very sick."

They were the last words Mertz wrote. He remained in his bag for three days, sinking deeper into despair, gloom, and periodic irritation. Mawson tried to persuade him to make an attempt to walk. He placated and tolerated his mounting revulsion against dog flesh by making over their entire stock of powdered milk, only to find Mertz turn away from food entirely. He even rejected an offering of their "supreme luxury," a biscuit and a knob of their last piece of butter.

It was part of an inexplicable pattern of confusing moods that marked the wasted hours while the blizzard drift whirled above their tent. Trapped on the exposed ice hill, unable to move, Mawson's anxiety deepened. He tried to build his companion's fading strength, and out of kindness fed him a half-share of his own piece of Ginger's liver, arguing in his compassion that it would be easily chewed and digested. Mertz slipped rapidly into deeper lassitude, into disregard of his plight. Mawson's talk of meals they would eat, of omelettes at the hut, of fine London restaurants was useless, so he filled the hours of dark gloom with dressing Mertz' splitting lips and the raw patches on his legs and groins with lanolin from the medical kit, persuading him to swallow hot drinks of cocoa and tea and, between times, stitching and repairing their clothes and drying socks over the primus flame. Nothing halted the progress of the illness and the slide into weakness of body and spirit. Desperate, Mawson induced him to swallow some dog stew, but, suddenly aware of the taste, Mertz flew into a feverish rage and flung the tin pannikin across the tent into the snow. "It is of the dogs," he yelled. "They make me ill because I eat their flesh!"

On the third afternoon of the year, Mawson enthused to the sick man: "Look, Xavier. Your sun has come! You said you believe in omens, remember? Here is the sun, calling you to march to the hut."

He aided him out of his bag and dressed him in his sledging gear. Mertz sat on the sledge as Mawson collapsed the tent and packed for the trail. Hopefully, with better visibility, they could make some distance— but again they made only a faltering, winding trek, slipping and falling, and after four miles Mertz stopped, hands hanging at his sides, panting heavily, head drooped. His fingers were again badly bitten by frost. They had to camp. He sank into ominous silence huddled in the wet bag. Mawson, perturbed, heated some cocoa and ate a piece of Ginger's liver. In his diary he entered:

"Xavier is in a very bad state: everything now depends on Providence."

In the following two days Mawson felt his own strength slipping away fast; he was nauseated, had pain in his side, and all movement made him dizzy. Acutely anxious at the passing time and their wasting food, he pressed Mertz constantly to resume marching. Mertz would not accept the argument that to rest in the sleeping bag and wait for good weather was to wait for death on the ice. Mawson wrote in his diary: "He practically refused my request that he should make an attempt to walk—even for a mile or two. He told me it would be suicide and that he would die if he tried to march in bad weather . . ." They had a short argument over the question of moving for the sake of keeping their blood flowing; then Mertz sank into gloom. He refused again to march when on January 5 the sun broke through, but Mawson won his promise that he would walk next day if the conditions were good.

January 6 brought cloud, a 25-mile wind and drift, but passable marching weather. At 7 a.m. Mawson climbed from the tent to start preparations for the trail. It was a three-hour struggle; he had to dress Mertz, feed him cocoa and biscuit, and help him don the sledging harness. The depredation of cold, hunger, exposure carved their faces, Mawson knew, but, once out of the softening green light of the tent in the stark cruel light of the plateau, Mertz' appearance was shocking. His beard was ragged tufts with patches of raw skin beneath, his mustache was a travesty, and his eyes deep-sunk pockets of gray beneath the protective goggles.

The march was a shambling, fearful trial of flesh and spirit. Weak and trembling, they felt their way through poor light in a slow meandering of which Mawson wrote: "The surface was slippery, and we both had frequent falls bruising our emaciated bodies. Quite dizzy from the long stay in our bags, I felt weak from the lack of food. But—to my surprise Xavier soon caved in. He went only two miles with many long halts; and then he refused to go any farther . . ."

Mawson was aghast at the implication; he threw an arm round the bent shoulders to help his comrade forward but Mertz slumped into the snow: "My mind goes forward, but my legs stay here," he moaned. Mawson hauled him to his feet. "We must go on! Our lives are at stake. We must walk while we can."

Mertz was beyond the reach of logic—beyond words or thoughts of a frozen death. He stood dumbly, unmoving. Mawson sought anxiously to avoid facing the awful fact that his companion was near the end. A week had gone by with few miles marched; a daily average of the ground they had covered in that time wouldn't save them. What could he do—his own body weakened by starvation and privation? Certainly he could not just camp and capitulate. No! He would not just lie down in the snow and wait out more days of agony as life slipped away.

"Get on the sledge. Xavier. The way is downhill, and we can go a little farther, and perhaps you'll feel like walking again." Mertz resisted. There was some affront for him riding the sledge; but Mawson insisted, pushing him onto the load, making him lie down, covering him with the sleeping bags.

The canvas harness cut into his shoulders. He leaned forward to haul the sledge, and the leather belt dug into the painful area of his right side; so he canted to the left. He could feel the draining drag of the runners through the snow and the sudden shudder as they struck the sastrugi and rode over the ice backs. He staggered as his feet slid on the wind-polished surfaces, and he heard Mertz moan with pain on the jolting sledge. The fearful thought crept into his mind—a sudden slip, a broken leg or ankle, and they would face the end. Better to go down on all fours on hands and knees. I can pull with the best of dogs, he told himself. I will do as well as Ginger—I can go on, and on!

The pounding of the steely ice jarred his knees, and he felt the skin split; snow crammed his gloves and crept into his clothing. He kept on crawling, lugging the weight across the snow, his whole concentration focused on making distance.

He covered two and a half miles this way. Then Mertz was calling out, in pain. He was very cold, with white spots of frost on his paper-brown cheeks. His condition was piteous; he uttered no word of complaint, but when Mawson helped him from the sledge he seemed unwilling to move his legs.

Mawson managed to erect the tent and get him inside within an hour; then he heated a thick cocoa and dog stew which he pressed on Mertz with the name of "Beef tea." The name deceived Mertz' mind, and he drank the hot liquid; yet his stomach soon rebelled, and he vomited into the snow. Anguish was a ball of lead inside Mawson. In his journal Mawson expressed his anxiety:

"Things are in a most serious state for both of us. If he cannot go on and make eight or 10 miles a day in the next day or two, then we are both doomed.

"I could perhaps pull through—with the provisions at hand—but I cannot leave him. His heart seems to have gone. It is very hard on me; to be within 100 miles of the hut and in such a position is awful."

Mertz seemed to fight out of his dark depression; he said he was sorry they had to stop. "How far did we go?" And then, brightening, he said he would ride the sledge again in the morning, and perhaps they could put up a sail with the tent. There was no more. He lapsed again into silence. Mawson turned in at 8 p.m. to face a "long and wearisome night." His last words for that day were: "If only I could get on! But I must stop with Xavier. He does not appear to be improving. Both our chances are going now."

Mawson woke from troubled dreaming of food to find the prospect of travel a shattered hope. Mertz was in a dire state. His trousers were fouled from an attack of dysentery, his eyes were wild and rolling, and he talked and babbled incoherently; he sounded demented. Mawson set to work cleaning Mertz' soiled clothing and was shocked to see his legs, his groin, stripped clean of skin, red, raw, rippled with painful folds. It was a long and tedious task before Mertz was restored to his sleeping bag. Mawson felt the cold badly and crawled back into his bag for an hour to try to recapture some warmth. At 10 a.m. that morning of January 7 he again rose when Mertz started shouting. His companion sat up, obsessed with a thought that Mawson wanted him to get out and ride on the sledge. His eyes were glaring.

Mawson was moved with deep pity. The affable, philosophical companion and friend had vanished, given way to this poor incontinent wretch, a shattered man who feared to move. Yet even in his deep compassion, Mawson could not imagine the terror Mertz might feel in riding the sledge as a passenger, that it could be an awful omen— a ride to slaughter as it had been for each of the beloved dogs. Mertz raged: "Am I a man—or a dog? You think I have no courage because I cannot walk—but I show you, I show . . ." He lifted his left hand; the little finger—yellowed from frostbite—was thrust into his mouth and Mawson watched in stupefied horror as Mertz crunched his teeth into the middle joint, savagely severing the skin, cartilage and sinew, tearing away with grimaces and groans of pain . . . then, in disdain, spitting the severed digit into the floor of the tent, the trace of thin coagulated blood turning the snow pink.

It opened a day of madness, of raving, and constant fits. Mawson dressed the stump of the finger and wrapped it in the bandages Mertz had used for his snowblindness. He now knew that Mertz would never walk again. Outside the tent the sun was showing through broken clouds; the conditions were good for marching:

"Obviously we can't go . . . this is terrible! I don't mind for myself, but it is for Paquita—for all others that are connected with the expedition—that I feel so deeply, and so sinfully.

"I pray to God to help us."

The babbling fits, the incoherent German and English, were followed by a quiet spell when Mawson again fed him cocoa. In the evening the raging became violence. Flinging his arms about, thrashing across the small space, Mertz broke one of their precious tent props and would have caused further damage but for Mawson sitting on his chest, holding his arms, struggling to quiet his dementia. Dysentery attacked him again; and he fell into unconsciousness. Mawson again cleaned him and his clothing. Once more, Mertz broke into raving; holding the side of his head he lay back in his bag, calling over, and over: *"Ohren, ohren! Ohrenweh!"* ("Ears, ears! Earache!")

The terrible day was done. At midnight Xavier Mertz lay in a coma; Mawson softly toggled the skin of the sleeping bag under his chin and wrapped the soft fur round his raw, skinned face. Drained physically and emotionally, he crawled into his own damp bag seeking relief in sleep.

His rest was troubled by disquiet and at 2 a.m. he woke. In dazed perplexity he searched for a reason for waking; there was no movement, no sound other than the ceaseless rattling tent. He reached out to touch his companion—and Xavier Mertz was stiff, cold, quite lifeless under his hand.

The awful truth was a blanket of cold fear, invisible, but falling over his entire world, filling the tent, flooding his mind with the terrible, haunting fact. He was alone. All that was human in this accursed place, all that had been alive—friends and dogs—were dead and gone. Lone-liness was in the vast wasted land outside in the soughing wind, in the corners of his mind, in his anguish and in the fear for his own safety.

He was himself, sick, famished and so weak he might collapse at any moment; and he lay stretched out on this floor of snow with the heart-rending truth pinning down his body and his mind. Mertz was dead.

What would he do? What chance had he of living? Very little, he decided. This spot was some 100 miles direct to the hut; ahead ranged the heaving wind-swept plateau ice, the great, broadly-fractured bed of the glacier, many miles of wicked winding crevasses, and then the long grinding, backbreaking climbs up the steep slopes and ice ramparts to the escarpment near The Crater—to be in sight of Aurora Peak, to leave some record there where they might come seeking his missing party. Yet he was so emaciated that the bitten, snow-clad peak seemed a million miles away.

Mertz was dead by his side; why then was he alive? In that question were hours of heart-searching, restless harking back over the weeks gone past. They had eaten, slogged the trail together, suffered the same cold and lack of food; and there were deep, hidden roots for the sense of sin that swept his being: fine, noble young men, and he had led them to their deaths. He could phrase a justification in his mind: "The accident to Ninnis, and its consequences are like fortunes of war—things always liable to happen, a risk that is part of the game and inseparable from pioneering in an ice-covered land." But why had Mertz died? Death was due to cold, constant weather exposure, and the effects of starvation culminating in fever and convulsions—that *had* to be the diagnosis. He could find no other. And there was relief in the thought that Xavier was now beyond the reach of pain and suffering. He could compose a eulogy for a comrade he had come to love like a brother. "Surely he had broken free from the fetters of this icy Antarctic plateau and has gone where a high mind and sterling quality meet true reward . . . Myself, I seem to stand on the wide lonely shores of the world with only a short step into my own unknown future . . ."

The outlook was gloomy. The gnawing pain in the stomach seemed to have developed into a permanent companion so that he could no longer stand erect—how could he pitch the tent single-handed in the strong winds?

In the early morning he heated some cocoa, and, covering Mertz' ravaged face with the sleeping-bag cowl, he wrote an entry in his diary:

"For many days—since January 1—Xavier's condition has prevented us going on; now I am afraid it has cooked my chances altogether—even of making a single journey north to the coast. Lying in the damp bag for a week on extremely low rations has reduced my condition seriously. However, I shall make an attempt. I shall do my utmost—to the last—for the sake of Paquita and all the members and supporters of the expedition to at least get some word through on how matters stand with me."

To get far enough toward Aurora Peak for his body and their diaries to be found, that was the aim. Over the slopes, crossing the glacier, up the terraces and ramparts on to the escarpment and past The Crater.

"Today I shall spend remodeling my gear for one-man travel. I shall cut down the sledge to carry half the load, and I shall doctor my own worn body and broken skin as best I can." It was time for action, a way to face the empty, lonely wasteland and to meet its trials.

He sat cross-legged in the tent for hours that morning. Mertz' waterproof coat was cut and trimmed and stitched into an old food bag to form a sail. Outside, defying the flying drift and wind, with his little saw he cut the sledge down to half its length and used parts of the discarded frame to mount a small mast and spar to carry his water-proof—thus windproof—sail.

More hours of crouching over the primus stove cooking the last meat from the dogs, scorching the remaining half of Ginger's liver. Reduce the need to cook down to the minimum, he argued, and you cut down the weight of fuel you need to carry on the sledge. In fact, he found he could leave two one-gallon cans behind.

In the afternoon lull the plateau wind fell away to a chill breeze, and he then faced his final duty to Dr. Xavier Mertz. On pages torn from his notebook he wrote his statement attesting Mertz' uncomplaining brav-ery, how the death of Ninnis had led to this second fatality, and how he himself was continuing westward. The note was placed in the sleeping bag, along with ten dozen exposed photographic plates, now accounted too heavy to carry in the final, bitter struggle toward Aurora Peak. He dragged the body from the tent.

The wind was rising again as he labored to cut the snow blocks for Xavier's burial cairn. The sky grew dark and threatening; he left the corpse in the stained sleeping bag—a shroud of reindeer skin—and soon drift and falling snowflakes covered it with purest white.

Building the cairn to shoulder level made his heart pound like a triphammer; he rested often. When it was done he took out his prayer book and for the second time on the journey stood bareheaded in the snow and read the burial service. They had stood together some four weeks before, and he had then named the Ninnis Glacier. The daunting glacier he had yet to cross would now carry the name on the world's maps—if his body and their diaries were ever found—of the Mertz Glacier.

He was dropping with fatigue, needing food and hot drink, but then it came to his mind that a fast-moving party of fit men might cross that gulf of country between him and the hut; there was need to mark the death cairn. The two halved runners, cut from the sledge, lay by the tent. He thrust them into the top of the cairn to form a simple cross in the snow.

The tent leaned drunkenly. Tiny in the white, horizonless immensity, stained and drab green, it sagged over the support broken in Xavier Mertz' final raving. Standing at the side of the burial cairn, bowed with sorrow, Mawson looked at his frail shelter and in its crookedness saw a symbol of Mertz' suffering and of his own vulnerability.

He crawled into the tent, utterly weary, aching from the toil of the burial, and his stomach creased with the pain he put down to hunger. He felt a deep desire for hot, richly fatty food and for a long warm sleep that would refresh his body and wash away fears of the perils ahead and the hopelessness of his plight. The wind was now rising, and the snowfall was thicker. The tent cover was flapping, and the broken ends of the strut were shaking. He forced himself to repair the fractured prop. If the ends pierced his cover, if the wind could rip through a tear, his shelter would soon be gone, and without it he would be finished. He fitted the little hammerhead to the Bonzer knife, foraged for nails and lampwick lashing in the repair bag, and set about splicing and binding the broken support.

His fingers fumbled, his hands trembled working above his head as he squatted in the snow. It was troublesome work, but it was a nostrum to his anxiety. When he had finished, he slumped where he sat. His whole body yearned to be in the reindeer bag, not to be moving, and he knew he could not yield. There were other tasks to claim his mind: light the primus and heat a pan of pemmican hoosh with dog-bone jelly, sew up the tears in his clothing, count up his food supplies—and write the diary entry; the last helped him to compose his mind:

"I read the burial service over poor Xavier . . ." and at once he was projected into his own predicament and the looming peril: "As there is now little chance of my reaching human aid alive, I greatly regret inability to set down the coastline as surveyed for the 300 miles we traveled; and the notes on glaciers and ice formations, most of which is, of course, committed to my head."

Time, his own collapsing condition, the reduced food reserve all urged him to make an early start on his long journey west. Should he march in brief spells, or just go on until he fell in his tracks? When and how soon should he pack and go?

The continent answered that question. A bustling river of deeply cold air burst down from the great icy canopy; booming gusts of wind above 50-mile strength soon surged over him and hurled a torrent of snow drift and flying crystals at his tent. The tent frame quivered and shook so menacingly that he squatted in the snow with his hands above his head to hold the struts into their ice holes.

Endlessly, it seemed, the gale stabbed and roared around his shelter, and he feared its raking blast might reach under the skirting and lift his cover from the snow grip and fling it to some unreachable distance. His hands were shot through with pain, his arms ached with leaden throbbing; not until late evening did it come to him to lash the struts with lampwick and hold them down with the weight of his body. It was some relief; but now his inert frame was filled with lassitude, and deep malaise flooded his mind with the crushing burdens of his problems. How could he hope, with this weakened body, to break camp, to march and erect the wretched tent in such wind? He was under pressure to yield, to surrender, to eat, rest easy, until the final sleep closed over his eyes with peace. Somewhere deep in the well of his being the primitive, powerful urge to survive, to exist at all costs, exerted pressure on his subconscious and raked his tiring memory for words of comfort, for motivation; and there came lines written by another man in a different world—to gird his resolve, to aid his fight—words from Robert Service:

> Buck up! Do your damndest and fight:
> It's the plugging away that will win you the day.

It rose in his consciousness like a call. It lifted him from despondency and was a challenge to his character—to attain some further westward point, to get beyond Aurora Peak where his body and their records might be found to tell the tale of his comrades and himself, for Paquita, for the search parties he was sure would be sent out to find him while the ship waited to sail west to relieve Frank Wild and his group. His love, his men, his ship and expedition: he owed them all a duty.

He had pontificated enough about character when he'd been promoting support for this expedition: the meetings of scientific groups, the public appeals, the huge audience in the brightly lit Melbourne Town Hall, resplendent for the occasion, the Governor-General, Lord Denman, glinting with decorations. Prime Minister Andrew Fisher, the Federal Opposition Leader. Alfred Deakin—pomp and power of the land under the one roof, and he could hear again his own voice:

"I have done my best to choose men of character. The important thing to look for in members of an expedition like this—is character. It is impossible to tell how men are going to act until circumstances arise . . . In that land of desolation, in that land of great loneliness, there are the conditions that measure a man at his true worth."

Character—when your own death looms over the tent, when all is against you, when all that seems sensible is to lie down and wait to die. It's the plugging away that will win the day; but outside the world was a chaos of drift flying in the wind, denying passage to the fittest, strongest, and the most resolute of men. The tent rocked and shuddered under the assault. "I am in the hands of Providence!" he consoled himself.

All the while the fear of losing his cover occupied his mind, and when the wind fell away later in the evening he crawled outside to cut more snow blocks to heap on the skirting. The snow was frozen, hard to pierce, and as he strained to lift one block a sudden squall took him off balance—and the spade handle broke in his hands.

Nearly four weeks had gone since the time Mertz had sat with these same tools over this same job—after the long march back from Black Crevasse. Now he repeated the tedious tacking and splicing and lashing of the handle, the same assessment of his pitiful stock of food. Mawson could not weigh what he had now; he could only assess that he might make this scanty provision last for a given time; and so he asked how long he could last? How far could he go on this diet of about 8 ounces a day? Say 25 miles to cross the glacier, 20 miles to Aurora Peak, and then the great curving ice dome beyond—and the allowance gave him 20 days of subsistence for the fight across the ice. Two biscuits a day; two little chocolate sticks and a few raisins as refreshment and thirst quenchers on the trail; thin pemmican, cocoa, dog meat—for the first 10 days; and the dog fragments, a small piece of liver, the sinews, and a set of paws.

What if the primus stove should break down? He would be dependent on provisions that did not need cooking; so he divided his food in two sections: that which had to be cooked—pemmican, cocoa, dog meat—for the first 10 days; and the biscuits, the bone jelly, half the chocolate, and the little bag of raisins and almonds for the second half.

Now his life was sectioned into 20 days—up to the end of the month. There was no future after that. And if he could march an average of five miles a day—taking all weather into account—he could come near to where he might find help. But where exactly was he now?

The sun glimmered through cloud in the evening sky. He set the theodolite on the cooker box. It was hard to get the instrument level, yet he felt the result to be near enough to put him roughly 100 air miles from the hut; but he had no wings, and he would walk many additional miles, wandering through the glacier and over the difficult land beyond. Still, it was a target; it answered his iron resolve to get as far as he could on what he had. It was grist for his deeper wish to survive.

He returned to his repair of the spade handle, and when the sky cleared and the sun lit his tent it roused a desperate urge to pack and walk—if only for a mile or two while the weather break lasted.

Somehow, he could not move. The spade had to be mended, and he argued that his raw scrotum, his stripped legs would be better for another night's healing rest; and, as well, he feared a return of the wind. Buck up! Do your damndest and fight! Yes, but with this poor body, how could he manage the toil of camping in a 50-mile wind, of securing the sledge, carting the gear inside, lighting the stove—with these bitten fingers?

They poked through the ends of his tattered woolen mitts— blackened at the tips from frost bruising, cracked round all the nails and festering on some. And what of the rest of this once powerful body? He untied his lampwick braces and belt and lowered his thick underpants—and a shower of skin fragments and hair fell into the snow at his feet. Strips of skin had completely vanished from his legs; his kneecaps were without cover, just roughly rippled flesh, his private parts were red and raw, scarified from the friction of work and walking. Around his waist, on his shoulders, the harness had laid a skinned pattern; and here and there he found eruptions breaking out like small boils with festering heads.

"My whole body is rotting from the want of proper nourishment," he lamented. "There is nothing to repair or replace my worn tissues."

The weather promised fair for the morning; so he turned in early. In the period before sleep his mind ranged across the facts of his predicament, and suddenly he no longer felt he was alone but that a presence was with him. A few yards away Xavier Mertz rested beneath the burial cairn, but Mawson felt his spirit still in the tent, by his side.

He woke to the gift of a peaceful morning; sunny, almost calm, with only wisps of cirrus cloud flying to the northern sky. Ice and snow fields stretched around in all directions into white-hazed horizons. In the still air it was very cold. He did not want to risk being chilled before breaking camp, so he went back into his bag again for an hour until the sunlight gained more strength. Every fiber in his being longed for him to be moving again. He counseled himself: "I must go slowly, steadily. I will not make a long day of today, but even so if the surface is good perhaps I might win ten miles." In three days he had walked no farther than the cairn; in the week before that, in the trauma of Mertz' sickness and dying, they had done no more than a dozen miles—in a dozen days! The need to march weighed on him, but his caution warned that his body would need time to be moving freely again, to unloosen his joints, to regain the rhythm of marching—and of pulling the sledge alone.

He rose at 8:30 a.m., and it took him more than two hours to heat a thin hoosh, collapse his tent, and lash and pack his possessions aboard the foreshortened sledge. The old food bag with Mertz' converted windproof stitched into it, was tied to the mast and the spar; the cooker box was loaded, and he was ready to go.

First he stood for a while by the cairn to pay last respects to the remains of a brave gentleman and a fine companion and murmured a short prayer for the dead man's soul—then added a plea for his own safety.

He turned away, donned the sledge harness, and bending to his left to ease the pain in his side, he pulled his load slowly onto a downhill slope. The slight breeze was from behind, and he felt its movement ease the pressure on his body. After trudging about one hundred steps he stopped and looked back, a deep sadness on him at leaving the forsaken, desolate spot where Mertz was buried. The death cairn was now rounded by the night winds, the cracks between blocks were filled with blown snow, and the whole had the shape of an elongated igloo. The cross of the two halved sledge runners stood stark against the frozen wilderness.

His trail led away to the northwest; soon the cairn was lost to his view. Very deliberately Mawson restricted his gait, shambling more than walking, leaning into the harness rather than pulling. Overhead the sky draped a peacock blue that fell into a misty meeting with the distant ice. The sun was clearly visible, and its warmth on his face stirred an idea in his mind. After covering about a mile he halted and filled his cooker tin with snow, then strapped it onto the sledge where the sunlight would fall on its outside and melt the contents to drinking water—to ease his thirst as he marched. At the same halt he rested the theodolite on the cooker box and took a reading to find his course heading was 44 degrees west of north. He had two sticks of chocolate in his pouch, and he ate one of these as he resumed his pulling, moving into his northwest trail.

Every step was painful; the raw areas between his groins, the skin-stripped scrotum, induced him to walk with his legs apart. It shortened his step but he found that on the snow-covered ice it made his tread more secure, and in this way he walked another downhill mile. The hard backs of sastrugi started to show from beneath the snowy cover; he slipped and staggered and in the jarring of his legs he felt a new disturbing pain in his feet spreading discomfort through his ankles into his legs. Persisting with the target of 10 miles that day, he went down on all fours and crawled across the ice waves. The new pressure and the pounding on his knees wiped away the new pain for a while and masked his mind against the awkward, lumpy, squelching feeling in his feet, as though he was treading in treacle; there was also a deep-rooted ache in his ankles. Soon a new sense of apprehension filled his mind; the sun was bright and there was little wind as he stopped again to find the cause of this fresh affliction. He sat on the edge of the sledge and took off his finnesko and the two pairs of socks.

The sight of his feet was a hammerblow to the heart. The lumpy, awkward feeling came from underneath—where both his soles had separated into casts of dead skin. The thick pads of the feet had come away leaving abraded, raw tissue. His soles and heels were stripped; an abundant, watery fluid filled his socks, and it was that which had caused the squelching feeling. A wave of despair rode over him. He sat aghast, staring at the ruined feet he had trusted to carry him to Aurora Peak. He was to write later: "All that could be done was to heavily smear the red inflamed exposed flesh with lanolin—and luckily I had a good supply—and then replace the separated soles and bind them into position with bandages. They were the softest things I had available to put next to the raw tissue." He took all the socks in his bag—six pairs in all—and pulled them over the bandages, then forced his soft finnesko over the top.

The shock told heavily on him. He could not at once start marching again. He felt the sun's light falling on his face and found it refreshing; suddenly he was seized with the idea that solar energy would benefit his body. He spread his sail in the snow and took down his trousers, pulled up his vest and, defying the cold air, lay down to expose his body to the light streaming from the sky. Later that night he noted: "I bathed in the glorious kiss of the sun and an almost instant feeling of well-being went tingling through my body. It was exhilarating, a sensation that flooded my senses." The sunlight's energy seemed to glow under his skin to stimulate restorative processes that eased the deep anxiety roused by the state of his feet made him feel stronger and more confident.

He lay in the sun's light as long as he could bear the cold; then he covered his body and renewed walking, avoiding hard ice where he could and treading in soft snow. Each step was a controlled movement to avoid too much pressure on his feet. Sometimes he walked on the outside edge of the finnesko, sometimes reaching on to his toes; in between he dropped to his hands and knees to rest his feet. Through the afternoon he continued, pausing to sip a drink from the melting snow in his cooker, nibbling his second stick of chocolate, edging his way northwest.

The pain wore deeply into his nerves. In the early evening, though the air was clear and the sun still shone, he gave in and camped. By the reading of the sledge meter he had gone six and a quarter miles that day of January 11. His strength was exhausted; he scribbled in his diary: "I am nerve-worn from the pain in my feet. Had I gone any farther I should not have found strength to erect the tent."

It took him all of 90 minutes to set up his shelter and stow his gear ready for cooking his pemmican and the last set of dog paws—he no longer knew from which animal they came. "With long stewing," he noted, "they came down to digestible softness." The hours of this evening were given over mainly to attention to his body. Unwrapping his sore feet, he found them in a "much more deplorable condition." The trouble had spread round his ankles. "The whole skin has burst into blisters—almost the whole of both feet." As well, he noticed his toes were blackened from frostbite, and like his fingers were also festering. He spent hours with the dressings on his body and bandaging his loose skin soles back into place.

As he ate his meal, he became aware that he could no longer taste food and had lost his sense of smell. "The membranes of my nasal canals have gone wrong, and my saliva glands are refusing duty—for want of proper nourishment." But, despite the lack of taste and smell, his hunger was razor-edged, and he looked at his food stock and wished intently that it was twice the size. "Then I could set to and have a fine meal, whether I would taste it or not." The longing now was to feel the bulk and the warmth in his stomach, and his only satisfaction came in the vivid dreams of food which pursued him in sleep.

The sun shone brightly through the tent fabric. He crawled outside to enjoy the light. "I am sure the sunshine will have set much right in me; I felt the good of the sun as I have never done before. Sunshine is the elixir of life for those who have been without it for weeks, never taking off their clothing in the snows and winds of the Antarctic plateau. I am determined I will be a sun-worshipper—for as long as I can live!" The thought helped him back to the reality of his plight.

He stood by his tent in the dazzling white scene, the land dipping downhill away from him—into a valley of ice. All at once he saw he was on the edge of the frozen chaos of the main stream of the great glacier he had named for Mertz, with its daunting upheavals and depressions; and there, some 30 miles farther on—rising in the cold hazy air—he saw the dark rocky summit of Aurora Peak. And beyond that, he knew, the great ice plateau rose and rolled away into distance—to Aladdin's Cave and the hut. He lifted his face toward the sun, and a silent prayer formed in him:

"Oh! If Providence will give me 20 days of weather like this and will heal my feet—surely I can reach succour."

For more than 30 hours a snow-laden, angry wind had lashed his camp; now, suddenly, sharply, it had passed. It was ominous silence, the quiet of the grave, and Douglas Mawson sat bolt upright in his tent, his ears straining, his mind hungry for sound. No wind, no movement, not even the rustle of whispering snowflakes broke the frozen calm.

He put his head through the tent entrance and saw cold, featureless desolation; and in this setting, in this instant, his solitude became utterly consuming. The feeling of the presence of Xavier Mertz had gone; loneliness was a chilling fact, almost a pain in itself. He thought: "Oh God! I could be all alone in this whole world, a poor creature, a solitary man of pre-Cambrian times . . . or a lost soul on the surface of Mars!"

His sense of isolation increased and weighed more heavily on his spirit when he found he did not know the real time. He had again forgotten to wind his watch.

He guessed the time to be around 7 a.m., but until he could sight the sun that was uncertain. His world outside the tent was filled with diffuse and treacherous light; the land was exactly the same color as the sky, and conditions were too dangerous for him to march. Impatient as he was to be mobile, he had to bide his time and to use work for his hands as a panacea against worry, against the anxiety of the burdensome hours of waiting and knowing the passing of time reduced his food supply—and his chances. So he rebandaged his sore feet, dressed the inflamed areas of his body with soothing lanolin, applied iodine to the eruptions and to his festering fingers; he cooked a half ration of pemmican and then, hoping to build strength for the journeying ahead, added some of his dwindling stock of dog jelly with half a biscuit; then he boiled up an old tea bag. He relashed the tent prop and tightened the binding on the spade handle; he dressed himself for the trail, packing a layer of dried grass into his finnesko to ease the pressure on his feet—all done steadily to while away the hours as he waited for the sun, hoping the enforced rest would help to heal his tattered body.

On this fuzzy, bleak Monday January 13, the sun broke through a little after midday, and he balanced his theodolite on the cooker box, took his readings, and found his watch to be 2 hours 40 minutes fast. By the time this was done it was 1 p.m. Overhead the clouds were fragmenting, and the growing strength of the sun was dispersing the haze, promising a clear, calm afternoon. Hurriedly he broke camp. Soon after 2 p.m. he tied the 20-feet alpine rope, knotted every three feet, to the back of his harness, adjusted his goggles over his snow helmet, and, leaning forward to take the drag of the runners on his shoulders and midriff, he moved down into the tortured valley of the glacier, facing many days of glaring light, snow falls, and showers of frozen crystals—and underfoot, the hidden perils of snow-topped crevasses and sudden, sheer precipices in the hard, blue ice.

Almost at once the downhill run of the glacial ice broke into sharp-edged corrugations, ridges that butted through the protection of his fur boots. He tried all his tricks of walking, shuffling flat-footed, on the sides of his soles, bending out the ankles—and the iron-hard ice still took its toll. He could feel the abraded skin bursting and the fluid filling his socks. The pain and the fear of severe damage forced him to seek patches of virgin snow—and he knew he invited danger. "I am just blundering forward," he told himself. Yet, he had no other course but direct across the Mertz glacial valley. Fit and well-provisioned, he would have detoured far to the southern highlands to escape the trials in front of him.

In mid-afternoon, the sky cleared as though some magical hand swept the cloud away to the north. Risking the blight of snow blindness he lifted his goggles from his straining eyes—and an awesome landscape rolled before him. At once his heart was uplifted. In the far distance beyond the western banks of the Mertz Glacier, the black-topped rocky mass of Aurora Peak was sharp against a sky of pale blue; it called him on and stirred him to fresh effort. It was a signpost to winter quarters, he had told his now-dead companions. Now it was symbolic to his struggling body, a citadel to be achieved.

But was there an easier road than his hazardous direct course? In the south the highlands rose in massive banks, and he could see the sun glinting gold on the frozen falls that fed the glacier. Too far, too exhausting for his frail body! Could he go down the glacier, follow the rolling banks of ice downhill, until he reached the sea? There he might find food, seal meat, or penguin, or eggs, and regain some strength. But would there be any likelihood the search parties would come seeking him along the coast? He could see no real option to his chosen path through this deadly, crevassed region.

He battled on ahead. Now and again he stopped to sip water from the snow melting in his cooker; he nibbled on a chocolate stick. Down and still downward the course ran. With each shambling step forward he felt the immensity of the river of ice cracking and grinding its way to the sea, of the titanic power needed to push the huge floating tongue, some 2,000 feet thick, across the bedrock until 60 miles or so offshore it floated. He was puny against this vast setting, but will power pushed him onward.

In the low light of evening, shadows sharpened the contours and etched out the ridges of the snow lids above a network of crevasses. He paused and stared unbelieving at his watch. It was 8 p.m.; he had walked for six hours covering a distance of five and a half miles. In the deceptive light Aurora Peak seemed no nearer to his eye than when he first saw it loom through the distance. Rather than face the crisscross peril of the crevasse network in this light, he decided to camp where he stood, among the snow-filled mouths of the icy pits.

There was very little wind so that, with frequent rests, he had his tent pitched and was inside cooking his supper by 10 p.m.—pemmican and his last piece of dog liver, with biscuit and cocoa. He gulped the food, and only when the last trace was licked from his pannikin did he tend to his wounds. When he pulled off his boots and socks he was again downcast. All the rest he had given his feet was undone, all the treatment had been nullified. The mess in his socks, the blood-soaked bandages appalled him; the raw areas had abraded and bled, and copious fluid flowed from his insteps. He cleaned his feet and rebound them for the night. In his diary he wrote of his concern:

"My feet are worse than ever—very painful. Things look bad—but, I shall persevere."

Every bone and sinew in his being ached for the peace of sleep in the reindeer bag; but, again, the glacier denied him.

Soon after 11 p.m.—as though resenting the weight of his wasting body on its mighty back—the river of ice opened a resounding cannon-ade. Booming, echoing volleys of sharp explosions went reverberating down the length of the glacier bed, and Mawson could feel the solid ice under his snowy floor rebound and quake with the fierce eruptions. Disturbed by the outburst, overpowering to him in his loneliness, he looked out from his shelter to peer into the night scene. In the south the sun rimmed the highlands toward which the Mertz Glacier serpented, and from there the outburst seemed to roll down toward the sea, passing under him. He believed there was large scale cracking and a rending of the body of the glacier. He reasoned that enormous pressure from the vast plateau and the result of the sun's warmth on the back of the frozen river was the cause. He wrote his observations: "In the chill cold of the night it seemed that great volumes of compressed air were released with every explosion . . . due to the splitting of the ice."

Into the night the frozen bombardment rocked the ice under his sleeping bag; and that night he did not hunger for sound. In the small hours of the morning the wind took over, with 45-mile gusts bringing flying drift in whirling clouds that killed his hope for an early start into the depths of the glacier's valley.

The wind held him down until early next afternoon. He spent the time in fixing his position by dead reckoning and calculated he was some 82 air miles from Aladdin's Cave, south of the headland they had discovered on their way out and southeast of the vast depression he had named The Crater. He cut his rations that morning because he could not march. He had half a helping of pemmican and a half of a biscuit.

When the sun broke through and the wind dropped, he resumed his winding course through the shattered ice. Snow walls, banks of drift, small patches of white cover were all potential traps. He carried a tent prop to probe his forward path and it was slow, grinding progress. When he came to hard, exposed ice, he donned a pair of crampons to aid his footing and made some headway—but that did not last long. In the still air the sun's light caused little trickles of water, which ran into the cracks and turned the snow into the consistency of heavy mud. The weight of the sledge, its drag through the half-frozen snow made him giddy with exertion. Exhausted after six hours, he had covered a bare five miles, and could go no farther that day.

Weakness, debility, the pain of starvation all attacked his determination again, and when he saw the state of his feet he considered a more perilous course: "If my feet do not improve I must turn down the bed of the glacier—to try and reach the sea." Wisely, he slept on the idea.

The fracturing explosions in the glacier again broke his sleep. This night he questioned whether the refreezing theory was correct. There could be far more complex causes. "The sounds are so loud I think some other cause might be involved. The noise resembles explosions of heavy guns, but they come at random, and usually start high up in the glacier and end down toward the sea. There is no real visible evidence of how they are produced."

The frozen bombardment caused him to sleep late. When he woke at 9:30 a.m. it was an overcast morning; and at once came the stabbing realization: "We should all be back at the hut by now." This was the deadline date—January 15—end of the second week in the month, and the Aurora by now should have pulled up the anchor and be sailing out of Commonwealth Bay, the main base party aboard, and on her way to pick up Frank Wild and his group to return to Hobart. He had made the date firm in his declaration at the hut. How well he could recall that evening in the lamplight, the atmosphere full of expectation of high adventure, and serious exploration: "At all costs we have to be ready to go home by then!" What had happened to them all? Had their plans crashed—like his own—into disaster and death? He hoped above all that none of them had known the cruel agony of hopelessness. And when none of his party appeared—what would they do? How long would Davis keep the *Aurora* there? How long dare he wait to sail to Wild and avoid being trapped in the pack ice? In his illness and his hunger, obligation crowded down on his conscience; he was leader, founder, promoter of this expedition. He had brought all these fine men to this terrible land. Please, God! Let them all be safely back.

Concern forced him into rash, urgent action. He broke camp and tried to walk into the snowy morass. The soft mess underfoot and the wind beat down his resolve to make another five miles that day. He was stopped in his tracks after two hours of hauling, amid signs of snow-coated crevasses. Another wasted day hung over him. Two miles of slogging, and he was again compelled to pitch his tent, to lie in his bag and wait for evening to bring the cold that would make the going easier. Also, he had to steel his mind against temptation to eat a warming pannikin of hoosh—not to march was not to eat.

Evening brought further disappointment. When the glacier opened its nightly bombardment, he went outside for a few minutes; he came back to make a diary entry: "10 p.m. Snow still soft. Much snow falling. Impossible to see crevasses or steer a correct course." At 2 a.m. it was the same; and in the end his restlessness for distance brought him from his bag at 5 a.m. when he cooked a weak pemmican and packed his sledge. The wind now blew in cat's paws from the southeast, and the sky was heavily overcast, the air full of snow flurries. The light was bad for traveling, and in normal circumstances he would not have budged. Now he donned his harness and trod into the new snow, desperate to cover ground, to try to get free from the menacing clutch of this glacier.

The conditions were abominable. The glare was such that no detail of the ice or snow could be distinguished. The soft snow built into soggy plates over the sledge runners; it formed a clogging ball over the measuring meter and the turning wheel at the rear of his load. Again, and again he stopped to free his gear from the cloying snow; frequently he clambered over drift heaps, or felt his way along ice ridges that were the lips of crevasses, and all the while he prodded and probed with his tent prop, feeling a blind way through a hazardous, shattered area. "I believe that Providence walks with me," he exclaimed after several escapes from danger.

Once he felt the shock of falling feet first through the snow; luckily it was frozen below the surface and, because his outstretched arms and the tent prop kept him above ground, he was able to clamber out. He would not rest while the compulsion to keep going west burned in him—until 3 p.m.

He had fought his way forward for eight taxing hours, switching directions when the crevasses were too wide or too dangerous, virtually edging his way across the frozen valley. The light southeast breeze had all day filled his sail with no more than gentle pressure. He came up a slope of hard ice onto a rolling brow in the glacial bed, and then there came the first sudden surge of a battering wind from the southwest. It took his sledge from behind him, swung it across the ice, round him and to his front, the tow rope catching his knees and bringing him down. Both sledge and Mawson were being blown down the slope when he dug his crampons into the ice and checked his own descent. Then, horror-struck, he could see his load, all his hope of life, all his possessions, teetering on the open maw of a great hole in the hard blue ice. It had steep precipitous sides, like a frigid quarry, dropping down out of his sight. Instantly he hauled on the tow rope and his sledge was braked on the very lip of the ice with the wind still yanking its weight against his straining arms. For a full minute he could do no more than hold the weight. It was eternity to him. Then, slowly, he hauled back, and, inch by inch, the sledge came against the wind up the slope. He backtracked to a flat snowy area and, with many rests, put up his tent.

Exhausted and faint, he lay on the snowy floor for a while before lighting his stove and preparing his food. This evening the need for nourishment was a sharp and vivid pain, and his only palliative was to crouch over the cooker and see the steam rise from the weak pemmican mixed with a little dog jelly; so acute was his hunger, his crying desire for food, he drooled as he ate the tasteless, odorless mixture.

He was shaken by toil and by his narrow escape from disaster; yet, he had to recapture in his diary the moment when his sledge "was a yard from the edge of a great yawning crevasse." His hand shook as he scribbled with his pencil: "I don't know what lies on ahead at all . . . I do hope the sky will clear, and that frost will come. It takes quite a while dressing my feet each day now."

He ended his entry there for January 16; the meticulous notes on meteorology, wind direction and strength, temperature and altitude, the cloud formations—all omitted now in this bitter fight to win ground against the glacier. He had forgotten his heartfelt prayer for fair days; now he spent restless nights and met and accepted dismal overcast weather as the normal thing. He was coming closer to Adélie Land, and he no longer prayed for good conditions.

On the morning of January 17, ignoring the falling snow and the virtual white-out, he tramped on a course 20 degrees west of north, grimly set on covering at least another five miles. A plain of ice and snow, on the spine of the Mertz Glacier, rose in front of him. He could feel the ascent, but not see it. The pressure underfoot was on his toes as, bent almost double, he carted his burden into the morning.

He toiled a long, rising slope, heavily covered with snow. The sun was hidden, but its light and warmth filtered through the low cloud. He took off his waterproof jacket for easier movement and, along with his gloves, tied it on the back of the sledge. He strained his eyes to find the safest path in the horrible, deceptive glare. Several times he stopped short of open-mouthed crevasses; twice he actually scraped past gaping cracks he had not seen. He then came on smooth snow, and the sledge was running well when without any sign—he went through to his thighs. He clambered out with some effort and resumed his climb up the slope. Peering out from under his goggles, he made out the line of the crevasse on the edge of which he had just fallen through. It went to the south beyond vision; he turned to the north, and, 50 yards farther on, all trace had vanished into a field of flat, clear snow that offered him a path back to his westering course.

In the next instant, he felt himself falling, his stomach a plummeting lead weight. Then the rope yanked viciously, cutting the harness into his body, bringing a sea of bright-colored pain. He was suspended over a black, bottomless chasm. Now he could feel the sledge, pulled by his weight, sliding across the snow toward the edge of this icy pit—nearer and nearer. In seconds the bulk of the sledge would rush over the broken snow bridge, and then he would fall into the abyss. The thought flashed to his mind: "So—this is the end!"

The movement stopped. Against some unseen ridge or roll of snowdrift, the sledge halted; and now he swung fourteen feet down between sheer walls of steely-blue ice, six feet apart.

Slowly he spun in the crevasse, drooping with despair, at the end of the rope. Above, the lowering sky was a narrow band of light; below him were unseen black depths. Cautiously lifting his arms, he could just touch the crevasse walls. Smooth and cold, they offered no fingerhold. Overhead the light showed the line of the rope cutting deep into the broken snow bridge, and he was fearful that sudden movement could again start the sledge sliding toward the edge. He held his position; the sledge did not move when he swung his legs in a wide arc. Gratitude filled his heart: "God has given me another chance . . ." A small, slim chance. Yet, how could he haul his weight directly upward on 14 feet of rope with his bare hands, his clothing full of snow, his body weak from starvation? Despairing, he turned his mind to the sledge propped in the snow above. How much did it weigh? Would it hold his weight if he tried to climb? He pictured his possessions on the abbreviated sledge, and instantly he saw the bag of food stacked on the mid-platform, and in the fear that clouded his brain he knew that he must make every effort to reach the bag.

The thought of wasted food galvanized him to action, and he was reaching a long skinny arm above his head, closing his bare fingers around the first knot in the rope. Shutting his mind against pain and stress, he lunged upward with his other hand and pulled his chin level. Again the reach—and he was six feet nearer the ledge; once more, and then again, holding the rope between his knees, feeling for the knots with his feet now—and he was level with the broken snow bridge. The treacherous, compacted snow was crumbling. Several times he tried to crawl to safety, and he was halfway to solid ice when the whole ledge fragmented under him. Again he crashed to the full length of the rope.

Once more the sledge held its grip in the snow. Once more he dangled, limp, drained, suspended in the chill half light. His hands were bleeding, all the skin of his palms had gone, his fingertips were black, and his body was freezing fast from the snow clogging his clothing, the deep cold of the ice walls shutting him in. He asked— why just hang here waiting for a frozen death? Why not end it all quickly, be done with the pain, the suffering, the struggle? Later he would write: "It was a moment of rare temptation. To quit small things for great, to pass from petty exploration of this world to vaster worlds beyond . . ." At the back of his belt was the razor-sharp sheath-knife. A good slash, a moment or two of breathless rush, and then, final peace—and no one would ever know how it ended, what had happened to him. He could see the sorrowing face of his beloved Paquita, the faces of his comrades—and he pictured again the food waiting on the surface—and Robert Service—Buck up! Do your damndest and fight. Try again!

His strength was draining fast, he was growing deadly cold. Soon it would be all over and done with. But Providence still had him at the end of the rope that was a way back to the surface. By what he later called a "supreme effort," he scaled the rope, knot after knot, and, with a wild, flailing kick, thrust himself into the snow above the solid ice. He fell into a faint and lay unconscious, his face toward the sky, his hands bleeding into the snow.

For the rest of his life he could not recall how he made that final climb from the crevasse; nor did he truly know how long he lay unconscious—he believed it to be well over an hour. When he came back to awareness, it was in answer to the eye of the sun staring down at him from a clearing sky.

He camped near the edge of the cold pit which had almost claimed him. He could not march. His battered hands fumbled and trembled as he lashed the rough frame together, and, as he struggled to draw the cover over his shelter, he thanked Providence again and again, for restoring him to life, to his mission.

He filled his pannikin with hot steaming hoosh and cooked some fragments of dog meat and ate it all with a biscuit, still shaking from the experience, living it over in his mind. Sitting in his bag and with the stub of pencil held in his painful fingers he wrote his story of that day, and ended: "It is impossible . . . the light gives no chance, and I sincerely hope that something will happen to change the state of the weather, else how can I manage to keep up my average. I trust in Providence, however, who has already helped me so many times."

A Bad Time

by Nancy Mitford

The story of Scott's last and fatal expedition to Antarctica has been told many times. This short secondhand account is among the best of its type. Written 50 years after Scott's death, it delivers no new information to the seasoned armchair explorer. Instead, it offers the crisp style of Nancy Mitford (1904–1973), with her humor and her sensibility.

Apsley Cherry-Garrard has said that 'polar exploration is at once the cleanest and most isolated way of having a bad time that has yet been devised'.* Nobody could deny that he and the twenty-four other members of Captain Scott's expedition to the South Pole had a bad time; in fact, all other bad times, embarked on by men of their own free will, pale before it. Theirs is the last of the great classic explorations; their equipment, though they lived in our century, curiously little different from that used by Captain Cook. Vitamin pills would probably have saved the lives of the Polar party, so would a wireless transmitter; an electric torch have mitigated the misery of the Winter Journey. How many things which we take completely as a matter of course had not yet been invented, such a little time ago! Scott's *Terra Nova* had the advantage over Cook's *Resolution* of steam as well as sail. Even this was a mixed blessing, as it involved much hateful shovelling, while the coal occupied space which could have been put to better account in the little wooden barque (764

* Unless otherwise stated, the quotations in this essay are from *The Worst Journey in the World* by Cherry-Garrard.

tons). Three motor-sledges lashed to the deck seemed marvellously up-to-date and were the pride and joy of Captain Scott.

The *Terra Nova* sailed from London 15th June 1910 and from New Zealand 26th November. She was fearfully overloaded; on deck, as well as the motor-sledges in their huge crates, there were 30 tons of coal in sacks, 21/2 tons of petrol in drums, 33 dogs, and 19 ponies. She rode out a bad storm by a miracle. 'Bowers and Campbell were standing upon the bridge and the ship rolled sluggishly over until the lee combings of the main hatch were under the sea . . . as a rule, if a ship goes that far over she goes down.' It took her thirty-eight days to get to McMurdo Sound, by which time the men were in poor shape. They had slept in their clothes, lucky if they got five hours a night, and had had no proper meals. As soon as they dropped anchor they began to unload the ship. This entailed dragging its cargo over ice floes which were in constant danger of being tipped up by killer whales, a very tricky business, specially when it came to moving ponies, motor- sledges and a pianola. Then they built the Hut which was henceforward to be their home. Scott, tireless himself, always drove his men hard and these things were accomplished in a fortnight. The *Terra Nova* sailed away; she was to return the following summer, when it was hoped that the Polar party would be back in time to be taken off before the freezing up of the sea forced her to leave again. If not, they would be obliged to spend a second winter on McMurdo Sound. Winter, of course, in those latitudes, happens during our summer months and is perpetual night, as the summer is perpetual day. The stunning beauty of the scenery affected the men deeply. When the sun shone the snow was never white, but brilliant shades of pink, blue and lilac; in winter the aurora australis flamed across the sky and the summit of Mount Erebus glowed.

The Hut, unlike so much of Scott's equipment, was a total success. It was built on the shore, too near the sea, perhaps, for absolute security in the cruel winter storms, under the active volcano Mount Erebus, called after the ship in which Ross discovered these regions in 1839. It was 50 feet by 25, 9 feet high. The walls had double boarding inside and outside the frames, with layers of quilted seaweed between the boards. The roof had six layers of alternate wood, rubber and seaweed. Though 109 degrees of frost was quite usual, the men never suffered from cold indoors; in fact, with twenty-five of them living there, the cooking range at full blast and a stove at the other end, they sometimes complained of stuffiness.

Life during the first winter was very pleasant. Before turning in for good they had done several gruelling marches, laying stores in depots along the route of the Polar journey; they felt they needed and had earned a rest. Their only complaint was that there were too many lectures; Scott insisted on at least three a week and they seem to have bored the others considerably—except for Ponting's magic lantern slides of Japan. A gramophone and a pianola provided background music and there was a constant flow of witticisms which one assumes to have been unprintable until one learns that Dr Wilson would leave the company if a coarse word were spoken. In the Hut they chiefly lived on flesh of seals, which they killed without difficulty, since these creatures are friendly and trustful by nature. 'A sizzling on the fire and a smell of porridge and seal liver heralded breakfast which was at 8 a.m. in theory and a good deal later in practice.' Supper was at 7. Most were in their bunks by 10 p.m., sometimes with a candle and a book; the acetylene was turned off at 10:30 to economize the fuel. Cherry-Garrard tells us that the talk at meals was never dull. Most of these men were from the Royal Navy, and sailors are often droll, entertaining fellows possessing much out-of-the-way information. (Nobody who heard them can have forgotten the performances of Commander Campbell on the B.B.C.—he was one of the greatest stars they ever had, in my view.) Heated arguments would break out on a diversity of subjects, to be settled by recourse to an encyclopedia or an atlas or sometimes a Latin dictionary. They wished they had also brought a *Who's Who*. One of their discussions, which often recurred, concerned 'Why are we here? What is the force that drives us to undergo severe, sometimes ghastly hardships of our own free will?' The reply was The Interests of Science— it is important that man should know the features of the world he lives in, but this was not a complete answer. Once there was a discussion as to whether they would continue to like Polar travel if, by the aid of modern inventions, it became quite easy and comfortable. They said no, with one accord. It seems as if they really wanted to prove to themselves how much they could endure. Their rewards were a deep spiritual satisfaction and relationships between men who had become more than brothers.

Their loyalty to each other was fantastic—there was no jealousy, bickering, bullying or unkindness. Reading between the lines of their diaries and records it is impossible to guess whether anybody disliked anybody else. As for The Owner, as they called Scott, they all worshipped and blindly followed him. Cherry-Garrard, the only one who could be called an intellectual and who took a fairly objective view of the others, gives an interesting account of Scott's character: subtle, he says, full of light and shade. No sense of humour—peevish by nature, highly strung, irritable, melancholy and moody. However, such was his strength of mind that he overcame these faults, though he could not entirely conceal long periods of sadness. He was humane, so fond of animals that he refused to take dogs on long journeys, hauling the sledge himself rather than see them suffer. His idealism and intense patriotism shone through all he wrote. Of course, he had the extraordinary charm without which no man can be a leader. In his diaries he appears as an affectionate person, but shyness or the necessary isolation of a sea-captain prevented him from showing this side to the others. He was poor; he worried about provision for his family when it became obvious that he would never return to them. Indeed, he was always hampered by lack of money and never had enough to finance his voyages properly. Lady Kennet, his widow, once told me that Scott only took on Cherry-Garrard because he subscribed £2,000 to the expedition. He thought him too young (23), too delicate and too shortsighted, besides being quite inexperienced; he was the only amateur in the party. It is strange and disgraceful that Scott, who was already a world-famous explorer, should have had so little support from the Government for this prestigious voyage.

These men had an enemy, not with them in the Hut but ever present in their minds. His shadow fell across their path before they left New Zealand, when Captain Scott received a telegram dated from Madeira, with the laconic message Am going South Amundsen. Now, Amundsen was known to be preparing Nansen's old ship, the Fram, for a journey, having announced that he intended to do some further exploring in the Arctic. Only when he was actually at sea did he tell his crew that he was on his way to try and reach the South Pole. There seemed something underhand and unfair about this. Scott's men were furious; they talked of finding the Amundsen party and having it out with them, but Scott put a good face on it and pretended not to mind at all. The two leaders could hardly have been more different. Amundsen was cleverer than Scott, 'an explorer of a markedly intellectual type rather Jewish than Scandinavian'. There was not much humanity or idealism about him, he was a tough, brave professional. He had a sense of humour and his description of flying over the North Pole in a dirigible with General Nobile is very funny indeed. Nobile was forever in tears and Amundsen on the verge of striking him, the climax coming when, over the Pole, Nobile threw out armfuls of huge Italian flags which caught in the propeller and endangered their lives. All the same, Amundsen died going to the rescue of Nobile in 1928.

No doubt the knowledge that 'the Norskies' were also on their way to the Pole was a nagging worry to Scott all those long, dark, winter months, though he was very careful to hide his feelings and often re-marked that Amundsen had a perfect right to go anywhere at any time. 'The Pole is not a race,' he would say. He (Scott) was going in the interests of science and not in order to 'get there first'. But he knew that everybody else would look on it as a race; he was only human, he longed to win it.

The chief of Scott's scientific staff and his greatest friend was Dr. Wilson. He was to Scott what Sir Joseph Hooker had been to Ross. (Incredible as it seems, Hooker only died that very year, 1911. Scott knew him well.) Wilson was a doctor of St George's Hospital and a zoo-logist specializing in vertebrates. He had published a book on whales, penguins and seals and had prepared a report for the Royal Comm-ission on grouse disease. While he was doing this Cherry-Garrard met him, at a shooting lodge in Scotland, and became fired with a longing to go south. Wilson was an accomplished water-colourist. Above all, he was an adorable person: 'The finest character I ever met,' said Scott. Now Dr Wilson wanted to bring home the egg of an Emperor Penguin. He had studied these huge creatures when he was with Scott on his first journey to the Antarctic and thought that their embryos would be of paramount biological interest, possibly proving to be the missing link between bird and fish. The Emperors, who weigh 61/2 stone, look like sad little men and were often taken by early explorers for human natives of the South Polar regions, are in a low state of evolution (and of spirits). They lay their eggs in the terrible mid-winter, because only thus can their chicks, which develop with a slowness abnormal in birds, be ready to survive the next winter. They never step on shore, even to breed; they live in rookeries on sea-ice. To incubate their eggs, they balance them on their enormous feet and press them against a patch of bare skin on the abdomen protected from the cold by a lappet of skin and feathers. Paternity is the only joy known to these wretched birds and a monstrous instinct for it is implanted in their breasts; male and female hatch out the eggs and nurse the chicks, also on their feet, indiscriminately. When a penguin has to go in the sea to catch his dinner he leaves egg or chick on the ice; there is then a mad scuffle as twenty childless birds rush to adopt it, quite often breaking or killing it in the process. They will nurse a dead chick until it falls to pieces and sit for months on an addled egg or even a stone. All this happens in darkness and about a hundred degrees of frost. I often think the R.S.P.C.A. ought to do something for the Emperor Penguins.

Dr Wilson had reason to suppose that there was a rookery of Emperors at Cape Crozier, about sixty miles along the coast. When the ghastly winter weather had properly set in he asked for two volunteers to go with him and collect some eggs. It was one of the rules in the Hut that everybody volunteered for everything, so Wilson really chose his own companions: 'Birdie' Bowers, considered by Scott to be the hardest traveller in the world, and Cherry-Garrard. The three of them left the light and warmth and good cheer of the Hut to embark upon the most appalling nightmare possible to imagine. The darkness was profound and invariable. (They steered by Jupiter.) The temperature was generally in the region of 90 degrees of frost, unless there was a blizzard, when it would rise as high as 40 degrees of frost, producing other forms of discomfort and the impossibility of moving. The human body exudes a quantity of sweat and moisture, even in the lowest temperatures, so the men's clothes were soon frozen as stiff as boards and they were condemned to remain in the bending position in which they pulled their sleigh. It was as though they were dressed in lead. The surface of the snow was so bad that they had to divide their load and bring it along by relays. They could never take off their huge gloves for fear of losing their hands by frostbite; as it was, their fingers were covered with blisters in which the liquid was always frozen, so that their hands were like bunches of marbles. The difficulty of performing the simplest action with them may be imagined; it sometimes took over an hour to light a match and as much as nine hours to pitch their tent and do the work of the camp. Everything was slow, slow. When they had a discussion it lasted a week. If Cherry-Garrard had written his book in a more uninhibited age he would no doubt have told us how they managed about what the Americans call going to the bathroom.* As it is, this interesting point remains mysterious. Dr Wilson insisted on them spending seven hours out of the twenty-four (day and night in that total blackness were quite arbitrary) in their sleeping-bags. These were always frozen up, so that it took at least an hour to worm their way in and then they suffered the worst of all the tortures. Normally on such journeys the great comfort was sleep. Once in their warm dry sleeping-bags the men went off as if they were drugged and nothing, neither pain nor worry, could keep them awake. But now the cold was too intense for Wilson and Cherry-Garrard to close an eye. They lay shivering until they thought their backs would break, enviously listening to the regular snores of Birdie. They had got a spirit lamp—the only bearable moments they knew were when they had just swallowed a hot drink; for a little while it was like a hot-water bottle on their hearts; but the effect soon wore off. Their teeth froze and split to pieces. Their toe-nails came away. Cherry-Garrard began to long for death. It never occurred to any of them to go back. The penguin's egg assumed such importance in their minds, as they groped and plodded their four or five miles a day, that the whole future of the human race might have depended on their finding one.

At last, in the bleakest and most dreadful place imaginable, they heard the Emperors calling. To get to the rookery entailed a long, dangerous feat of mountaineering, since it was at the foot of an immense

* They [the savages] go to the bathroom in the street.' (Report from a member of the Peace Corps in the Congo).

cliff. Dim twilight now glowed for an hour or two at midday, so they were able to see the birds, about a hundred of them, mournfully huddled together, trying to shuffle away from the intruders without losing the eggs from their feet and trumpeting with curious metallic voices. The men took some eggs, got lost on the cliff, were nearly killed several times by falling into crevasses and broke all the eggs but two. That night there was a hurricane and their tent blew away, carried out to sea, no doubt. Now that they faced certain death, life suddenly seemed more attractive. They lay in their sleeping-bags for two days waiting for the wind to abate and pretending to each other that they would manage somehow to get home without a tent, although they knew very well that they must perish. When it was possible to move again Bowers, by a miracle, found the tent. 'We were so thankful we said nothing.' They could hardly remember the journey home—it passed like a dreadful dream, and indeed they often slept while pulling their sleigh. When they arrived, moribund, at the Hut, exactly one month after setting forth, The Owner said: 'Look here, you know, this is the hardest journey that has ever been done.'

I once recounted this story to a hypochondriac friend, who said, horrified, 'But it must have been so bad for them.' The extraordinary thing is that it did them no harm. They were quite recovered three months later, in time for the Polar journey, from which, of course, Wilson and Bowers did not return, but which they endured longer than any except Scott himself. Cherry-Garrard did most of the Polar journey; he went through the 1914 war, in the trenches much of the time, and lived until 1959.

As for the penguins' eggs, when Cherry-Garrard got back to London the first thing he did was to take them to the Natural History Museum. Alas, nobody was very much interested in them. The Chief Custodian, when he received Cherry-Garrard after a good long delay, simply put them down on an ink stand and went on talking to a friend. Cherry-Garrard asked if he could have a receipt for the eggs? 'It's not necessary. It's all right. You needn't wait,' he was told.

The Winter Journey was so appalling that the journey to the Pole, which took place in daylight and in much higher temperatures seemed almost banal by comparison; but it was terribly long (over seven hundred miles each way) and often very hard. Scott left the Hut at 11 p.m. on 1st November. He soon went back, for a book; was undecided what to take, but finally chose a volume of Browning. He was accompanied by a party of about twenty men with two motor-sledges (the third had fallen into the sea while being landed), ponies and dogs. Only four men were to go to the Pole, but they were to be accompanied until the dreaded Beardmore glacier had been climbed. The men in charge of the motors turned back first, the motors having proved a failure. They delayed the party with continual breakdowns and only covered fifty miles. The dogs and their drivers went next. The ponies were shot at the foot of the glacier. The men minded this; they had become attached to the beasts, who had done their best, often in dreadful conditions. So far the journey had taken longer than it should have. The weather was bad for travelling, too warm, the snow too soft; there were constant blizzards. Now they were twelve men, without ponies or dogs, manhauling the sledges. As they laboured up the Beardmore, Scott was choosing the men who would go to the Pole with him. Of course, the disappointment of those who were sent home at this stage was acute; they had done most of the gruelling journey and were not to share in the glory. On 20th December Cherry-Garrard wrote: 'This evening has been rather a shock. As I was getting my finesko on to the top of my ski Scott came up to me and said he had rather a blow for me. Of course, I knew what he was going to say, but could hardly grasp that I was going back—tomorrow night. . . . Wilson told me it was a toss-up whether Titus [Oates] or I should go on; that being so I think Titus will help him more than I can. I said all I could think of—he seemed so cut up about it, saying "I think somehow it is specially hard on you." I said I hoped I had not disappointed him and he caught hold of me and said "No, no— no", so if that is the case all is well.'

There was still one more party left to be sent back after Cherry-Garrard's. Scott said in his diary: 'I dreaded this necessity of choosing, nothing could be more heartrending.' He added: 'We are struggling on, considering all things against odds. The weather is a constant anxiety.' The weather was against them; the winter which succeeded this disappointing summer set in early and was the worst which hardened Arctic travellers had ever experienced.

Scott had always intended to take a party of four to the Pole. He now made the fatal decision to take five. Oates was the last-minute choice; it is thought that Scott felt the Army ought to be represented. So they were: Scott aged 43, Wilson 39, Seaman Evans 37, Bowers 28, and Oates 32. The extra man was *de trop* in every way. There were only four pairs of skis; the tent was too small for five, so that one man was too near the outside and always cold; worst of all, there were now five people to eat rations meant for four. It was an amazing mistake, but it showed that Scott thought he was on a good wicket. The returning parties certainly thought so; it never occurred to them that he would have much difficulty, let alone that his life might be in danger. But they were all more exhausted than they knew and the last two parties only got home by the skin of their teeth, after hair-raising experiences on the Beardmore. Scott still had 150 miles to go.

On 10th January, only a few miles from the Pole, Bowers spied something in the snow—an abandoned sledge. Then they came upon dog tracks. Man Friday's footsteps on the sand were less dramatic. They knew that the enemy had won. 'The Norwegians have forestalled us,' wrote Scott, 'and are first at the Pole. . . . All the day dreams must go; it will be a wearisome return'. And he wrote at the Pole itself: 'Great God! This is an awful place!'

Amundsen had left his base on 20th October with three other men, all on skis, and sixty underfed dogs to pull his sleighs. He went over the Axel Herberg glacier, an easier climb than the Beardmore, and reached the Pole on 16th December with no more discomfort than on an ordinary Antarctic journey. His return only took thirty-eight days, by which time he had eaten most of the dogs, beginning with his own favourite. When the whole story was known there was a good deal of feeling in England over these animals. At the Royal Geographical Society's dinner to Amundsen the President, Lord Curzon, infuriated his guest by ending his speech with the words, 'I think we ought to give three cheers for the dogs.'

And now for the long pull home. Evans was dying, of frostbite and concussion from a fall. He never complained, just staggered along, sometimes wandering in his mind. The relief when he died was tremendous, as Scott had been tormented by feeling that perhaps he ought to abandon him, for the sake of the others. When planning the Winter Journey, Wilson had told Cherry-Garrard that he was against taking seamen on the toughest ventures—he said they simply would not look after themselves. Indeed, Evans had concealed a wound on his hand which was the beginning of his troubles. A month later, the party was again delayed, by Oates's illness; he was in terrible pain from frostbitten feet. He bravely committed suicide, but too late to save the others. Scott wrote: 'Oates's last thoughts were of his mother, but imm-ediately before he took pride in thinking that his regiment would be pleased at the bold way in which he met his death. . . . He was a brave soul. He slept through the night, hoping not to wake; but he woke in the morning, yesterday. It was blowing a blizzard. He said "I am just going outside and may be some time."'

All, now, were ill. Their food was short and the petrol for their spirit lamp, left for them in the depots, had mostly evaporated. The horrible pemmican, with its low vitamin content, which was their staple diet was only bearable when made into a hot stew. Now they were eating it cold, keeping the little fuel they had to make hot cocoa. (This business of the petrol was very hard on the survivors. When on their way home, the returning parties had made use of it, carefully taking much less than they were told was their share. They always felt that Scott, who never realized that it had evaporated, must have blamed them in his heart for the shortage.) Now the weather changed. 'They were in evil case but they would have been all right if the cold had not come down upon them; unexpected, unforetold and fatal. The cold in itself was not so tremendous until you realize that they had been out four months, that they had fought their way up the biggest glacier in the world, in feet of soft snow, that they had spent seven weeks under plateau conditions of rarified air, big winds and low temperatures.' They struggled on and might just have succeeded in getting home if they had had ordinary good luck. But, eleven miles from the depot which would have saved them, a blizzard blew up so that they could not move. It blew for a week, at the end of which there was no more hope. On 29th March Scott wrote: 'My dear Mrs Wilson. If this reaches you, Bill and I will have gone out together. We are very near it now and I should like you to know how splendid he was at the end—everlastingly cheerful and ready to sacrifice himself for others, never a word of blame to me for leading him into this mess. He is suffering, luckily, only minor discomforts.

His eyes have a comfortable blue look of hope and his mind is peaceful with the satisfaction of his faith, in regarding himself as part of the great scheme of the Almighty. I can do no more to comfort you than to tell you that he died, as he lived, a brave, true man—the best of comrades and staunchest of friends. My whole heart goes out to you in pity.

Yours R. Scott.'

And to Sir James Barrie:

'We are pegging out in a very comfortless spot . . . I am not at all afraid of the end but sad to miss many a humble pleasure which I had planned for the future on our long marches. . . . We have had four days of storm in our tent and nowhere's food or fuel. We did intend to finish ourselves when things proved like this but we have decided to die naturally in the track.'

On 19th March Cherry-Garrard and the others in the Hut, none of them fit, began to be worried. The *Terra Nova* had duly come back, with longed-for mails and news of the outer world. They had to let her go again, taking those who were really ill. On 27th March Atkinson, the officer in charge, and a seaman went a little way to try and meet the Polar party, but it was a hopeless quest, and they were 100 miles from where Scott was already dead when they turned back. They now prepared for another winter in the Hut, the sadness of which can be imagined. Long, long after they knew all hope was gone they used to think they heard their friends coming in, or saw shadowy forms that seemed to be theirs. They mourned them and missed their company. Scott, Wilson and Bowers had been the most dynamic of them all, while 'Titus' or 'Farmer Hayseed' (Oates) was a dear, good-natured fellow whom everybody loved to tease. The weather was unimaginably awful. It seemed impossible that the Hut could stand up to the tempests which raged outside for weeks on end and the men quite expected that it might collapse at any time. When at last the sun reappeared they set forth to see if they could discover traces of their friends. They hardly expected any results, as they were firmly convinced that the men must have fallen down a crevasse on the Beardmore, a fate they had all escaped by inches at one time or another. Terribly soon, however, they came upon what looked like a cairn; it was, in fact, Scott's tent covered with snow.

'We have found them. To say it has been a ghastly day cannot express it. Bowers and Wilson were sleeping in their bags. Scott had thrown the flaps of his bag open at the end. His left hand was stretched over Wilson, his lifelong friend.' Everything was tidy, their papers and records in perfect order. Atkinson and Cherry-Garrard read enough to find out what had happened and packed up the rest of the papers unopened. They built a cairn over the tent, which was left as they found it. Near the place where Oates disappeared they put up a cross with the inscription: 'Hereabouts died a very gallant gentleman, Captain E. G. Oates of the Inniskilling Dragoons. In March 1912, returning from the Pole, he walked willingly to his death in a blizzard to try and save his comrades, beset by hardship.'

In due course Cherry-Garrard and the others were taken off by the *Terra Nova*. When they arrived in New Zealand Atkinson went ashore to send cables to the dead men's wives. 'The Harbour Master came out in the tug with him. "Come down here a minute," said Atkinson to me and "It's made a tremendous impression. I had no idea it would make so much," he said.' Indeed it had. The present writer well remembers this impression, though only seven at the time.

Amundsen had won the race, but Scott had captured his fellow countrymen's imagination. It is one of our endearing qualities, perhaps unique, that we think no less of a man because he has failed—we even like him better for it. In any case, Amundsen complained that a year later a Norwegian boy at school in England was being taught that Captain Scott discovered the South Pole.

I don't quite know why I have felt the need to write down this well-known story, making myself cry twice, at the inscription on Oates's cross and when Atkinson said, 'It has made a tremendous impression.' Perhaps the bold, bald men who get, smiling, into cupboards, as if they were playing sardines, go a little way (about as far as from London to Manchester) into the air and come out of their cupboards again, a few hours later, smiling more than ever, have put me in mind of other adventurers. It is fifty years to the day, as I write this, that Scott died. Most of the wonderful books which tell of his expedition are out of print now, but they can easily be got at second hand. I should like to feel that I may have induced somebody to read them again.

from The Worst Journey
in the World
by Apsley Cherry-Garrard

Apsley Cherry-Garrard's account of Scott's last expedition is named after the side trip that youthful expedition member Cherry-Garrard (1886–1959) took to obtain eggs of the emperor penguin in June 1911. This passage recounts that trip. His companions included two of the men who died with Scott the following March, Henry ("Birdie") Bowers and William ("Uncle Bill") Wilson. Cherry-Garrard accompanied the search party that found their bodies in November 1912.

June 22. Midwinter Night

A hard night: clear, with a blue sky so deep that it looks black: the stars are steel points: the glaciers burnished silver. The snow rings and thuds to your footfall. The ice is cracking to the falling temperature and the tide crack groans as the water rises. And over all, wave upon wave, fold upon fold, there hangs the curtain of the aurora. As you watch, it fades away, and then quite suddenly a great beam flashes up and rushes to the zenith, an arch of palest green and orange, a tail of flaming gold. Again it falls, fading away into great searchlight beams which rise behind the smoking crater of Mount Erebus. And again the spiritual veil is drawn—

> Here at the roaring loom of Time I ply
> And weave for God the garment thou seest him by.

Inside the hut are orgies. We are very merry—and indeed why not? The sun turns to come back to us tonight, and such a day comes only once a year.

After dinner we had to make speeches, but instead of making a speech Bowers brought in a wonderful Christmas tree, made of split bamboos and a ski stick, with feathers tied to the end of each branch; candles, sweets, preserved fruits, and the most absurd toys of which Bill was the owner. Titus got three things which pleased him immensely, a sponge, a whistle, and a pop-gun which went off when he pressed the butt. For the rest of the evening he went round asking whether you were sweating. 'No.' 'Yes, you are,' he said, and wiped your face with the sponge. 'If you want to please me very much you will fall down when I shoot you,' he said to me, and then he went round shooting everybody. At intervals he blew the whistle.

He danced the Lancers with Anton, and Anton, whose dancing puts that of the Russian Ballet into the shade, continually apologized for not being able to do it well enough. Ponting gave a great lecture with slides which he had made since we arrived, many of which Meares had coloured. When one of these came up one of us would shout, 'Who coloured that,' and another would cry, 'Meares,'—then uproar. It was impossible for Ponting to speak. We had a milk punch, when Scott proposed the Eastern Party, and Clissold, the cook, proposed Good Old True Milk. Titus blew away the ball of his gun. 'I blew it into the cerulean—how doth Homer have it?—cerulean azure—hence Erebus.' As we turned in he said, 'Cherry, are you responsible for your actions?' and when I said Yes, he blew loudly on his whistle, and the last thing I remembered was that he woke up Meares to ask him whether he was fancy free.

It was a magnificent bust.

Five days later and three men, one of whom at any rate is feeling a little frightened, stand panting and sweating out in McMurdo Sound. They have two sledges, one tied behind the other, and these sledges are piled high with sleeping-bags and camping equipment, six weeks' provisions, and a venesta case full of scientific gear for pickling and preserving. In addition there is a pickaxe, ice-axes, an Alpine rope, a large piece of green Willesden canvas and a bit of board. Scott's amazed remark when he saw our sledges two hours ago, 'Bill, why are you taking all this oil?' pointing to the six cans lashed to the tray on the second sledge, had a bite in it. Our weights for such travelling are enormous—253 lbs. a man.

It is midday but it is pitchy dark, and it is not warm.

As we rested my mind went back to a dusty, dingy office in Victoria Street some fifteen months ago. 'I want you to come' said Wilson to me, and then, 'I want to go to Cape Crozier in the winter and work out the embryology of the Emperor penguins, but I'm not saying much about it—it might never come off.' Well! this was better than Victoria Street, where the doctors had nearly refused to let me go because I could only see the people across the road as vague blobs walking. Then Bill went and had a talk with Scott about it, and they said I might come if I was prepared to take the additional risk. At that time I would have taken anything.

After the Depot Journey, at Hut Point, walking over that beastly, slippery, sloping ice-foot which I always imagined would leave me some day in the sea, Bill asked me whether I would go with him—and who else for a third? There can have been little doubt whom we both wanted, and that evening Bowers had been asked. Of course he was made to come. And here we were. 'This winter travel is a new and bold venture,' wrote Scott in the hut that night, 'but the right men have gone to attempt it.'

I don't know. There never could have been any doubt about Bill and Birdie. Probably Lashly would have made the best third, but Bill had a prejudice against seamen for a journey like this—'They don't take enough care of themselves, and they *will* not look after their clothes.' But Lashly was wonderful—if Scott had only taken a four-man party and Lashly to the Pole!

What is this venture? Why is the embryo of the Emperor penguin so important to Science? And why should three sane and common-sense explorers be sledging away on a winter's night to a Cape which has only been visited before in daylight, and then with very great difficulty?

The Emperor is a bird which cannot fly, lives on fish and never steps on land even to breed. It lays its eggs on the bare ice during the winter and carries out the whole process of incubation on the sea-ice, resting the egg upon its feet, pressed closely to the lower abdomen. But it is because the Emperor is probably the most primitive bird in existence that the working out of his embryology is so important. The embryo shows remains of the development of an animal in former ages and former states; it recapitulates its former lives. The embryo of an

Emperor may prove the missing link between birds and the reptiles from which birds have sprung.

Only one rookery of Emperor penguins had been found at this date, and this was on the sea-ice inside a little bay of the Barrier edge of Cape Crozier, which was guarded by miles of some of the biggest pressure in the Antarctic. Chicks had been found in September, and Wilson reckoned that the eggs must be laid in the beginning of July. And so we started just after midwinter on the weirdest bird's-nesting expedition that has ever been or ever will be.

But the sweat was freezing in our clothing and we moved on. All we could see was a black patch away to our left which was Turk's Head: when this disappeared we knew that we had passed Glacier Tongue which, unseen by us, eclipsed the rocks behind. And then we camped for lunch.

That first camp only lives in my memory because it began our education of camp work in the dark. Had we now struck the blighting temperature which we were to meet. . .

There was just enough wind to make us want to hurry: down harness, each man to a strap on the sledge—quick with the floor cloth—the bags to hold it down—now a good spread with the bamboos and the tent inner lining—hold them, Cherry, and over with the outer covering—snow on to the skirting and inside with the cook with his candle and a box of matches. . . . .

That is how we tied it: that is the way we were accustomed to do it, day after day and night after night when the sun was still high or at any rate only setting, sledging on the Barrier in spring and summer and autumn; pulling our hands from our mitts when necessary—plenty of time to warm up afterwards; in the days when we took pride in getting our tea boiling within twenty minutes of throwing off our harness: when the man who wanted to work in his fur mitts was thought a bit too slow.

But now it *didn't* work. 'We shall have to go a bit slower,' said Bill, and 'we shall get more used to working in the dark.' At this time, I remember, I was still trying to wear spectacles.

We spent that night on the sea-ice, finding that we were too far in towards Castle Rock; and it was not until the following afternoon that we reached and lunched at Hut Point. I speak of day and night, though they were much the same, and later on when we found that we could not get the work into a twenty-four-hour day; we decided to carry on as though such a convention did not exist; as in actual fact it did not. We had already realized that cooking under these conditions would be a bad job, and that the usual arrangement by which one man was cook for the week would be intolerable. We settled to be cook alternately day by day. For food we brought only pemmican and biscuit and butter; for drink we had tea, and we drank hot water to turn in on.

Pulling out from Hut Point that evening we brought along our heavy loads on the two 9-ft sledges with comparative ease; it was the first, and though we did not know it then, the only bit of good pulling we were to have. Good pulling to the sledge traveller means easy pulling. Away we went round Cape Armitage and eastwards. We knew that the Barrier edge was in front of us and also that the break-up of the sea-ice had left the face of it as a low perpendicular cliff. We had therefore to find a place where the snow had formed a drift. This we came right up against and met quite suddenly a very keen wind flowing, as it always does, from the cold Barrier down to the comparatively warm sea-ice. The temperature was −47° F., and I was a fool to take my hands out of my mitts to haul on the ropes to bring the sledges up. I started away from the Barrier edge with all ten fingers frost-bitten. They did not really come back until we were in the tent for our night meal, and within a few hours there were two or three large blisters, up to an inch long, on all of them. For many days those blisters hurt frightfully.

We were camped that night about half a mile in from the Barrier edge. The temperature was −56°. We had a baddish time, being very glad to get out of our shivering bags next morning (29 June). We began to suspect, as we knew only too well later, that the only good time of the twenty-four hours was breakfast, for then with reasonable luck we need not get into our sleeping-bags again for another seventeen hours.

The horror of the nineteen days it took us to travel from Cape Evans to Cape Crozier would have to be re-experienced to be appreciated; and any one would be a fool who went again: it is not possible to describe it. The weeks which followed them were comparative bliss, not because later our conditions were better—they were far worse—but because we were callous. I for one had come to that point of suffering at which I did not really care if only I could die without much pain. They talk of the heroism of the dying—they little know—it would be so easy to die, a dose of morphia, a friendly crevasse, and blissful sleep. The trouble is to go on . . .

It was the darkness that did it. I don't believe minus seventy temperatures would be bad in daylight, not comparatively bad, when you could see where you were going, where you were stepping, where the sledge straps were, the cooker, the primus, the food; could see your footsteps lately trodden deep into the soft snow that you might find your way back to the rest of your load; could see the lashings of the food bags; could read a compass without striking three or four different boxes to find one dry match; could read your watch to see if the blissful moment of getting out of your bag was come without groping in the snow all about; when it would not take you five minutes to lash up the door of the tent, and five hours to get started in the morning . . .

But in these days we were never less than four hours from the moment when Bill cried 'Time to get up' to the time when we got into our harness. It took two men to get one man into his harness, and was all they could do, for the canvas was frozen and our clothes were frozen until sometimes not even two men could bend them into the required shape.

The trouble is sweat and breath. I never knew before how much of the body's waste comes out through the pores of the skin. On the most bitter days, when we had to camp before we had done a four-hour march in order to nurse back our frozen feet, it seemed that we must be sweating. And all this sweat, instead of passing away through the porous wool of our clothing and gradually drying off us, froze and accumulated. It passed just away from our flesh and then became ice: we shook plenty of snow and ice down from inside our trousers every time we changed our foot-gear, and we could have shaken it from our vests and from between our vests and shirts, but of course we could not strip to this extent. But when we got into our sleeping-bags, if we were fortunate, we became warm enough during the night to thaw this ice: part remained in our clothes, part passed into the skins of our sleeping-bags, and soon both were sheets of armour-plate.

As for our breath—in the daytime it did nothing worse than cover the lower parts of our faces with ice and solder our balaclavas tightly to our heads. It was no good trying to get your balaclava off until you had had the primus going quite a long time, and then you could throw your breath about if you wished. The trouble really began in your sleeping-bag, for it was far too cold to keep a hole open through which to breathe. So all night long our breath froze into the skins, and our respiration became quicker and quicker as the air in our bags got fouler and fouler: it was never possible to make a match strike or burn inside our bags!

Of course we were not iced up all at once: it took several days of this kind of thing before we really got into big difficulties on this score. It was not until I got out of the tent one morning fully ready to pack the sledge that I realized the possibilities ahead. We had had our breakfast, struggled into our foot-gear, and squared up inside the tent, which was comparatively warm. Once outside, I raised my head to look round and found I could not move it back. My clothing had frozen hard as I stood—perhaps fifteen seconds. For four hours I had to pull with my head stuck up, and from that time we all took care to bend down into a pulling position before being frozen in.

By now we had realized that we must reverse the usual sledging routine and do everything slowly, wearing when possible the fur mitts which fitted over our woollen mitts, and always stopping whatever we were doing, directly we felt that any part of us was getting frozen, until the circulation was restored. Henceforward it was common for one or other of us to leave the other two to continue the camp work while he stamped about in the snow, beat his arms, or nursed some exposed part. But we could not restore the circulation of our feet like this—the only way then was to camp and get some hot water into ourselves before we took our foot-gear off. The difficulty was to know whether our feet were frozen or not, for the only thing we knew for certain was that we had lost all feeling in them. Wilson's knowledge as a doctor came in here: many a time he had to decide from our descriptions of our feet whether to camp or to go on for another hour. A wrong decision meant disaster, for if one of us had been crippled the whole party would have been placed in great difficulties. Probably we should all have died.

On 29 June the temperature was −50° all day and there was sometimes a light breeze which was inclined to frost-bite our faces and
hands. Owing to the weight of our two sledges and the bad surface our
pace was not more than a slow and very heavy plod: at our lunch camp
Wilson had the heel and sole of one foot frost-bitten, and I had two big
toes. Bowers was never worried by frost-bitten feet.

That night was very cold, the temperature falling to −66°, and it was
−55° at breakfast on 30 June. We had not shipped the eider-down
linings to our sleeping-bags, in order to keep them dry as long as
possible. My own fur bag was too big for me, and throughout this
journey was more difficult to thaw out than the other two: on the other
hand, it never split, as did Bill's.

We were now getting into that cold bay which lies between the Hut
Point Peninsula and Terror Point. It was known from old Discovery
days that the Barrier winds are deflected from this area, pouring out
into McMurdo Sound behind us, and into the Ross Sea at Cape Crozier
in front. In consequence of the lack of high winds the surface of the
snow is never swept and hardened and polished as elsewhere: it was
now a mass of the hardest and smallest snow crystals, to pull through
which in cold temperatures was just like pulling through sand. I have
spoken elsewhere of Barrier surfaces, and how, when the cold is very
great, sledge runners cannot melt the crystal points but only advance by
rolling them over and over upon one another. That was the surface we
met on this journey, and in soft snow the effect is accentuated. Our feet
were sinking deep at every step.

And so when we tried to start on 30 June we found we could not
move both sledges together. There was nothing for it but to take one on
at a time and come back for the other. This has often been done in
daylight when the only risks run are those of blizzards which may
spring up suddenly and obliterate tracks. Now in darkness it was more
complicated. From 11 a.m. to 3 p.m. there was enough light to see the
big holes made by our feet, and we took on one sledge, trudged back in
our tracks, and brought on the second. Bowers used to toggle and
untoggle our harnesses when we changed sledges. Of course in this
relay work we covered three miles in distance for every one mile
forward, and even the single sledges were very hard pulling. When we

lunched the temperature was –61°. After lunch the little light had gone, and we carried a naked lighted candle back with us when we went to find our second sledge. It was the weirdest kind of procession, three frozen men and a little pool of light. Generally we steered by Jupiter, and I never see him now without recalling his friendship in those days.

We were very silent, it was not very easy to talk: but sledging is always a silent business. I remember a long discussion which began just now about cold snaps—was this the normal condition of the Barrier, or was it a cold snap?—what constituted a cold snap? The discussion lasted about a week. Do things slowly, always slowly, that was the burden of Wilson's leadership: and every now and then the question, Shall we go on? and the answer Yes. 'I think we are all right as long as our appetites are good,' said Bill. Always patient, self-possessed, unruffled, he was the only man on earth, as I believe, who could have led this journey.

That day we made 31/4 miles, and travelled 10 miles to do it. The temperature was –66° when we camped, and we were already pretty badly iced up. That was the last night I lay (I had written slept) in my big reindeer bag without the lining of eider-down which we each carried. For me it was a very bad night: a succession of shivering fits which I was quite unable to stop, and which took possession of my body for many minutes at a time until I thought my back would break, such was the strain placed upon it. They talk of chattering teeth: but when your body chatters you may call yourself cold. I can only compare the strain to that which I have been unfortunate enough to see in a case of lock-jaw. One of my big toes was frost-bitten, but I do not know for how long. Wilson was fairly comfortable in his smaller bag, and Bowers was snoring loudly. The minimum temperature that night as taken under the sledge was –69°; and as taken on the sledge was –75°. That is a hundred and seven degrees of frost.

We did the same relay work on 1 July, but found the pulling harder still; and it was all that we could do to move the one sledge forward. From now onwards Wilson and I, but not to the same extent as Bowers, experienced a curious optical delusion when returning in our tracks for the second sledge. I have said that we found our way back by the light of a candle, and we found it necessary to go back in our same footprints. These holes became to our tired brains not depressions but elevations: hummocks over which we stepped, raising our feet painfully and draggingly. And then we remembered, and said what fools we were, and for a while we compelled ourselves to walk through these phantom hills. But it was no lasting good, and as the days passed we realized that we must suffer this absurdity, for we could not do anything else. But of course it took it out of us.

During these days the blisters on my fingers were very painful. Long before my hands were frost-bitten, or indeed anything but cold, which was of course a normal thing, the matter inside these big blisters, which rose all down my fingers with only a skin between them, was frozen into ice. To handle the cooking gear or the food bags was agony; to start the primus was worse; and when, one day, I was able to prick six or seven of the blisters after supper and let the liquid matter out, the relief was very great. Every night after that I treated such others as were ready in the same way until they gradually disappeared. Sometimes it was difficult not to howl.

I *did* want to howl many times every hour of these days and nights, but I invented a formula instead, which I repeated to myself continually. Especially, I remember, it came in useful when at the end of the march with my feet frost-bitten, my heart beating slowly, my vitality at its lowest ebb, my body solid with cold, I used to seize the shovel and go on digging snow on to the tent skirting while the cook inside was trying to light the primus. 'You've got it in the neck—stick it—stick it—you've got it in the neck,' was the refrain, and I wanted every little bit of encouragement it would give me: then I would find myself repeating 'Stick it—stick it—stick it—stick it,' and then 'You've got it in the neck.' One of the joys of summer sledging is that you can let your mind wander thousands of miles away for weeks and weeks. Oates used to provision his little yacht (there was a pickled herring he was going to have): I invented the compactest little revolving bookcase which was going to hold not books, but pemmican and chocolate and biscuit and cocoa and sugar, and have a cooker on the top, and was going to stand always ready to quench my hunger when I got home: and we visited restaurants and theatres and grouse moors, and we thought of a pretty girl; or girls, and. . . . But now that was all impossible. Our conditions forced themselves upon us without pause:

it was not possible to think of anything else. We got no respite. I found it best to refuse to let myself think of the past or the future—to live only for the job of the moment, and to compel myself to think only how to do it most efficiently. Once you let yourself imagine. . . .

This day also (1 July) we were harassed by a nasty little wind which blew in our faces. The temperature was −66°, and in such temperatures the effect of even the lightest airs is blighting, and immediately freezes any exposed part. But we all fitted the bits of wind-proof lined with fur, which we had made in the hut, across our balaclavas in front of our noses and these were of the greatest comfort. They formed other places upon which our breath could freeze, and the lower parts of our faces were soon covered with solid sheets of ice, which was in itself an additional protection. This was a normal and not uncomfortable condition during the journey: the hair on our faces kept the ice away from the skin, and for myself I would rather have the ice than be without it, until I want to get my balaclava off to drink my hoosh. We only made 21/4 miles, and it took 8 hours.

It blew force 3 that night with a temperature of −65.2°, and there was some drift. This was pretty bad, but luckily the wind dropped to a light breeze by the time we were ready to start the next morning (2 July). The temperature was then −60°, and continued so all day, falling lower in the evening. At 4 p.m. we watched a bank of fog form over the peninsula to our left and noticed at the same time that our frozen mitts thawed out on our hands, and the outlines of the land as shown by the stars became obscured. We made 21/2 miles with the usual relaying, and camped at 8 p.m. with the temperature −65°. It really was a terrible march, and parts of both my feet were frozen at lunch. After supper I pricked six or seven of the worst blisters, and the relief was considerable.

I have met with amusement people who say, 'Oh, we had minus fifty temperatures in Canada; they didn't worry *me*,' or 'I've been down to minus sixty something in Siberia.' And then you find that they had nice dry clothing, a nice night's sleep in a nice aired bed, and had just walked out after lunch for a few minutes from a nice warm hut or an overheated train. And they look back upon it as an experience to be remembered. Well of course as an experience of cold this can only be compared to eating a vanilla ice with hot chocolate cream after an excellent dinner at Claridge's. But in our present state we began to look upon minus fifties as a luxury which we did not often get.

That evening, for the first time, we discarded our naked candle in favour of the rising moon. We had started before the moon on purpose, but as we shall see she gave us little light. However, we owed our escape from a very sticky death to her on one occasion.

It was a little later on when we were among crevasses, with Terror above us, but invisible, somewhere on our left, and the Barrier pressure on our right. We were quite lost in the darkness, and only knew that we were running downhill, the sledge almost catching our heels. There had been no light all day, clouds obscured the moon, we had not seen her since yesterday. And quite suddenly a little patch of clear sky drifted, as it were, over her face, and she showed us three paces ahead a great crevasse with just a shining icy lid not much thicker than glass. We should all have walked into it, and the sledge would certainly have followed us down. After that I felt we had a chance of pulling through: God could not be so cruel as to have saved us just to prolong our agony.

But at present we need not worry about crevasses; for we had not reached the long stretch where the moving Barrier, with the weight of many hundred miles of ice behind it, comes butting up against the slopes of Mount Terror, itself some eleven thousand feet high. Now we were still plunging ankle-deep in the mass of soft sandy snow which lies in the windless area. It seemed to have no bottom at all, and since the snow was much the same temperature as the air, our feet, as well as our bodies, got colder and colder the longer we marched: in ordinary sledging you begin to warm up after a quarter of an hour's pulling, here it was just the reverse. Even now I find myself unconsciously kicking the toes of my right foot against the heels of my left: a habit I picked up on this journey by doing it every time we halted. Well no. Not always. For there was one halt when we just lay on our backs and gazed up into the sky, where, so the others said, there was blazing the most wonderful aurora they had ever seen. I did not see it, being so near-sighted and unable to wear spectacles owing to the cold. The aurora was always before us as we travelled east, more beautiful than any seen by previous expeditions wintering in McMurdo Sound, where Erebus must have hidden the most brilliant displays. Now most of the sky was covered with swinging, swaying curtains which met in a great whirl overhead: lemon yellow, green and orange.

The minimum this night was −65°, and during 3 July it ranged between −52° and −58°. We got forward only 21/2 miles, and by this time I had silently made up my mind that we had not the ghost of a chance of reaching the penguins. I am sure that Bill was having a very bad time these nights, though it was an impression rather than anything else, for he never said so. We knew we did sleep, for we heard one another snore, and also we used to have dreams and nightmares; but we had little consciousness of it, and we were now beginning to drop off when we halted on the march.

Our sleeping-bags were getting really bad by now, and already it took a long time to thaw a way down into them at night. Bill spread his in the middle, Bowers was on his right, and I was on his left. Always he insisted that I should start getting my legs into mine before *he* started: we were rapidly cooling down after our hot supper, and this was very unselfish of him. Then came seven shivering hours and first thing on getting out of our sleeping-bags in the morning we stuffed our personal gear into the mouth of the bag before it could freeze: this made a plug which when removed formed a frozen hole for us to push into as a start in the evening.

We got into some strange knots when trying to persuade our limbs into our bags, and suffered terribly from cramp in consequence. We would wait and rub, but directly we tried to move again down it would come and grip our legs in a vice. We also, especially Bowers, suffered agony from cramp in the stomach. We let the primus burn on after supper now for a time—it was the only thing which kept us going—and when one who was holding the primus was seized with cramp we hastily took the lamp from him until the spasm was over. It was horrible to see Birdie's stomach cramp sometimes: he certainly got it much worse than Bill or I. I suffered a lot from heartburn, especially in my bag at nights: we were eating a great proportion of fat and this was probably the cause. Stupidly I said nothing about it for a long time. Later when Bill found out, he soon made it better with the medical case.

Birdie always lit the candle in the morning—so called, and this was an heroic business. Moisture collected on our matches if you looked at them. Partly I suppose it was bringing them from outside into a comparatively warm tent; partly from putting boxes into pockets in our clothing. Sometimes it was necessary to try four or five boxes before a match struck. The temperature of the boxes and matches was about a hundred degrees of frost, and the smallest touch of the metal on naked flesh caused a frost-bite. If you wore mitts you could scarcely feel anything—especially since the tips of our fingers were already very callous. To get the first light going in the morning was a beastly cold business, made worse by having to make sure that it was at last time to get up. Bill insisted that we must lie in our bags seven hours every night.

In civilization men are taken at their own valuation because there are so many ways of concealment, and there is so little time, perhaps even so little understanding. Not so down South. These two men went through the Winter Journey and lived: later they went through the Polar Journey and died. They were gold, pure, shining, unalloyed. Words cannot express how good their companionship was.

Through all these days, and those which were to follow, the worst I suppose in their dark severity that men have ever come through alive, no single hasty or angry word passed their lips. When, later, we were sure, so far as we can be sure of anything, that we must die, they were cheerful, and so far as I can judge their songs and cheery words were quite unforced. Nor were they ever flurried, though always as quick as the conditions would allow in moments of emergency. It is hard that often such men must go first when others far less worthy remain.

There are those who write of Polar Expeditions as though the whole thing was as easy as possible. They are trusting, I suspect, in a public who will say, 'What a fine fellow this is! we know what horrors he has endured, yet see, how little he makes of all his difficulties and hard-ships.' Others have gone to the opposite extreme. I do not know that there is any use in trying to make a $-18°$ temperature appear formidable to an uninitiated reader by calling it fifty degrees of frost. I want to do neither of these things. I am not going to pretend that this was anything but a ghastly journey, made bearable and even pleasant to look back upon by the qualities of my two companions who have gone. At the same time I have no wish to make it appear more horrible than it actually was: the reader need not fear that I am trying to exaggerate.

During the night of 3 July the temperature dropped to –65°, but in the morning we wakened (we really did wake that morning) to great relief. The temperature was only –27° with the wind blowing some 15 miles an hour with steadily falling snow. It only lasted a few hours, and we knew it must be blowing a howling blizzard outside the windless area in which we lay, but it gave us time to sleep and rest, and get thoroughly thawed, and wet, and warm, inside our sleeping-bags. To me at any rate this modified blizzard was a great relief, though we all knew that our gear would be worse than ever when the cold came back. It was quite impossible to march. During the course of the day the temperature dropped to –44°: during the following night to –54°.

The soft new snow which had fallen made the surface the next day (5 July) almost impossible. We relayed as usual, and managed to do eight hours' pulling, but we got forward only 11/2 miles. The temperature ranged between –55° and –61°, and there was at one time a considerable breeze, the effect of which was paralysing. There was the great circle of a halo round the moon with a vertical shaft, and mock moons. We hoped that we were rising on to the long snow cape which marks the beginning of Mount Terror. That night the temperature was –75°; at breakfast –70°; at noon nearly –77°. The day lives in my memory as that on which I found out that records are not worth making. The thermometer as swung by Bowers after lunch at 5.51 p.m. registered –77.5°, which is 1091/2 degrees of frost, and is I suppose as cold as any one will want to endure in darkness and iced-up gear and clothes. The lowest temperature recorded by a *Discovery* Spring Journey party was –67.7°,* and in those days fourteen days was a long time for a Spring Party to be away sledging, and they were in daylight. This was our tenth day out and we hoped to be away for six weeks.

Luckily we were spared wind. Our naked candle burnt steadily as we trudged back in our tracks to fetch our other sledge, but if we touched

---

* The thermometer which registered -77° at the Winter Quarters of H.M.S. *Alert* on 4 March 1876 is preserved by Royal Geographical Society. I do not know whether it was screened.

metal for a fraction of a second with naked fingers we were frost-bitten. To fasten the strap buckles over the loaded sledge was difficult: to handle the cooker, or mugs, or spoons, the primus or oil can was worse. How Bowers managed with the meteorological instruments I do not know, but the meteorological log is perfectly kept. Yet as soon as you breathed near the paper it was covered with a film of ice through which the pencil would not bite.

To handle rope was always cold and in these very low temperatures dreadfully cold work. The toggling up of our harnesses to the sledge we were about to pull, the untoggling at the end of the stage, the lashing up of our sleeping-bags in the morning, the fastening of the cooker to the top of the instrument box, were bad, but not nearly so bad as the smaller lashings which were now strings of ice. One of the worst was round the weekly food bag, and those round the pemmican, tea and butter bags inside were thinner still. But the real devil was the lashing of the tent door: it was like wire, and yet had to be tied tight. If you had to get out of the tent during the seven hours spent in our sleeping-bags you must tie a string as stiff as a poker, and re-thaw your way into a bag already as hard as a board. Our paraffin was supplied at a flash point suitable to low temperatures and was only a little milky: it was very difficult to splinter bits off the butter.

The temperature that night was −75.8°, and I will not pretend that it did not convince me that Dante was right when he placed the circles of ice below the circles of fire. Still we slept sometimes, and always we lay for seven hours. Again and again Bill asked us how about going back, and always we said no. Yet there was nothing I should have liked better: I was quite sure that to dream of Cape Crozier was the wildest lunacy. That day we had advanced 11/2 miles by the utmost labour, and the usual relay work. This was quite a good march—and Cape Crozier is 67 miles from Cape Evans!

More than once in my short life I have been struck by the value of the man who is blind to what appears to be a common-sense certainty: he achieves the impossible. We never spoke our thoughts: we discussed the Age of Stone which was to come, when we built our cosy warm rock hut on the slopes of Mount Terror, and ran our stove with penguin blubber, and pickled little Emperors in warmth and dryness. We were quite intelligent people, and we must all have known that we were not going to see the penguins and that it was folly to go forward. And yet with quiet perseverance, in perfect friendship, almost with gentleness those two men led on. I just did what I was told.

It is desirable that the body should work, feed and sleep at regular hours, and this is too often forgotten when sledging. But just now we found we were unable to fit 8 hours marching and 7 hours in our sleeping-bags into a 24-hour day: the routine camp work took more than 9 hours, such were the conditions. We therefore ceased to observe the quite imaginary difference between night and day, and it was noon on Friday (7 July) before we got away. The temperature was –68° and there was a thick white fog: generally we had but the vaguest idea where we were, and we camped at 10 p.m. after managing 13/4 miles for the day. But what a relief. Instead of labouring away, our hearts were beating more naturally: it was easier to camp, we had some feeling in our hands, and our feet had not gone to sleep. Birdie swung the thermometer and found it only –55°. 'Now if we tell people that to get only 87 degrees of frost an be an enormous relief they simply won't believe us,' I remember saying. Perhaps you won't, but it was, all the same: and I wrote that night: 'There is something after all rather good in doing something never done before.' Things were looking up, you see.

Our hearts were doing very gallant work. Towards the end of the march they were getting beaten and were finding it difficult to pump the blood out to our extremities. There were few days that Wilson and I did not get some part of our feet frost-bitten. As we camped, I suspect our hearts were beating comparatively slowly and weakly. Nothing could be done until a hot drink was ready—tea for lunch, hot water for supper. Directly we started to drink then the effect was wonderful: it was, said Wilson, like putting a hot-water bottle against your heart. The beats became very rapid and strong and you felt the warmth travelling outwards and downwards. Then you got your foot-gear off—puttees (cut in half and wound round the bottom of the trousers), finnesko, saennegrass, hair socks, and two pairs of woollen socks. Then you nursed back your feet and tried to believe you were glad—a frost-bite does not hurt until it begins to thaw. Later came the blisters, and then the chunks of dead skin.

Bill was anxious. It seems that Scott had twice gone for a walk with him during the Winter, and tried to persuade him not to go, and only finally consented on condition that Bill brought us all back unharmed: we were Southern Journey men. Bill had a tremendous respect for Scott, and later when we were about to make an effort to get back home over the Barrier, and our case was very desperate, he was most anxious to leave no gear behind at Cape Crozier, even the scientific gear which could be of no use to us and of which we had plenty more at the hut. 'Scott will never forgive me if I leave gear behind,' he said. It is a good sledging principle, and the party which does not follow it, or which leaves some of its load to be fetched in later is seldom a good one: but it is a principle which can be carried to excess.

And now Bill was feeling terribly responsible for both of us. He kept on saying that he was sorry, but he had never dreamed it was going to be as bad as this. He felt that having asked us to come he was in some way chargeable with our troubles. When leaders have this kind of feeling about their men they get much better results, if the men are good: if men are bad or even moderate they will try and take advantage of what they consider to be softness.

The temperature on the night of 7 July was −59°.

On 8 July we found the first sign that we might be coming to an end of this soft, powdered, arrowrooty snow. It was frightfully hard pulling; but every now and then our finnesko pierced a thin crust before they sank right in. This meant a little wind, and every now and then our feet came down on a hard slippery patch under the soft snow. We were surrounded by fog which walked along with us, and far above us the moon was shining on its roof. Steering was as difficult as the pulling, and four hours of the hardest work only produced 11/4 miles in the morning, and three more hours 1 mile in the afternoon—and the temperature was −57° with a breeze—horrible!

In the early morning of the next day snow began to fall and the fog was dense: when we got up we could see nothing at all anywhere. After the usual four hours to get going in the morning we settled that it was impossible to relay, for we should never be able to track ourselves back to the second sledge. It was with very great relief that we found we could move both sledges together, and I think this was mainly due to the temperature which had risen to –36°.

This was our fourth day of fog in addition to the normal darkness, and we knew we must be approaching the land. It would be Terror Point, and the fog is probably caused by the moist warm air coming up from the sea through the pressure cracks and crevasses; for it is supposed that the Barrier here is afloat.

I wish I could take you on to the great Ice Barrier some calm evening when the sun is just dipping in the middle of the night and show you the autumn tints on Ross Island. A last look round before turning in, a good day's march behind, enough fine fat pemmican inside you to make you happy, the homely smell of tobacco from the tent, a pleasant sense of soft fur and the deep sleep to come. And all the softest colours God has made are in the snow; on Erebus to the west, where the wind can scarcely move his cloud of smoke; and on Terror to the east, not so high, and more regular in form. How peaceful and dignified it all is.

That was what you might have seen four months ago had you been out on the Barrier plain. Low down on the extreme right or east of the land there was a black smudge of rock peeping out from great snow-drifts: that was the Knoll, and close under it were the cliffs of Cape Crozier, the Knoll looking quite low and the cliffs invisible, although they are eight hundred feet high, a sheer precipice falling to the sea.

It is at Cape Crozier that the Barrier edge, which runs for four hundred miles as an ice-cliff up to 200 feet high, meets the land. The Barrier is moving against this land at a rate which is sometimes not much less than a mile in a year. Perhaps you can imagine the chaos which it piles up: there are pressure ridges compared to which the waves of the sea are like a ploughed field. These are worst at Cape Crozier itself, but they extend all along the southern slopes of Mount Terror, running parallel with the land, and the disturbance which Cape Crozier makes is apparent at Corner Camp some forty miles back on the Barrier in the crevasses we used to find and the occasional ridges we had to cross.

In the *Discovery* days the pressure just where it hit Cape Crozier formed a small bay, and on the sea-ice frozen in this bay the men of the

Discovery found the only Emperor penguin rookery which had ever been seen. The ice here was not blown out by the blizzards which cleared the Ross Sea, and open water or open leads were never far away. This gave the Emperors a place to lay their eggs and an opportunity to find their food. We had therefore to find our way along the pressure to the Knoll, and thence penetrate *through* the pressure to the Emperors' Bay. And we had to do it in the dark.

Terror Point, which we were approaching in the fog, is a short twenty miles from the Knoll, and ends in a long snow-tongue running out into the Barrier. The way had been travelled a good many times in *Discovery* days and in daylight, and Wilson knew there was a narrow path, free from crevasses, which skirted along between the mountain and the pressure ridges running parallel to it. But it is one thing to walk along a corridor by day, and quite another to try to do so at night, especially when there are no walls by which you can correct your course—only crevasses. Anyway, Terror Point must be somewhere close to us now, and vaguely in front of us was that strip of snow, neither Barrier nor mountain, which was our only way forward.

We began to realize, now that our eyes were more or less out of action, how much we could do with our feet and ears. The effect of walking in finnesko is much the same as walking in gloves, and you get a sense of touch which nothing else except bare feet could give you. Thus we could feel every small variation in surface, every crust through which our feet broke, every hardened patch below the soft snow. And soon we began to rely more and more upon the sound of our footsteps to tell us whether we were on crevasses or solid ground. From now onwards we were working among crevasses fairly constantly. I loathe them in full daylight when much can be done to avoid them, and when if you fall into them you can at any rate see where the sides are, which way they run and how best to scramble out; when your companions can see how to stop the sledge to which you are all attached by your harness; how most safely to hold the sledge when stopped, how, if you are dangling fifteen feet down in a chasm, to work above you to get you up to the surface again. And then our clothes were generally something like clothes. Even under the ideal conditions of good light, warmth and no wind, crevasses are beastly, whether you are pulling over a level and uniform snow surface, never knowing what moment will find you dropping into some bottomless pit, or whether you are rushing for the Alpine rope and the sledge, to help some companion who has disappeared. I dream sometimes now of bad days we had on the Beardmore and elsewhere, when men were dropping through to be caught up and hang at the full length of the harnesses and toggles many times in an hour. On the same sledge as myself on the Beardmore one man went down once head first, and another eight times to the length of his harness in 25 minutes. And always you wondered whether your harness was going to hold when the jerk came. But those days were a Sunday School treat compared to our days of blind-man's-buff with the Emperor penguins among the crevasses of Cape Crozier.

Our troubles were greatly increased by the state of our clothes. If we had been dressed in lead we should have been able to move our arms and necks and heads more easily than we could now. If the same amount of icing had extended to our legs I believe we should still be there, standing unable to move: but happily the forks of our trousers still remained movable. To get into our canvas harness was the most absurd business. Quite in the early days of our journey we met with this difficulty, and somewhat foolishly decided not to take off our harness for lunch. The harnesses thawed in the tent, and froze back as hard as boards. Likewise our clothing was hard as boards and stuck out from our bodies in every imaginable fold and angle. To fit one board over the other required the united efforts of the would-be wearer and his two companions, and the process had to be repeated for each one of us twice a day. Goodness knows how long it took; but it cannot have been less than five minutes' thumping at each man.

As we approached Terror Point in the fog we sensed that we had risen and fallen over several rises. Every now and then we felt hard slippery snow under our feet. Every now and then our feet went through crusts in the surface. And then quite suddenly, vague, indefinable, monstrous, there loomed a something ahead. I remember having a feeling as of ghosts about as we untoggled our harnesses from the sledge, tied them together, and thus roped walked upwards on that ice. The moon was showing a ghastly ragged mountainous edge above us in the fog, and as we rose we found that we were on a pressure ridge. We stopped, looked at one another, and then *bang*—right under our feet. More bangs, and creaks and groans; for that ice was moving and splitting like glass. The cracks went off all round us, and some of them ran along for hundreds of yards. Afterwards we got used to it, but at first the effect was very jumpy. From first to last during this journey we had plenty of variety and none of that monotony which is inevitable in sledging over long distances of Barrier in summer. Only the long shivering fits following close one after the other all the time we lay in our dreadful sleeping-bags, hour after hour and night after night in those temperatures—they were as monotonous as could be. Later we got frost-bitten even as we lay in our sleeping-bags. Things are getting pretty bad when you get frost-bitten in your bag.

There was only a glow where the moon was; we stood in a moonlit fog, and this was sufficient to show the edge of another ridge ahead, and yet another on our left. We were utterly bewildered. The deep booming of the ice continued, and it may be that the tide has something to do with this, though we were many miles from the ordinary coastal ice. We went back, toggled up to our sledges again and pulled in what we thought was the right direction, always with that feeling that the earth may open underneath your feet which you have in crevassed areas. But all we found were more mounds and banks of snow and ice, into which we almost ran before we saw them. We were clearly lost. It was near midnight, and I wrote, 'it may be the pressure ridges or it may be Terror, it is impossible to say,—and I should think it is impossible to move till it clears. We were steering N.E. when we got here and returned S.W. till we seemed to be in a hollow and camped.'

The temperature had been rising from –36° at 11 a.m. and it was now –27°; snow was falling and nothing whatever could be seen. From under the tent came noises as though some giant was banging a big empty tank. All the signs were for a blizzard, and indeed we had not long finished our supper and were thawing our way little by little into our bags when the wind came away from the south. Before it started we got a glimpse of black rock, and knew we must be in the pressure ridges where they nearly join Mount Terror.

It is with great surprise that in looking up the records I find that blizzard lasted three days, the temperature and wind both rising till it was +9° and blowing force 9 on the morning of the second day (11 July). On the morning of the third day (12 July) it was blowing storm force (10). The temperature had thus risen over eighty degrees.

It was not an uncomfortable tune. Wet and warm, the risen temperature allowed all our ice to turn to water, and we lay steaming and beautifully liquid, and wondered sometimes what we should be like when our gear froze up once more. But we did not do much wondering, I suspect: we slept. From that point of view these blizzards were a perfect Godsend.

We also revised our food rations. From the moment we started to prepare for this journey we were asked by Scott to try certain experiments in view of the Plateau stage of the Polar Journey the following summer. It was supposed that the Plateau stage would be the really rough part of the Polar Journey, and no one then dreamed that harder conditions could be found in the middle of the Barrier in March than on the Plateau, ten thousand feet higher, in February. In view of the extreme conditions we knew we must meet on this winter journey, far harder of course in point of weather than anything experienced on the Polar Journey, we had determined to simplify our food to the last degree. We only brought pemmican, biscuit, butter and tea; and tea is not a food, only a pleasant stimulant, and hot: the pemmican was excellent and came from Beauvais, Copenhagen.

The immediate advantage of this was that we had few food bags to handle for each meal. If the air temperature is 100 degrees of frost, then everything in the air is about 100 degrees of frost too. You have only to untie the lashings of one bag in a −70° temperature, with your feet frozen and your fingers just nursed back after getting a match to strike for the candle (you will have tried several boxes—metal), to realize this as an advantage.

The immediate and increasingly pressing disadvantage is that you have no sugar. Have you ever had a craving for sugar which never leaves you, even when asleep? It is unpleasant. As a matter of fact the craving for sweet things never seriously worried us on this journey, and there must have been some sugar in our biscuits which gave a pleasant sweetness to our midday tea or nightly hot water when broken up and soaked in it. These biscuits were specially made for us by Huntley and Palmer: their composition was worked out by Wilson and that firm's chemist, and is a secret. But they are probably the most satisfying biscuit ever made, and I doubt whether they can be improved upon. There were two kinds, called Emergency and Antarctic, but there was I think little difference between them except in the baking. A well-baked biscuit was good to eat when sledging if your supply of food was good: but if you were very hungry an underbaked one was much preferred.

By taking individually different quantities of biscuit, pemmican and butter we were able roughly to test the proportions of proteins, fats and carbohydrates wanted by the human body under such extreme circumstances. Bill was all for fat, starting with 8 oz. butter, 12 oz. pemmican and only 12 oz. biscuit a day. Bowers told me he was going for proteids, 16 oz. pemmican and 16 oz. biscuit, and suggested I should go the whole hog on carbohydrates. I did not like this, since I knew I should want more fat, but the rations were to be altered as necessary during the journey, so there was no harm in trying. So I started with 20 oz. of biscuit and 12 oz. of pemmican a day.

Bowers was all right (this was usual with him), but he did not eat all his extra pemmican. Bill could not eat all his extra butter, but was satisfied. I got hungry, certainly got more frost-bitten than the others, and wanted more fat. I also got heartburn. However, before taking more fat I increased my biscuits to 24 oz., but this did not satisfy me; I wanted fat. Bill and I now took the same diet, he giving me 4 oz. of butter which he could not eat, and I giving him 4 oz. of biscuit which did not satisfy my wants. We both therefore had 12 oz. pemmican, 16 oz. biscuit and 4 oz. butter a day, but we did not always finish our butter. This is an extremely good ration, and we had enough to eat during most of this journey. We certainly could not have faced the conditions without.

I will not say that I was entirely easy in my mind as we lay out that blizzard somewhere off Terror Point; I don't know how the others were feeling. The unearthly banging going on underneath us may have had something to do with it. But we were quite lost in the pressure and it might be the deuce and all to get out in the dark. The wind eddied and swirled quite out of its usual straightforward way, and the tent got badly snowed up: our sledge had disappeared long ago. The position was not altogether a comfortable one.

Tuesday night and Wednesday it blew up to force 10, temperature from −7° to +2°. And then it began to modify and get squally. By 3 a.m. on Thursday (13 July) the wind had nearly ceased, the temperature was falling and the stars were shining through detached clouds. We were soon getting our breakfast, which always consisted of tea, followed by pemmican. We soaked our biscuits in both. Then we set to work to dig out the sledges and tent, a big job taking several hours. At last we got started. In that jerky way in which I was still managing to jot a few sentences down each night as a record, I wrote:

'Did 71/2 miles during day—seems a marvellous run—rose and fell over several ridges of Terror—in afternoon suddenly came on huge crevasse on one of these—we were quite high on Terror—moon saved us walking in—it might have taken sledge and all.'

To do seven miles in a day, a distance which had taken us nearly a week in the past, was very heartening. The temperature was between −20° and −30° all day, and that was good too. When crossing the undulations which ran down out of the mountain into the true pressure ridges on our right we found that the wind which came down off the mountain struck along the top of the undulation, and flowing each way, caused a N.E. breeze on one side and a N.W. breeze on the other. There seemed to be wind in the sky, and the blizzard had not cleared as far away as we should have wished.

During the time through which we had come it was by burning more oil than is usually allowed for cooking that we kept going at all. After each meal was cooked we allowed the primus to burn on for a while and thus warmed up the tent. Then we could nurse back our frozen feet and do any necessary little odd jobs. More often we just sat and nodded for a few minutes, keeping one another from going too deeply to sleep. But it was running away with the oil. We started with 6 one-gallon bins (those tins Scott had criticized), and we had now used four of them. At first we said we must have at least two one-gallon tins with which to go back; but by now our estimate had come down to one full gallon tin, and two full primus lamps. Our sleeping-bags were awful. It took me, even as early in the journey as this, an hour of pushing and thumping and cramp every night to thaw out enough of mine to get into it at all. Even that was not so bad as lying in them when we got there.

Only −35° but 'a very bad night' according to my diary. We got away in good time, but it was a ghastly day and my nerves were quivering at the end, for we could not find that straight and narrow way which led between the crevasses on either hand. Time after time we found we were out of our course by the sudden fall of the ground beneath our feet—in we went and then—'are we too far right?'—nobody knows—'well let's try nearer in to the mountain,' and so forth!

> By hard slogging 23/4 miles this morning—then on in thick gloom which suddenly lifted and we found ourselves under a huge great mountain of pressure ridge looking black in shadow. We went on, bending to the left, when Bill fell and put his arms into a crevasse. We went over this and another, and some time after got somewhere up to the left, and both Bill and I put a foot into a crevasse. We sounded all about and everywhere was hollow, and so we ran the sledge down over it and all was well.*

Once we got right into the pressure and took a longish time to get out again. Bill lengthened his trace out with the Alpine rope now and often afterwards, so he found the crevasses well ahead of us and the sledge: nice for us but not so nice for Bill. Crevasses in the dark do put your nerves on edge.

When we started next morning (15 July) we could see on our left front and more or less on top of us the Knoll, which is a big hill whose precipitous cliffs to seaward form Cape Crozier. The sides of it sloped down towards us, and pressing against its ice-cliffs on ahead were miles and miles of great pressure ridges, along which we had travelled, and which hemmed us in. Mount Terror rose ten thousand feet high on our left, and was connected with the Knoll by a great cup-like drift of wind-polished snow. The slope of this in one place runs gently out on to the

* My own diary.

corridor along which we had sledged, and here we turned and started to pull our sledges up. There were no crevasses, only the great drift of snow, so hard that we used our crampons just as though we had been on ice, and as polished as the china sides of a giant cup which it resembled. For three miles we slogged up, until we were only 150 yards from the moraine shelf where we were going to build our hut of rocks and snow. This moraine was above us on our left, the twin peaks of the Knoll were across the cup on our right; and here, 800 feet up the mountain side, we pitched our last camp.

We had arrived.

What should we call our hut? How soon could we get our clothes and bags dry? How would the blubber stove work? Would the penguins be there? 'It seems too good to be true, 19 days out. Surely seldom has anyone been so wet; our bags hardly possible to get into, our wind-clothes just frozen boxes. Birdie's patent balaclava is like iron—it is wonderful how our cares have vanished.'*

It was evening, but we were so keen to begin that we went straight up to the ridge above our camp, where the rock cropped out from the snow. We found that most of it *was in situ* but that there were plenty of boulders, some gravel, and of course any amount of the icy snow which fell away below us down to our tent, and the great pressure about a mile beyond. Between us and that pressure, as we were to find out afterwards, was a great ice-cliff. The pressure ridges, and the Great Ice Barrier beyond, were at our feet; the Ross Sea edge but some four miles away. The Emperors must be somewhere round that shoulder of the Knoll which hides Cape Crozier itself from our view.

Our scheme was to build an igloo with rock walls, banked up with snow, using a nine-foot sledge as a ridge beam, and a large sheet of green Willesden canvas as a roof. We had also brought a board to form a lintel over the door. Here with the stove, which was to be fed with blubber from the penguins, we were to have a comfortable warm home whence we would make excursions to the rookery perhaps four miles away. Perhaps we would manage to get our tent down to the rookery

* My own diary.

itself and do our scientific work there on the spot, leaving our nice hut for a night or more. That is how we planned it.

That same nightwe started to dig in under a great boulder on the top of the hill, hoping to make this a large part of one of the walls of the hut, but the rock came close underneath and stopped us. We then chose a moderately level piece of moraine about twelve feet away, and just under the level of the top of the hill, hoping that here in the lee of the ridge we might escape a good deal of the tremendous winds which we knew were common. Birdie gathered rocks from over the hill, nothing was too big for him; Bill did the banking up outside while I built the wall with the boulders. The rocks were good, the snow, however, was blown so hard as to be practically ice; a pick made little impression upon it, and the only way was to chip out big blocks gradually with the small shovel. The gravel was scanty, but good when there was any. Altogether things looked very hopeful when we turned in to the tent some 150 yards down the slope, having done about half one of the long walls.*

The view from eight hundred feet up the mountain was magnificent and I got my spectacles out and cleared the ice away time after time to look. To the east a great field of pressure ridges below, looking in the moonlight as if giants had been ploughing with ploughs which made furrows fifty or sixty feet deep: these ran right up to the Barrier edge, and beyond was the frozen Ross Sea, lying flat, white and peaceful as though such things as blizzards were unknown. To the north and north-east the Knoll. Behind us Mount Terror on which we stood, and over all the grey limitless Barrier seemed to cast a spell of cold immensity, vague, ponderous, a breeding-place of wind and drift and darkness. God! What a place!

> There was now little moonlight or daylight, but for the next
> forty-eight hours we used both to their utmost, being up at
> all times by day and night, and often working on when there
> was great difficulty in seeing anything; digging by the light of

* My own diary.

the hurricane lamp. By the end of two days we had the walls built, and banked up to one or two feet from the top; we were to fit the roof cloth close before banking up the rest. The great difficulty in banking was the hardness of the snow, it being impossible to fill in the cracks between the blocks which were more like paving-stones than anything else. The door was in, being a triangular tent doorway, with flaps which we built close in to the walls, cementing it with snow and rocks. The top folded over a plank and the bottom was dug into the ground.*

• • •

Birdie was very disappointed that we could not finish the whole thing that day: he was nearly angry about it, but there was a lot to do yet and we were tired out. We turned out early the next morning (Tuesday 18th) to try and finish the igloo, but it was blowing too hard. When we got to the top we did some digging but it was quite impossible to get the roof on, and we had to leave it. We realized that day that it blew much harder at the top of the slope than where our tent was. It was bitterly cold up there that morning with a wind force 4–5 and a minus thirty temperature.

The oil question was worrying us quite a lot. We were now well in to the fifth of our six tins, and economizing as much as possible, often having only two hot meals a day. We had to get down to the Emperor penguins somehow and get some blubber to run the stove which had been made for us in the hut. The 19th being a calm fine day we started at 9.30, with an empty sledge, two ice-axes, Alpine rope, harnesses and skinning tools.

Wilson had made this journey through the Cape Crozier pressure ridges several times in the *Discovery* days. But then they had daylight, and they had found a practicable way close under the cliffs which at the present moment were between us and the ridges.

As we neared the bottom of the mountain slope, farther to the north

* My own diary.

than we had previously gone, we had to be careful about crevasses, but we soon hit off the edge of the cliff and skirted along it until it petered out on the same level as the Barrier. Turning left handed we headed towards the sea-ice, knowing that there were some two miles of pressure between us and Cape Crozier itself. For about half a mile it was fair going, rounding big knobs of pressure but always managing to keep more or less on the flat and near the ice-cliff which soon rose to a very great height on our left. Bill's idea was to try and keep close under this cliff, along that same *Discovery* way which I have mentioned above. They never arrived there early enough for the eggs in those days: the chicks were hatched. Whether we should now find any Emperors, and if so whether they would have any eggs, was by no means certain.

However, we soon began to get into trouble, meeting several crevasses every few yards, and I have no doubt crossing scores of others of which we had no knowledge. Though we hugged the cliffs as close as possible we found ourselves on the top of the first pressure ridge, separated by a deep gulf from the ice-slope which we wished to reach. Then we were in a great valley between the first and second ridges: we got into huge heaps of ice pressed up in every shape on every side, crevassed in every direction: we slithered over snow-slopes and crawled along drift ridges, trying to get in towards the cliffs. And always we came up against impossible places and had to crawl back. Bill led on a length of Alpine rope fastened to the toggle of the sledge; Birdie was in his harness also fastened to the toggle, and I was in my harness fastened to the rear of the sledge, which was of great use to us both as a bridge and a ladder.

Two or three times we tried to get down the ice-slopes to the comparatively level road under the cliffs, but it was always too great a drop. In that dim light every proportion was distorted; some of the places we actually did manage to negotiate with ice-axes and Alpine rope looked absolute precipices, and there were always crevasses at the bottom if you slipped. On the way back I did slip into one of these and was hauled out by the other two standing on the wall above me.

We then worked our way down into the hollow between the first and second large pressure ridges, and I believe on to the top of the second. The crests here rose fifty or sixty feet. After this I don't know where we went. Our best landmarks were patches of crevasses, sometimes three or four in a few footsteps. The temperatures were lowish (−37°), it was impossible for me to wear spectacles, and this was a tremendous difficulty to me and handicap to the party: Bill would find a crevasse and point it out; Birdie would cross; and then time after time, in trying to step over or climb over on the sledge, I put my feet right into the middle of the cracks. This day I went well in at least six times; once, when we were close to the sea, rolling into and out of one and then down a steep slope until brought up by Birdie and Bill on the rope.

We blundered along until we got into a great cul-de-sac which probably formed the end of the two ridges, where they butted on to the sea-ice. On all sides rose great walls of battered ice with steep snow-slopes in the middle, where we slithered about and blundered into crevasses. To the left rose the huge cliff of Cape Crozier, but we could not tell whether there were not two or three pressure ridges between us and it, and though we tried at least four ways, there was no possibility of getting forward.

And then we heard the Emperors calling.

Their cries came to us from the sea-ice we could not see, but which must have been a chaotic quarter of a mile away. They came echoing back from the cliffs, as we stood helpless and tantalized. We listened and realized that there was nothing for it but to return, for the little light which now came in the middle of the day was going fast, and to be caught in absolute darkness there was a horrible idea. We started back on our tracks and almost immediately I lost my footing and rolled down a slope into a crevasse. Birdie and Bill kept their balance and I clambered back to them. The tracks were very faint and we soon began to lose them. Birdie was the best man at following tracks that I have ever known, and he found them time after time. But at last even he lost them altogether and we settled we must just go ahead. As a matter of fact, we picked them up again, and by then were out of the worst: but we were glad to see the tent.

The next morning (Thursday, 20 June) we started work on the igloo at 3 a.m. and managed to get the canvas roof on in spite of a wind which harried us all that day. Little did we think what that roof had in store for us as we packed it in with snow blocks, stretching it over our second sledge, which we put athwartships across the middle of the longer walls. The windward (south) end came right down to the ground and we tied it securely to rocks before packing it in. On the other three sides we had a good two feet or more of slack all round, and in every case we tied it to rocks by lanyards at intervals of two feet. The door was the difficulty, and for the present we left the cloth arching over the stones, forming a kind of portico. The whole was well packed in and over with slabs of hard snow, but there was no soft snow with which to fill up the gaps between the blocks. However, we felt already that nothing could drag that roof out of its packing, and subsequent events proved that we were right.

It was a bleak job for three o'clock in the morning before breakfast, and we were glad to get back to the tent and a meal, for we meant to have another go at the Emperors that day. With the first glimpse of light we were off for the rookery again.

But we now knew one or two things about that pressure which we had not known twenty-four hours ago; for instance, that there was a lot of alteration since the *Discovery* days and that probably the pressure was bigger. As a matter of fact it has been since proved by photographs that the edges now ran out three-quarters of a mile farther into the sea than they did ten years before. We knew also that if we entered the pressure at the only place where the ice-cliffs came down to the level of the Barrier, as we did yesterday, we could neither penetrate to the rookery nor get in under the cliffs where formerly a possible way had been found. There was only one other thing to do—to go over the cliff. And this was what we proposed to try and do.

Now these ice-cliffs are some two hundred feet high, and I felt uncomfortable, especially in the dark. But as we came back the day before we had noticed at one place a break in the cliffs from which there hung a snow-drift. It *might* be possible to get down that drift.

And so, all harnessed to the sledge, with Bill on a long lead out in front and Birdie and myself checking the sledge behind, we started down the slope which ended in the cliff, which of course we could not see. We crossed a number of small crevasses, and soon we knew we must be nearly there. Twice we crept up to the edge of the cliff with no success, and then we found the slope: more, we got down it without great difficulty and it brought us out just where we wanted to be, between the land cliffs and the pressure.

Then began the most exciting climb among the pressure that you can imagine. At first very much as it was the day before—pulling ourselves and one another up ridges, slithering down slopes, tumbling into and out of crevasses and holes of all sorts, we made our way along under the cliffs which rose higher and higher above us as we neared the black lava precipices which form Cape Crozier itself. We straddled along the top of a snow ridge with a razor-backed edge, balancing the sledge between us as we wriggled: on our right was a drop of great depth with crevasses at the bottom, on our left was a smaller drop also crevassed. We crawled along, and I can tell you it was exciting work in the more than half darkness. At the end was a series of slopes full of crevasses, and finally we got right in under the rock on to moraine, and here we had to leave the sledge.

We roped up, and started to worry along under the cliffs, which had now changed from ice to rock, and rose 800 feet above us. The tumult of pressure which climbed against them showed no order here. Four hundred miles of moving ice behind it had just tossed and twisted those giant ridges until Job himself would have lacked words to reproach their Maker. We scrambled over and under, hanging on with our axes, and cutting steps where we could not find a foothold with our crampons. And always we got towards the Emperor penguins, and it really began to look as if we were going to do it this time, when we came up against a wall of ice which a single glance told us we could never cross. One of the largest pressure ridges had been thrown, end on, against the cliff. We seemed to be stopped, when Bill found a black hole, something like a fox's earth, disappearing into the bowels of the ice. We looked at it: 'Well, here goes!' he said, and put his head in, and disappeared. Bowers likewise. It was a longish way, but quite possible to wriggle along, and presently I found myself looking out of the other side with a deep gully below me, the rock face on one hand and the ice on the other. 'Put your back against the ice and your feet against the rock and lever yourself along,' said Bill, who was already standing on firm ice at the far end in a snow pit. We cut some fifteen steps to get out of that hole. Excited by now, and thoroughly enjoying ourselves, we found the way ahead easier, until the penguins' call reached us again and we stood, three crystallized ragamuffins, above the Emperors' home. They were there all right, and we were going to reach them, but where were all the thousands of which we had heard?

We stood on an ice-foot which was really a dwarf cliff some twelve feet high, and the sea-ice, with a good many ice blocks strewn upon it, lay below. The cliff dropped straight, with a bit of an overhang and no snow-drift. This may have been because the sea had only frozen recently; whatever the reason may have been it meant that we should have a lot of difficulty in getting up again without help. It was decided that someone must stop on the top with the Alpine rope, and clearly that one should be I, for with short sight and fogged spectacles which I could not wear I was much the least useful of the party for the job immediately ahead. Had we had the sledge we could have used it as a ladder, but of course we had left this at the beginning of the moraine miles back.

We saw the Emperors standing all together huddled under the Barrier cliff some hundreds of yards away. The little light was going fast: we were much more excited about the approach of complete darkness and the look of wind in the south than we were about our triumph. After indescribable effort and hardship we were witnessing a marvel of the natural world, and we were the first and only men who had ever done so; we had within our grasp material which might prove of the utmost importance to science: we were turning theories into facts with every observation we made,—and we had but a moment to give.

The disturbed Emperors made a tremendous row, trumpeting with their curious metallic voices. There was no doubt they had eggs, for they tried to shuffle along the ground without losing them off their feet. But when they were hustled a good many eggs were dropped and left lying on the ice, and some of these were quickly picked up by eggless Emperors who had probably been waiting a long time for the opportunity. In these poor birds the maternal side seems to have necessarily swamped the other functions of life. Such is the struggle for existence that they can only live by a glut of maternity, and it would be interesting to know whether such a life leads to happiness or satisfaction.

The men of the *Discovery* found this rookery where we now stood.*

* My own diary.

They made journeys in the early spring but never arrived early enough to get eggs and only found parents and chicks. They concluded that the Emperor was an impossible kind of bird who, for some reason or other, nests in the middle of the Antarctic winter with the temperature anywhere below seventy degrees of frost, and the blizzards blowing, always blowing, against his devoted back. And they found him holding his precious chick balanced upon his big feet, and pressing it maternally, or paternally (for both sexes squabble for the privilege) against a bald patch in his breast. And when at last he simply must go and eat something in the open leads near by, he just puts the child down on the ice, and twenty chickless Emperors rush to pick it up. And they fight over it, and so tear it that sometimes it will die. And, if it can, it will crawl into any ice-crack to escape from so much kindness, and there it will freeze. Likewise many broken and addled eggs were found, and it is clear that the mortality is very great. But some survive, and summer comes; and when a big blizzard is going to blow (they know all about the weather), the parents take the children out for miles across the sea-ice, until they reach the threshold of the open sea. And there they sit until the wind comes, and the swell rises, and breaks that ice-floe off; and away they go in the blinding drift to join the main pack-ice, with a private yacht all to themselves.

You must agree that a bird like this is an interesting beast, and when, seven months ago, we rowed a boat under those great black cliffs, and found a disconsolate Emperor chick still in the down, we knew definitely why the Emperor has to nest in mid-winter. For if a June egg was still without feathers in the beginning of January, the same egg laid in the summer would leave its produce without practical covering for the following winter. Thus the Emperor penguin is compelled to undertake all kinds of hardships because his children insist on developing so slowly, very much as we are tied in our human relationships for the same reason. It is of interest that such a primitive bird should have so long a childhood.

But interesting as the life history of these birds must be, we had not travelled for three weeks to see them sitting on their eggs. We wanted the embryos, and we wanted them as young as possible, and fresh and unfrozen, that specialists at home might cut them into microscopic sections and learn from them the previous history of birds throughout the evolutionary ages. And so Bill and Birdie rapidly collected five eggs, which we hoped to carry safely in our fur mitts to our igloo upon Mount Terror, where we could pickle them in the alcohol we had brought for the purpose. We also wanted oil for our blubber stove, and they killed and skinned three birds—an Emperor weighs up to 61/2 stones.

The Ross Sea was frozen over, and there were no seal in sight. There were only 100 Emperors as compared with 2000 in 1902 and 1903. Bill reckoned that every fourth or fifth bird had an egg, but this was only a rough estimate, for we did not want to disturb them unnecessarily. It is a mystery why there should have been so few birds, but it certainly looked as though the ice had not formed very long. Were these the first arrivals? Had a previous rookery been blown out to sea and was this the beginning of a second attempt? Is this bay of sea-ice becoming unsafe?

Those who previously discovered the Emperors with their chicks saw the penguins nursing dead and frozen chicks if they were unable to obtain a live one. They also found decomposed eggs which they must have incubated after they had been frozen. Now we found that these birds were so anxious to sit on something that some of those which had no eggs were sitting on ice! Several times Bill and Birdie picked up eggs to find them lumps of ice, rounded and about the right size, dirty and hard. Once a bird dropped an ice nest egg as they watched, and again a bird returned and tucked another into itself, immediately forsaking it for a real one, however, when one was offered.

Meanwhile a whole procession of Emperors came round under the cliff on which I stood. The light was already very bad and it was well that my companions were quick in returning: we had to do everything in a great hurry. I hauled up the eggs in their mitts (which we fastened together round our necks with lampwick lanyards) and then the skins, but failed to help Bill at all. 'Pull,' he cried, from the bottom: 'I am pulling,' I said. 'But the line's quite slack down here,' he shouted. And when he had reached the top by climbing up on Bowers's shoulders, and we were both pulling all we knew Birdie's end of the rope was still slack in his hands. Directly we put on a strain the rope cut into the ice edge and jammed—a very common difficulty when working among crevasses. We tried to run the rope over an ice-axe without success, and things began to look serious when Birdie, who had been running about prospecting and had meanwhile put one leg through a crack into the sea, found a place where the cliff did not overhang. He cut steps for himself, we hauled, and at last we were all together on the top—his foot being by now surrounded by a solid mass of ice.

We legged it back as hard as we could go: five eggs in our fur mitts, Birdie with two skins tied to him and trailing behind, and myself with one. We were roped up, and climbing the ridges and getting through the holes was very difficult. In one place where there was a steep rubble and snow slope down I left the ice-axe half-way up; in another it was too dark to see our former ice-axe footsteps, and I could see nothing, and so just let myself go and trusted to luck. With infinite patience Bill said: 'Cherry, you *must* learn how to use an ice-axe.' For the rest of the trip my wind-clothes were in rags.

We found the sledge, and none too soon, and now had three eggs left, more or less whole. Both mine had burst in my mitts: the first I emptied out, the second I left in my mitt to put into the cooker; it never got there, but on the return journey I had my mitts far more easily thawed out than Birdie's (Bill had none) and I believe the grease in the egg did them good. When we got into the hollows under the ridge where we had to cross, it was too dark to do anything but feel our way. We did so over many crevasses, found the ridge and crept over it. Higher up we could see more, but to follow our tracks soon became imposs- ible, and we plugged straight ahead and luckily found the slope down which we had come. All day it had been blowing a nasty cold wind with a temperature between −20° and −30°, which we felt a good deal. Now it began to get worse. The weather was getting thick and things did not look very nice when we started up to find our tent. Soon it was blowing force 4, and soon we missed our way entirely. We got right up above the patch of rocks which marked our igloo and only found it after a good deal of search.

I have heard tell of an English officer at the Dardanelles who was left, blinded, in No Man's Land between the English and Turkish trenches. Moving only at night, and having no sense to tell him which were his own trenches, he was fired at by Turk and English alike as he groped his ghastly way to and from them. Thus he spent days and nights until, one night, he crawled towards the English trenches, to be fired at as usual. 'Oh God! what can I do!' someone heard him say, and he was brought in.

Such extremity of suffering cannot be measured: madness or death may give relief. But this I know: we on this journey were already beginning to think of death as a friend. As we groped our way back that night, sleeples, icy, and dog-tired in the dark and the wind and the drift, a crevasse seemed almost a friendly gift.

'Things must improve,' said Bill next day, 'I think we reached bed-rock last night.' We hadn't, by a long way.

from Scott's Last Expedition:
The Journals
by Robert Falcon Scott

Robert Falcon Scott's (1868–1912) party of five men arrived at the South Pole in January 1912 to discover that the great Norwegian explorer Roald Amundsen and his men had arrived just 21 days before. Disappointed, weary, short of food, the British retraced their steps across a chain of supply depots, set up with the help of support parties who had turned back short of the Pole. Here the polar party has dwindled to four with the death from exhaustion of Petty Officer Edgar Evans.

S*unday, February 18* R 32. Temp. –5.5°. At Shambles Camp. We gave ourselves five hours' sleep at the lower glacier depot after the horrible night, and came on at about three today to this camp, coming fairly easily over the divide. Here with plenty of horsemeat we have had a fine supper, to be followed by others such, and so continue a more plentiful era if we can keep good marches up. New life seems to come with greater food almost immediately, but I am anxious about the Barrier surfaces.

Monday, February 19 Lunch T. –16°. It was late (past noon) before we got away today, as I gave nearly eight hours sleep, and much camp work was done shifting sledges and fitting up new one with mast, etc., packing horsemeat and personal effects. The surface was every bit as bad as I expected, the sun shining brightly on it and its covering of soft loose sandy snow. We have come out about 2′ on the old tracks. Perhaps lucky to have a fine day for this and our camp work, but we shall want wind or change of sliding conditions to do anything on such a surface as we have got. I fear there will not be much change for the next three or four days.

R 33 Temp. −17°. We have struggled out 4.6 miles in a short day over a really terrible surface—it has been like pulling over desert sand, not the least glide in the world. If this goes on we shall have a bad time, but I sincerely trust it is only the result of this windless area close to the coast and that, as we are making steadily outwards, we shall shortly escape it. It is perhaps premature to be anxious about covering distance. In all other respects things are improving. We have our sleeping-bags spread on the sledge and they are drying out, but, above all, we have our full measure of food again. Tonight we had a sort of stew fry of pemmican and horseflesh, and voted it the best hoosh we had ever had on a sledge journey. The absence of poor Evans is a help to the commissariat, but if he had been here in a fit state we might have got along faster. I wonder what is in store for us, with some little alarm at the lateness of the season.

Monday, February 20 R 34. Lunch Temp. −13°; Supper Temp. −15°. Same terrible surface; four hours' hard plodding in morning brought us to our Desolation Camp, where we had the four-day blizzard. We looked for more pony meat, but found none. After lunch we took to ski with some improvement of comfort. Total mileage for day, seven—the ski tracks pretty plain and easily followed this afternoon. We have left another cairn behind. Terribly slow progress, but we hope for better things as we clear the land. There is a tendency to cloud over in the S.E. tonight, which may turn to our advantage. At present our sledge and ski leave deeply ploughed tracks which can be seen winding for miles behind. It is distressing, but as usual trials are forgotten when we camp, and good food is our lot. Pray God we get better travelling as we are not so fit as we were, and the season is advancing apace.

Tuesday, February 21 R 35. Lunch Temp. +91/2 ; Supper Temp. −11°. Gloomy and overcast when we started; a good deal warmer. The marching almost as bad as yesterday. Heavy toiling all day, inspiring gloomiest thoughts at times. Rays of comfort when we picked up tracks and cairns. At lunch we seemed to have missed the way, but an hour or two after we passed the last pony walls, and since, we struck a tent ring, ending the march actually on our old pony-tracks. There is a critical spot here with a long stretch between cairns. If we can tide that over we get on the regular cairn route, and with luck should stick to it; but everything depends on the weather. We never won a march of 81/2 miles with greater difficulty, but we can't go on like this. We are drawing away from the land and perhaps may get better things in a day or two. I devoutly hope so.

Wednesday, February 22 R 36. Supper Temp. −2°. There is little doubt we are in for a rotten critical time going home, and the lateness of the season may make it really serious. Shortly after starting today the wind grew very fresh from the S.E. with strong surface drift. We lost the faint track immediately, though covering ground fairly rapidly. Lunch came without sight of the cairn we had hoped to pass. In the afternoon, Bowers being sure we were too far to the west, steered out. Result, we have passed another pony camp without seeing it. Looking at the map tonight there is no doubt we are too far to the east. With clear weather we ought to be able to correct the mistake, but will the weather get clear? It's a gloomy position, more especially as one sees the same difficulty recurring even when we have corrected this error. The wind is dying down tonight and the sky is clearing in the south, which is hopeful. Meanwhile it is satisfactory to note that such untoward events fail to damp the spirit of the party. Tonight we had a pony hoosh so excellent and filling that one feels really strong and vigorous again.

Thursday, February 23 R 37. Lunch Temp. −9.8°; Supper Temp. −12°. Started in sunshine, wind almost dropped. Luckily Bowers took a round of angles and with help of the chart we fogged out that we must be inside rather than outside tracks. The data were so meagre that it seemed a great responsibility to march out and we were none of us happy about it. But just as we decided to lunch, Bowers' wonderful sharp eyes detected an old double lunch cairn, the theodolite telescope confirmed it, and our spirits rose accordingly. This afternoon we marched on and picked up another cairn; then on and camped only 21/2 miles from the depot. We cannot see it, but, given fine weather, we cannot miss it. We are, therefore, extraordinarily relieved. Covered 8.2 miles in seven hours, showing we can do 10 to 12 on this surface.

Things are again looking up, as we are on the regular line of cairns, with no gaps right home, I hope.

Friday, February 24 Lunch. Beautiful day—too beautiful—an hour after starting loose ice crystals spoiling surface. Saw depot and reached it middle forenoon. Found store in order except shortage oil—shall have to be very saving with fuel—otherwise have ten full days' provision from tonight and shall have less than 70 miles to go. Note from Meares who passed through December 15, saying surface bad; from Atkinson, after fine marching (21/4 days from pony depot), reporting Keohane better after sickness. Short note from Evans, not very cheerful, saying surface bad, temperature high. Think he must have been a little anxious. It is an immense relief to have picked up this depot and, for the time, anxieties are thrust aside. There is no doubt we have been rising steadily since leaving the Shambles Camp. The coastal Barrier descends except where glaciers press out. Undulation still, but flattening out. Surface soft on top, curiously hard below. Great difference now between night and day temperatures. Quite warm as I write in tent. We are on tracks with half-march cairn ahead; have covered 41/2 miles. Poor Wilson has a fearful attack snow blindness consequent on yesterday's efforts. Wish we had more fuel.

   Night Camp R 38 Temp. –17°. A little despondent again. We had a really terrible surface this afternoon and only covered 4 miles. We are on the track just beyond a lunch cairn. It really will be a bad business if we are to have this pulling all through. I don't know what to think, but the rapid closing of the season is ominous. It is great luck having the horsemeat to add to our ration. Tonight we have had a real fine hoosh. It is a race between the season and hard conditions and our fitness and good food.

Saturday, February 25 Lunch Temp. –12°. Managed just six miles this morning. Started somewhat despondent; not relieved when pulling seemed to show no improvement. Bit by bit surface grew better, less sastrugi, more glide, slight following wind for a time. Then we began to travel a little faster. But the pulling is still very hard; undulations disappearing but inequalities remain.

Camp 26 walls about two miles ahead, all tracks in sight—Evans' track very conspicuous. There is something in favour, but the pulling is tiring us, though we are getting into better ski drawing again. Bowers hasn't quite the trick and is a little hurt at my criticisms, but I never doubted his heart. Very much easier—write diary at lunch—excellent meal—now one pannikin very strong tea—four biscuits and butter.

Hope for better things this afternoon, but no improvement apparent. Oh! for a little wind—E. Evans evidently had plenty.

R 39 Temp. –20°. Better march in afternoon. Day yields 11.4 miles— the first double figure of steady dragging for a long time, but it meant and will mean hard work if we can't get a wind to help us. Evans evidently had a strong wind here, S.E. I should think. The temperature goes very low at night now when the sky is clear as at present. As a matter of fact this is wonderfully fine weather—the only drawback the spoiling of the surface and absence of wind. We see all tracks very plain, but the pony walls have evidently been badly drifted up. Some kind people had substituted a cairn at last camp 27. The old cairns do not seem to have suffered much.

Sunday, February 26 Lunch Temp. –17°. Sky overcast at start, but able see tracks and cairn distinct at long distance. Did a little better, 61/2 miles to date. Bowers and Wilson now in front. Find great relief pulling behind with no necessity to keep attention on track. Very cold nights now and cold feet starting march, as day foot-gear doesn't dry at all. We are doing well on our food, but we ought to have yet more. I hope the next depot, now only 50 miles, will find us with enough surplus to open out. The fuel shortage still an anxiety.

R 40 Temp. –21°. Nine hours' solid marching has given us 111/2 miles. Only 43 miles from the next depot. Wonderfully fine weather but cold, very cold. Nothing dries and we get our feet cold too often. We want more food yet and especially more fat. Fuel is woefully short. We can scarcely hope to get a better surface at this season, but I wish we could have some help from the wind, though it might shake us up badly if the temp. didn't rise.

Monday, February 27 Desperately cold last night: –33° when we got up, with −37° minimum. Some suffering from cold feet, but all got good rest. We must open out on food soon. But we have done seven miles this morning and hope for some five this afternoon. Overcast sky and good surface till now, when sun shows again. It is good to be marching the cairns up, but there is still much to be anxious about. We talk of little but food, except after meals. Land disappearing in satisfactory manner. Pray God we have no further set-backs. We are naturally always discussing possibility of meeting dogs, where and when, etc. It is a critical position. We may find ourselves in safety at next depot, but there is a horrid element of doubt.

Camp R 41 Temp. −32°. Still fine clear weather but very cold—absolutely calm tonight. We have got off an excellent march for these days (12.2) and are much earlier than usual in our bags. Thirty-one miles to depot, three days' fuel at a pinch, and six days' food. Things begin to look a little better; we can open out a little on food from tomorrow night, I think.

Very curious surface—soft recent sastrugi which sink underfoot, and between, a sort of flaky crust with large crystals beneath.

Tuesday, February 28 Lunch. Thermometer went below −40° last night; it was desperately cold for us, but we had a fair night. I decided to slightly increase food; the effect is undoubtedly good. Started marching in −32° with a slight north-westerly breeze—blighting. Many cold feet this morning; long time over foot-gear, but we are earlier. Shall camp earlier and get the chance of a good night, if not the reality. Things must be critical till we reach the depot, and the more I think of matters, the more I anticipate their remaining so after that event. Only 241/2 miles from the depot. The sun shines brightly, but there is little warmth in it. There is no doubt the middle of the Barrier is a pretty awful locality.

Camp R 42 Splendid pony hoosh sent us to bed and sleep happily after a horrid day, wind continuing; did 111/2 miles. Temp. not quite so low, but expect we are in for cold night (Temp. −27°).

Wednesday, February 29 Lunch. Cold night. Minimum Temp. −37 .5°; −30° with north-west wind, force four, when we got up. Frightfully cold starting; luckily Bowers and Oates in their last new finnesko; keeping my old ones for present. Expected awful march and for first hour got it. Then things improved and we camped after 51/2 hours marching close to lunch camp—221/2 . Next camp is our depot and it is exactly 13 miles. It ought not to take more than 11/2 days; we pray for another fine one. The oil will just about spin out in that event, and we arrive three clear days' food in hand. The increase of ration has had an enormously beneficial result. Mountains now looking small. Wind still very light from west—cannot understand this wind.

Thursday, March 1 Lunch. Very cold last night—minimum –41.5°. Cold start to march, too, as usual now. Got away at eight and have marched within sight of depot; flag something under three miles away. We did 111/2 yesterday and marched six this morning. Heavy dragging yesterday and very heavy this morning. Apart from sledging considerations the weather is wonderful. Cloudless days and nights and the wind trifling. Worse luck, the light airs come from the north and keep us horribly cold. For this lunch hour the exception has come. There is a bright and comparatively warm sun. All our gear is out drying.

• • •

Friday, March 2 Lunch. Misfortunes rarely come singly. We marched to the [Middle Barrier] depot fairly easily yesterday afternoon, and since that have suffered three distinct blows which have placed us in a bad position. First we found a shortage of oil; with most rigid economy it can scarce carry us to the next depot on this surface [71 miles away]. Second, Titus Oates disclosed his feet, the toes showing very bad indeed, evidently bitten by the late temperatures. The third blow came in the night, when the wind, which we had hailed with some joy, brought dark overcast weather. It fell below –40° in the night, and this morning it tool 11/2 hours to get our foot-gear on, but we got away before eight. We lost cairn and tracks together and made as steady as we could N. by W., but have seen nothing. Worse was to come—the surface is simply awful. In spite of strong wind and full sail we have only done 51/2 miles. We are in a very queer street since there is no doubt we cannot do the extra marches and feel the cold horribly.

Saturday, March 3 Lunch. We picked up the track again yesterday, finding ourselves to the eastward. Did close on 10 miles and things looked a trifle better; but this morning the outlook is blacker than ever. Started well and with good breeze; for an hour made good headway; then the surface grew awful beyond words. The wind drew forward; every circumstance was against us. After 4¼ hours things so bad that we camped, having covered 4½ miles. [R 46.] One cannot consider this a fault of our own—certainly we were pulling hard this morning—it was more than three parts surface which held us back—the wind at strongest, powerless to move the sledge. When the light is good it is easy to see the reason. The surface, lately a very good hard one, is coated with a thin layer of woolly crystals, formed by radiation no doubt. These are too firmly fixed to be removed by the wind and cause impossible friction on the runners. God help us, we can't keep up this pulling, that is certain. Amongst ourselves we are unendingly cheerful, but what each man feels in his heart I can only guess. Putting on foot-gear in the morning is getting slower and slower, therefore every day more dangerous.

Sunday, March 4 Lunch. Things looking very black indeed. As usual we forgot our trouble last night, got into our bags, slept splendidly on good hoosh, woke and had another, and started marching. Sun shining brightly, tracks clear, but surface covered with sandy frost-rime. All the morning we had to pull with all our strength, and in 41/2 hours we covered 31/2 miles. Last night it was overcast and thick, surface bad; this morning sun shining and surface as bad as ever. One has little to hope for except perhaps strong dry wind—an unlikely contingency at this time of year. Under the immediate surface crystals is a hard sastrugi surface, which must have been excellent for pulling a week or two ago. We are about 42 miles from the next depot and have a week's food, but only about three to four days' fuel—we are as economical of the latter as one can possibly be, and we cannot afford to save food and pull as we are pulling. We are in a very tight place indeed, but none of us despondent yet, or at least we preserve every semblance of good cheer, but one's heart sinks as the sledge stops dead at some sastrugi behind which the surface sand lies thickly heaped. For the moment the temperature is on the −20°—an improvement which makes us much more comfortable, but a colder snap is bound to come again soon. I fear that Oates at least will weather such an event very poorly. Providence to our aid! We can expect little from man now except the possibility of extra food at the next depot. It will be real bad if we get there and find the same shortage of oil. Shall we get there? Such a short distance it would have appeared to us on the summit! I don't know what I should do if Wilson and Bowers weren't so determinedly cheerful over things.

Monday, March 5 Lunch. Regret to say going from bad to worse. We got a slant of wind yesterday afternoon, and going on five hours we converted our wretched morning run of three and a half miles into something over nine. We went to bed on a cup of cocoa and pemmican solid with the chill off. (R 47.) The result is telling on all, but mainly on Oates, whose feet are in a wretched condition. One swelled up tremendously last night, and he is very lame this morning. We started march on tea and pemmican as last night—we pretend to prefer the pemmican this way. Marched for five hours this morning over a slightly better surface covered with high moundy sastrugi. Sledge capsized twice; we pulled on foot, covering about 51/2 miles. We are two pony marches and four miles about from our depot. Our fuel dreadfully low and the poor Soldier nearly done. It is pathetic enough because we can do nothing for him; more hot food might do a little, but only a little, I fear. We none of us expected these terribly low temperatures, and of the rest of us Wilson is feeling them most; mainly, I fear, from his self-sacrificing devotion in doctoring Oates' feet. We cannot help each other, each has enough to do to take care of himself. We get cold on the march when the trudging is heavy, and the wind pierces our warm garments. The others, all of them, are unendingly cheerful when in the tent. We mean to see the game through with a proper spirit, but it's tough work to be pulling harder than we ever pulled in our lives for long hours, and to feel that the progress is so slow. One can only say, 'God help us!' and plod on our weary way, cold and very miserable, though outwardly cheerful. We talk of all sorts of subjects in the tent, not much of food now, since we decided to take the risk of running a full ration. We simply couldn't go hungry at this time.

Tuesday, March 6 Lunch. We did a little better with help of wind yesterday afternoon, finishing 91/2 miles for the day, and 27 miles from depot. [R 48.] But this morning things have been awful. It was warm in the night and for the first time during the journey I overslept by more than an hour; then we were slow with foot-gear; then, pulling with all our might (for our lives) we could scarcely advance at rate of a mile an hour; then it grew thick and three times we had to get out of harness to search for tracks. The result is something less than 31/2 miles for the forenoon. The sun is shining now and the wind gone. Poor Oates is unable to pull, sits on the sledge when we are track-searching—he is wonderfully plucky, as his feet must be giving him great pain. He makes no complaint, but his spirits only come up in spurts now, and he grows more silent in the tent. We are making a spirit lamp to try and replace the primus when our oil is exhausted. It will be a very poor substitute and we've not got much spirit. If we could have kept up our nine-mile days we might have got within reasonable distance of the depot before running out, but nothing but a strong wind and good surface can help us now, and though we had quite a good breeze this morning, the sledge came as heavy as lead. If we were all fit I should have hopes of getting through, but the poor Soldier has become a terrible hindrance, though he does his utmost and suffers much I fear.

Wednesday, March 7 A little worse I fear. One of Oates' feet very bad this morning; he is wonderfully brave. We still talk of what we will do together at home.

We only made 61/2 miles yesterday. [R 49.] This morning in 41/2 hours we did just over four miles. We are 16 from our depot. If we only find the correct proportion of food there and this surface continues, we may get to the next depot [Mt Hooper, 72 miles farther] but not to One Ton Camp. We hope against hope that the dogs have been to Mt Hooper; then we might pull through. If there is a shortage of oil again we can have little hope. One feels that for poor Oates the crisis is near, but none of us are improving, though we are wonderfully fit considering the really excessive work we are doing. We are only kept going by good food. No wind this morning till a chill northerly air came ahead. Sun bright and cairns showing up well. I should like to keep the track to the end.

Thursday, March 8 Lunch. Worse and worse in morning; poor Oates' left foot can never last out, and time over foot-gear something awful. Have to wait in night foot-gear for nearly an hour before I start changing, and then am generally first to be ready. Wilson's feet giving trouble now, but this mainly because he gives so much help to others. We did 41/2 miles this morning and are now 81/2 miles from the depot—a ridiculously small distance to feel in difficulties, yet on this surface we know we cannot equal half our old marches, and that for that effort we expend nearly double the energy. The great question is: What shall we find at the depot? If the dogs have visited it we may get along a good distance, but if there is another short allowance of fuel, God help us indeed. We are in a very bad way, I fear, in any case.

Saturday, March 10 Things steadily downhill. Oates' foot worse. He has rare pluck and must know that he can never get through. He asked Wilson if he had a chance this morning, and of course Bill had to say he didn't know. In point of fact he has none. Apart from him, if he went under now, I doubt whether we could get through. With great care we might have a dog's chance, but no more. The weather conditions are awful, and our gear gets steadily more icy and difficult to manage. At the same time of course poor Titus is the greatest handicap. He keeps us waiting in the morning until we have partly lost the warming effect of our good breakfast, when the only wise policy is to be up and away at once; again at lunch. Poor chap! it is too pathetic to watch him; one cannot but try to cheer him up.

Yesterday we marched up the depot, Mt Hooper. Cold comfort. Shortage on our allowance all round. I don't know that anyone is to blame. The dogs which would have been our salvation have evidently failed. Meares had a bad trip home I suppose.

This morning it was calm when we breakfasted, but the wind came from the W.N.W. as we broke camp. It rapidly grew in strength. After travelling for half an hour I saw that none of us could go on facing such conditions. We were forced to camp and are spending the rest of the day in a comfortless blizzard camp, wind quite foul. [R 52.]

Sunday, March 11 Titus Oates is very near the end, one feels. What we or he will do, God only knows. We discussed the matter after breakfast; he is a brave fine fellow and understands the situation, but he practically asked for advice. Nothing could be said but to urge him to march as long as he could. One satisfactory result to the discussion; I practically ordered Wilson to hand over the means of ending our troubles to us, so that any one of us may know how to do so. Wilson had no choice between doing so and our ransacking the medicine case. We have 30 opium tabloids apiece and he is left with a tube of morphine. So far the tragical side of our story. [R 53.]

The sky completely overcast when we started this morning. We could see nothing, lost the tracks, and doubtless have been swaying a good deal since—3.1 miles for the forenoon—terribly heavy dragging—expected it. Know that six miles is about the limit of our endurance now, if we get no help from wind or surfaces. We have seven days' food and should be about 55 miles from One Ton Camp tonight, 6 3 7 = 42, leaving us 13 miles short of our distance, even if things get no worse. Meanwhile the season rapidly advances.

Monday, March 12 We did 6.9 miles yesterday, under our necessary average. Things are left much the same, Oates not pulling much, and now with hands as well as feet pretty well useless. We did four miles this morning in 4 hours 20 min—we may hope for three this afternoon, 7 3 6 = 42. We shall be 47 miles from the depot. I doubt if we can possibly do it. The surface remains awful, the cold intense, and our physical condition running down. God help us! Not a breath of favourable wind for more than a week, and apparently liable to head winds at any moment.

Wednesday, March 14 No doubt about the going downhill, but everything going wrong for us. Yesterday we woke to a strong northerly wind with temp. −37°. Couldn't face it, so remained in camp [R 54] till two, then did 51/4 miles. Wanted to march later, but party feeling the cold badly as the breeze (N.) never took off entirely, and as the sun sank the temp. fell. Long time getting supper in dark. [R 55.]

This morning started with southerly breeze, set sail and passed another cairn at good speed; half-way, however, the wind shifted to W.

by S. or W.S.W., blew through our wind clothes and into our mits. Poor Wilson horribly cold, could [not] get off ski for some time. Bowers and I practically made camp, and when we got into the tent at last we were all deadly cold. Then temp. now midday down –43° and the wind strong. We must go on, but now the making of every camp must be more difficult and dangerous. It must be near the end, but a pretty merciful end. Poor Oates got it again in the foot. I shudder to think what it will be like tomorrow. It is only with greatest pains rest of us keep off frostbites. No idea there could be temperatures like this at this time of year with such winds. Truly awful outside the tent. Must fight it out to the last biscuit, but can't reduce rations.

Friday, March 16 or Saturday 17 Lost track of dates, but think the last correct. Tragedy all along the line. At lunch, the day before yesterday, poor Titus Oates said he couldn't go on; he proposed we should leave him in his sleeping-bag. That we could not do and we induced him to come on, on the afternoon march. In spite of its awful nature for him he struggled on and we made a few miles. At night he was worse and we knew the end had come.

Should this be found I want these facts recorded. Oates' last thoughts were of his mother, but immediately before he took pride in thinking that his regiment would be pleased with the bold way in which he met his death. We can testify to his bravery. He has borne intense suffering for weeks without complaint, and to the very last was able and willing to discuss outside subjects. He did not—would not—give up hope till the very end. He was a brave soul. This was the end. He slept through the night before last, hoping not to wake; but he woke in the morning—yesterday. It was blowing a blizzard. He said, 'I am just going outside and may be some time.' He went out into the blizzard and we have not seen him since.

I take this opportunity of saying that we have stuck to our sick companions to the last. In case of Edgar Evans, when absolutely out of food and he lay insensible, the safety of the remainder seemed to demand his abandonment, but Providence mercifully removed him at this critical moment. He died a natural death, and we did not leave him till two hours after his death. We knew that poor Oates was walking to his death, but though we tried to dissuade him, we knew it was the act of a brave man and an English gentleman. We all hope to meet the end with a similar spirit, and assuredly the end is not far.

I can only write at lunch and then only occasionally. The cold is intense, –40° at midday. My companions are unendingly cheerful, but we are all on the verge of serious frostbites, and though we constantly talk of fetching through I don't think any one of us believes it in his heart.

We are cold on the march now, and at all times except meals. Yesterday we had to lay up for a blizzard and today we move dreadfully slowly. We are at No. 14 pony camp, only two pony marches from One Ton Depot. We leave here our theodolite, a camera, and Oates' sleeping-bags. Diaries, etc., and geological specimens carried at Wilson's special request, will be found with us or on our sledge.

Sunday, March 18 Today, lunch, we are 21 miles from the depot. Ill fortune presses, but better may come. We have had more wind and drift from ahead yesterday; had to stop marching; wind N.W., force four, temp. –35°. No human being could face it, and we are worn out nearly.

My right foot has gone, nearly all the toes—two days ago I was proud possessor of best feet. These are the steps of my downfall. Like an ass I mixed a small spoonful of curry powder with my melted pemmican— it gave me violent indigestion. I lay awake and in pain all night; woke and felt done on the march; foot went and I didn't know it. A very small measure of neglect and have a foot which is not pleasant to contemplate. Bowers takes first place in condition, but there is not much to choose after all. The others are still confident of getting through—or pretend to be—I don't know! We have the last half fill of oil in our primus and a very small quantity of spirit—this alone between us and thirst. The wind is fair for the moment, and that is perhaps a fact to help. The mileage would have seemed ridiculously small on our outward journey.

Monday, March 19 Lunch. We camped with difficulty last night, and were dreadfully cold till after our supper of cold pemmican and biscuit and a half a pannikin of cocoa cooked over the spirit. Then, contrary to expectation, we got warm and all slept well. Today we started in the usual dragging manner. Sledge dreadfully heavy. We are 151/2 miles from the depot and ought to get there in three days. What progress! We have two days' food but barely a day's fuel. All our feet are getting bad—Wilson's best, my right foot worst, left all right. There is no chance to nurse one's feet till we can get hot food into us. Amputation is the least I can hope for now, but will the trouble spread? That is the serious question. The weather doesn't give us a chance—the wind from N. to N.W. and −40° temp. today.

Wednesday, March 21 Got within 11 miles of depot Monday night; had to lay up all yesterday in severe blizzard. [R 60]. Today forlorn hope, Wilson and Bowers going to depot for fuel.

Thursday, March 22 and 23 Blizzard bad as ever—Wilson and Bowers unable to start—tomorrow last chance—no fuel and only one or two of food left—must be near the end. Have decided it shall be natural—we shall march for the depot with or without our effects and die in our tracks.

Thursday, March 29 Since the 21st we have had a continuous gale from W.S.W. and S.W. We had fuel to make two cups of tea apiece and bare food for two days on the 20th. Every day we have been ready to start for our depot 11 miles away, but outside the door of the tent it remains a scene of whirling drift. I do not think we can hope for any better things now. We shall stick it out to the end, but we are getting weaker, of course, and the end cannot be far.

It seems a pity, but I do not think I can write more.

R. Scott

Last entry.

For God's sake look after our people.

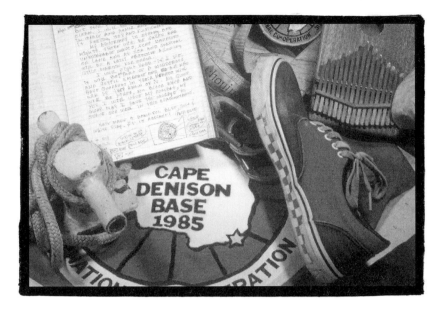

A Simple Quest

by Michael McRae

Most of us manage to resist Antarctica's powerful allure—thanks largely to the sheer difficulty of getting there. Those who do go usually go as sponsored professionals: scientists, explorers, journalists. Mel Fisher's 1985 trip south stands out in part because it wasn't a career move. Michael McRae's (born 1946) story of Fisher's adventure is a fine case study of what happens when stubborn desire meets implacable reality—as it often does in the polar regions.

In 1981, at age 47, Warren Pearson took stock of his life. He was married to a lovely, talented wife. He held a respectable job teaching college biology. He lived an hour from San Francisco in a comfortable home that the bank did not own. He had close friends. And he felt terribly unfulfilled—as if his life were slipping away without his ever having done something genuinely good.

There was only one solution: make a solitary pilgrimage to Antarctica and spend a winter there, alone and cut off.

His first plan was to buy a beat-up C-47 cargo plane and crashland it on a glacier. After some preliminary research, this seemed to be impractical. However, Plan B—to make the trip by sea and use the boat as an icebound base camp—struck him as eminently more feasible. Never mind that he had never captained a boat, that he wore a pacemaker, that such a voyage was without precedent, and that overwintering in Antarctica without a permit is illegal. Pearson began plotting in earnest and in total secrecy. Not even his wife was to know.

Four years later, on January 7, 1985, still having never piloted a boat a day in his life, Warren Pearson left port at Melbourne, Australia, bound for Cape Denison, a point of land near the south magnetic pole. His dreams had been realized.

This is his story. It is a tale of a spiritual quest and a scientific expedition, a test of limits and a grand political statement—and perhaps a way of salvaging a life of quiet desperation. Warren Pearson would appreciate your reading it. After all, he made the journey on behalf of all of us. And all of us, he would like to think, were with him in spirit on that terrible voyage.

Sipping coffee with him in his kitchen, you'd hardly think Warren Pearson the type to go haring off to Antarctica alone in a 37-foot ketch. Though he has an athletic, six-foot frame and a jaunty red beard, he has a gnomishness about him, and a shy reserve in his voice and manner. Warren Pearson is the guy next door: a somewhat colorless, scrupulously precise, rational, industrious man, not especially given to risking his life on foolhardy adventures. But if you listen to his story long enough, the pieces start to fall together, and the whole gambit begins to make perfect sense. Almost.

Pearson and his wife, Barbara, have a life of normalcy in suburban Benicia. He has taught at nearby Diablo Valley College for nearly 20 years. As well as teaching biology, he instructs nurses in human anatomy and has gained a reputation for his deftness in dissecting cadavers. His wife is a psychologist and artist, and teaches art to disturbed adults. Their home, which he built in his spare time, is a vision of California living: a dramatic, all-wood two-story, with a cavernous, mosaic-tiled spa, decks all around, and a magnificent view of the Carquinez Straits, the eastern gateway to the San Francisco Bay. The house is full of art: Pearson's whimsical junk sculptures made of brass fittings, his collection of penguins, Navajo rugs, Barbara's flamboyant, surrealistic canvases. The driveway harbors a decrepit 1955 Chevrolet sedan and a '57 Chevy pickup he is restoring.

If the Antarctic voyage has a genesis, it was probably Pearson's heart attack in 1979, which he says grew out of a long squabble with the college. In 1973 he took a paid sabbatical to study public health at the University of California at Berkeley, but when several courses were canceled he substituted a natural history field seminar in the Amazon. It was a time of high adventure and intellectual stimulation: He flew to

Leticia, Colombia, deep in the Amazon Basin, with a scientific team, and documented the expedition with a professional-quality Ariflex 16mm camera that he had taught himself to use. It took ten years to finish the half-hour documentary, but it was well received by his students. "It was not some bullshit thing," he says.

The college, however, was not impressed and sued him for the $12,000 in sabbatical salary. "It was Kafkaesque," he says, "six years in litigation." The stress led to the heart attack, but Pearson emerged from the ordeal a new man: "Material things became less important. It was as if I'd entered a spiritual phase of my life. Touching a part of nature that was dying—the rainforest—I became moved enough so that my perspective changed. My attention was directed to Antarctica. It was a pure place, and it hadn't been destroyed by man as the Amazon had."

He immersed himself in the literature of Antarctica, and finally the urge to go there overcame him. Over the new year of 1981–82 he booked passage on the Lindblad *Explorer*. He had invited his wife, but she decided to spend the holidays with her daughter from an earlier marriage and new granddaughter. The three-week Antarctic cruise cost $6,000, and because the college would not approve the trip as a sabbatical, he had to hire substitute teachers for his classes.

But the trip was worth every cent. Antarctica was a fantasy land, novel and unsullied. He brought his Ariflex and could hardly stop shooting. What struck him particularly was the air—so clear that mountains hundreds of miles distant would seem only half a day's walk away. There were other marvelous anomalies. Because of the absence of bacteria, food left out in a hut used by Sir Douglas Mawson's expedition was just as it had been left in 1914. The icebergs were more enormous than he imagined possible; the sun never set during the austral summer.

For all its difference and remoteness, though, Pearson felt at one with the strange new environment. The profusion of wildlife displayed an affecting innocence. "It's the damnedest thing to walk up to a penguin four feet high, and it isn't the slightest bit afraid of you," he recalls. "It's like walking in a primeval place of which you're a natural part, accepted into the community of living things."

In the book *Beyond Cape Horn* — one of Pearson's favorites—author Charles Neider discusses the syndrome of Antarctic addiction that struck a number of polar explorers, including himself. Pearson's sojourn seems to have affected him similarly, and he sits forward in his chair when he talks about his visit: "It casts a spell on you; it's so damn neat—like going back in time. Five million years ago it was the same as it is today. Talk about a wilderness experience, hey, that's it in spades.

"It's such a clean, innocent, symbolically pure, idyllic place that when you leave it and get back in the noisy, dirty city and see the human condition and the consequences of humanity, it makes you want to turn and go right back." This is pure hyperbole; Benicia is one of those all-American cities where a wino would appear as incongruous as a Martian. Nevertheless, Warren Pearson's Lindblad homecoming was less than joyous. And so he began to plot his return.

From the outset Pearson knew he would have to mount his own expedition. He stood no chance of qualifying for a National Science Foundation research grant, thus attaining eligibility for government transportation. Even if he had had a valid project, his pacemaker probably would have disqualified him. Not that he wanted help. Under the 1959 Antarctic Treaty each of the nations with voting power over activities in Antarctica—"The Club"—must be given advance notice about any expedition. That meant, as Pearson wrote in his three-volume journal of the expedition, "the countries would 'rescue' me against my will. My plans are meant to keep this from happening, if secrecy is not broached prematurely."

Pearson was vague with his wife about his plans, saying only that he intended to take a year off to sail the South Pacific. By doing so he kept his options open—he could have abandoned the Antarctic trip at any time—and spared her undue worry. The two interpret their marriage pact as allowing each other to be individuals. "I have a right to take a year off, to do any damn thing I want to," he says, "and so does she." Barbara Pearson, for example, once went to Huautla, Mexico, to visit a friend and wound up taking magic mushrooms in a ritualistic ceremony performed by a female shaman.

Barbara Pearson is fascinated by the school of Jungian myth interpretation, which explains human behavior in terms of mythological archetypes, and she saw his supposed island sojourn as a "spiritual quest, a seeking for the Holy Grail." She and Pearson share a private language that is charged with the symbols of medieval romances: grails, magicians, knights on white horses, unicorns—the same icons that inspire Californians from George Lucas to computer hackers with Dungeons and Dragons on the brain. Had she known his real plans, she would have despaired.

After abandoning the absurd C-47 crash-landing scheme, Pearson decided to buy a steel-hulled fishing trawler and motor his way south from Melbourne, Australia. If he succeeded, he reckoned, he would be the first man to make a solo voyage to the continent itself. (From 1972 to 1974 David Lewis, a retired physician living in Australia, sailed alone in a 32-foot sloop, the *Ice Bird* to the Antarctic peninsula and back to South Africa. "But that was the peninsula," Pearson explains. "It's farther north and much warmer there. Hell, on the mainland they refer to it as the 'Banana Belt.'" Lewis, whose boat was capsized and dismasted several times in waves cresting 60 feet, would probably scoff.)

In his journals, Pearson describes his expedition in terms far more grandiose and romantic than his wife's. He refers to Antarctica as "a wilderness emperor's palace" where his soul began to awaken, and "a Camelot" where good things happen and happiness reigns.

His heroic quest was to be a struggle with "the white soul of the planet. . . . It could be deadly but I am going to fight my guts out once in my life." The struggle, he was sure, would earn him "blessings from every god, king, savior, and spiritual force that ever existed in the minds and hearts of wellmeaning people." This adulation would be deserved because of the primary goal of the voyage: to publicize the value of Antarctica. It was this loftier motive that was to elevate the expedition above "self-indulgent escapism" and, he hoped, persuade the authorities to forgive his illegal scientific station.

In our kitchen conversation, Pearson became animated when he elaborated on his higher goal: "Antarctica brings out the best in people, and it's a hell of a nice example of people working together cooperatively. It's so easy to be hopeless about international relations, but the Argentines and the British would give each other the shirts off their backs down there. I wanted people to know that things are working for the collective good there, and that maybe it's possible to make it work elsewhere. I wanted to say that Antarctica is an unspoiled wilderness. It's important to know that there's a good, clean, wholesome place left. When people feel down and hopeless, just the mere knowledge of that is uplifting.

"My job is to be an informer. This was going to be an elaborate lecture to as many people as possible, and the message was: 'Antarctica is a good thing. Don't screw it up. Pat yourself on the back. You've done a good thing. We all have.' In a world full of negativity, that message was significant enough for me to risk my life."

Not long after he returned from the Lindblad trip, Pearson began working 14-hour days, substitute teaching and taking on night courses. The expedition would be expensive, and he intended to settle all his debts and have his insurance policies paid up before leaving. Between classes, he either worked on his Antarctica documentary or buried himself in the library. He read every book on Antarctica he could find and studied navigation, oceanography, meteorology—anything that might be useful on the voyage.

His first actual commitment came in December 1982 when he ordered 925 cloth patches that read HONORING THE SPIRIT OF ANTARCTIC INTERNATIONAL CO-OPERATION—CAPE DENNISON BASE 1985 (Antarctic teams collect and trade such emblems like baseball cards.) Pearson had them printed in each of the four official languages of the Antarctic Treaty: English, French, Spanish, and Russian. On each version, Denison was misspelled with two n's.

He had chosen Cape Denison with good reason. Though his vessel would be steel-hulled, pack ice that forms in the austral winter could easily crush the boat, as it did Ernest Shackleton's ship Endurance in 1914. One way to prevent this is to anchor in a narrow inlet, where the pressure of the ice cannot build up as much as it does in the open sea. Denison offers such an anchorage, and it is one of the few places on the ice-choked coastline accessible to a small boat. Perhaps more important, though, Pearson had stopped there on his Lindblad trip to visit the Mawson hut and to explore, and he had a deep sentimental attachment to the cape.

Unfortunately, that particular section of coastline has some of the harshest weather on the planet. Frigid air pouring off the continent's 10,000-foot-high central plateau creates 200-mile-per-hour winds there—the so-called katabatic winds. "They would have been a bitch," Pearson says, "but I would have dealt with them."

Had his boat's hull become crushed anyway, Pearson could have sought refuge from the otherworldly winter cold in the Mawson hut. (The lowest recorded Antarctic temperature is minus 88.3 degrees Celsius, minus 126 Fahrenheit without the wind.) Then, in the spring, he could have walked overland to DuMont d'Urville, the French outpost 80 miles away, and caught a supply ship home. In any case, he was aiming for another first: the only man to overwinter alone since Byrd in 1934 ("and he had major government support and maintained regular radio contact").

In spite of all his planning, Pearson never developed more than a vague idea of what he would do once he reached Antarctica. He wanted to film another documentary, do some creative writing, conduct modest research (perhaps collect meteorites or investigate sexual differences in the brain anatomy of dead or injured marine mammals). "Specifically I had no definite program," he says. "I wanted to expose myself to influences of an unforeseen nature-jumping out into the flow of life, experiencing the unknown. Why did Hillary want to climb Everest? The reason I wanted to go to Antarctica was to see what happened when I got to Antarctica.

"I also wanted to experience the inner changes I felt. If I died, that would have been part of the experience. I would have hoped if I had died that my 'lecture' would have gotten out, in which case my life would have had some meaning."

By the summer of 1984 Pearson had amassed almost $40,000. He had been so meticulous in putting his affairs in order that he had even written newspaper advertisements so that his wife could sell his cars if he were to die. To ensure that his lecture got out, he prepared a sealed box that she was to open March 31, 1985, three months after his projected departure date. By then, he figured, he would be either icebound and unreachable, or shipwrecked and dead. Inside were letters to the U.S. ambassadors of the 16 nations in The Club and to major newspapers in those countries. Each envelope also contained a number of patches. Barbara was to trundle these down to the Benicia post office and drop them in the slot, one by one: The Hon. Anatoly F. Dobrinyn, *Pravda, Le Monde, The London Times, El Mercurio, The New Zealand Herald* . . .

Another envelope contained an article—already typeset—for *Artwell* magazine, a guide to Benicia's annual spring art fair, which perhaps a thousand people might read. His wife would be editing the magazine in late March, and the piece would be her first inkling about his real destination.

Titled "Performance Peace," it presents his expedition as a kind of performance art in which the readers could participate by simply wishing him Godspeed. His only hope for success, he wrote, lay in "dancing with the forces of nature" and using the "supportive spiritual force coming from all humanity," whom he represented. "Without this force, or my belief in it," he wrote, "I would never undertake such an odyssey and doubt that I could survive it."

In late July, on a break between semesters, Pearson flew to Melbourne to find a boat. He had chosen Melbourne for its size and its proximity to Antarctica. Hobart, Tasmania, would have been closer, but a man buying a boat and tons of supplies in such a small city would arouse suspicion. In Melbourne he could maintain secrecy.

It was winter down under, and the day he arrived was gray and blustery. He checked into a modest hotel downtown. While the room was being prepared he took a walk, hoping to get his first glimpse of the Southern Ocean. His path led him to a lonely wharf, and when he looked over the edge, there at his feet, bobbing in the choppy, gray water, was a scruffy 37-foot steel-hulled cruising ketch: the *Finegold*. She was perfect.

Though the *Finegold* did not have a for sale sign on her, her owner was willing to give her up for $16,840. "When Cinderella put her foot in the shoe, it not only fit her perfectly but it was a moment of joy that I know about," Pearson wrote in his journal after closing the deal. Adding to his sense of predestination, the owner's name was Alan Pearson, and he had the same heart condition as Pearson did. Alan Pearson had bought her with his brother, intending to sail around the world, but his cardiac arrhythmia sabotaged the plans. Besides having a steel hull, the Finegold had a nearly new six-cylinder diesel engine; an insulated, self-bailing cockpit; and an enormous ballast, which would help prevent her from capsizing and right her if she did go over. Then there was the added feature of sail power.

"A.W. Pearson almost had another heart attack when J.W. Pearson walked up and bought his boat *without even stepping on it* or knowing if it had an engine," Pearson wrote gleefully back at his hotel.

For the next two weeks, with the start of the next semester rapidly approaching, Pearson worked like a madman. He figured he could motor all the way to Antarctica, but decided to rerig the *Finegold* with small, heavy-duty sails that would be easy to handle. Knowing little about rigging or sailing, he bought six books. ("So much to learn.") When he was not studying or working on the boat, he was building equipment: a ship's radio, compass and sextant, charts, flares, an emergency position-indicating radio beacon (EPIRB), used sails, hardware. He rode streetcars and, between stops, scribbled private thoughts in his journal. Little did the commuters around him know that the tan book contained a message to them:

"I am a wisp of love drifting through your life, an insignificant medium through which your kindness is rewarded. My destiny is to carry a torch of hope to the white kingdom for you. Your godly spirits will keep me from faltering in our journey, and I pledge my life that I will stay a worthy messenger."

For those four weeks in August, Warren Pearson was totally absorbed and content—an anonymous man on a top-secret mission for mankind. It was finally happening. Back home in California, Pearson's secret anticipation of weighing anchor for the "magnum opus" of his life carried him through the routine of teaching the fall semester.

In December Pearson left Benicia—for the last time, for all he knew—without even waiting for Christmas. On Christmas Eve, instead of carols and a crackling fire at home, he spent a solitary night aboard the *Finegold* in Melbourne. Short of cash until the banks reopened, and with his gear still in transit on a freighter, he washed up in a bucket of water heated on the stove, soaping up with some detergent and drying himself on old drapes. Afterward he went out to order sheet-metal hatch covers, wandered into a church, and sat alone listening to the choir and sermon. "Merry, merry. My soul has been fed," he wrote before going to sleep on a bunk without sheets.

It was not a melancholy time. He had concluded months earlier, with a curious logic, that by eliminating his sense of self-importance, he would not feel lonely. "I will realize a kind of joy by being as unimportant as a grain of sand on a storm-tossed beach," he rhapsodized in his diary. "Sadness, loneliness, and pain should remind me of my unimportance and then I might get a glimpse of that illusive thing I am seeking: a transcendent communion with myself as an infinitesimal fragment of the whole." Pearson was more put off by his lack of hair conditioner and towels than of companionship.

On Christmas morning he opened his present from Barbara: a tiny crystal chalice ("My grail!"); a letter opener with a unicorn on the handle, his sword; a hand harp; and a book titled We. The thin volume, by a Jungian analyst, recounts the epic story of Tristan and Iseult and explores the dynamics of romantic love. In one of Tristan's two voyages, he is "sick unto death" and drifts with only his harp, trusting the sea to bring him his cure. His inner journey eventually brings him to Iseult the Fair. Gazing at the chalice, Pearson felt a surge of warmth. Then, unaware of the symbolism of the letter opener, he opened a can of beans for breakfast with it and went straight to work rigging the mainsail.

Pearson pushed himself during the next two weeks in Melbourne, resuming his 14-hour schedule. He made a canvas retainer for his bunk, rigged the tiller in the aft cockpit so that he could steer from there or the cabin, studied his navigation books. Unable to find propane tanks for sale ("Just rentals, mate"), he bought a small wood stove in which he planned to burn leftover coal from Mawson's expedition for heat or, if necessary, seal blubber.

On January 4 he cleared through customs the ton and a half of equipment he had shipped and transferred it to his boat in a rental van. Sitting amid the jumble, he took stock. Though he claimed to have transcended materialism, you would never know it from the inventory: Chouinard ice-climbing equipment (for self-rescues from crevasses), a

Wilderness Experience Everest suit, a wet suit, Koflach Ultra Extreme mountaineering boots, vapor-barrier systems for himself and his sleeping bags, a mountain of polypropylene and wool clothing, a year's supply of survival rations supplying 6,000 calories a day, medical supplies, 8,000 feet of color movie film, his Ariflex, a 4-by-5 camera, two Canon A-1s, a 650-watt generator, a 13-foot Zodiac and outboard motor, 180 gallons of diesel and 40 of gas, and 10 propane tanks he had tracked down. He had spared no expense—nor bothered to keep track.

With his departure looming, his excitement gave way briefly to worry: "There has been so much frantic activity that I've had little time to realize the implications of what I am about to do," he wrote. But the timetable he had set for himself allowed no time for reflection and he plunged on, working each day until he dropped. On January 5 he filed customs clearance forms, listing Bluff, New Zealand, as his next port of call and January 24, 1985, as his arrival date. He felt some guilt over the deception, but wrote it off as a white lie: "If all goes well, I will arrive in Bluff on Jan. 24, 1986."

His real plan was to conduct his shakedown cruise on Port Phillip Bay below Melbourne and then streak to Kings Island off northwestern Tasmania, usually a three-day sail across the Bass Strait, notorious for its unpredictable weather. Just a week earlier, the Sydney-to-Hobart race over the strait had been a disaster. Only 40 boats in the field of 150 had finished; the rest had been disabled. Pearson wanted to put this part of the trip behind him as soon as possible. Not only is the weather generally miserable and the swells horrendous, the winds could drive him aground in the Furneaux Group, a cluster of islands off northeastern Tasmania. Once clear of Tasmania, there was nothing to run into for the next 1,500 miles. All he had to worry about were killer storms and rogue waves in the Roaring Forties, Furious Fifties, and Screaming Sixties—and, of course, the icebergs. But they would come later.

From the log of the *Finegold*:

"Monday, Jan. 7, 12:45 p.m.—Am now sailing! Lee helm, all canvas up. Light breeze. Bearing 220 degrees. Talk about excitement!"

The 60-mile shakedown cruise across the bay was marred only by a broken oil line—easily fixed—and a navigation blunder that put him aground in the shallows. "*Stupid, stupid, stupid,*" he berated himself in his journal. That evening, the rising tide freed him and he motored off toward the inlet of the bay, a treacherous spot called The Rip. A full moon rose over Melbourne and a dolphin jumped next to the boat—good omens. The evening was lovely, the papers had forecast fair weather, and Pearson decided to run The Rip.

"Mistake. Big mistake," is the next log entry. Huge swells beat the *Finegold*, turning the cabin into a tumble dryer full of flying gear. Twenty miles into the Bass Strait, with the swells still thrashing the boat, the engine quit. Pearson was terrified of being blown ashore, but took to his bunk. "Boat did crazy bobbing all night. Bad ass. Thought I was dead, really."

Tuesday morning, with the engine running again, a cup of coffee in him, and the sun shining, Pearson motored on. The wind subsided and he put up the main. "Really cooking with both sails and engine!" he wrote. The engine sputtered and died intermittently through the day, and the winds rose steadily, but he took heart that the *Finegold* was holding a steady course without his even touching the rudder. The bilge was taking on water, however, and the motorized pump was not working. He pumped the bilge by hand—750 strokes, 45 minutes—then got seasick and went below to rest.

By evening the winds were howling at 40 knots and Pearson left his bunk only long enough to lower the mainsail. With the dark closing around him and the boat holding a steady course, he planned to stay below all night, going up to check the situation every hour. "Why screw around with something that works?" he wrote.

That night—a "night of terror"—the *Finegold* heaved along, sliding into gaping, squarish troughs with 20-foot walls of water on all sides. Rogue waves thundered down on top of her, pitching her over 45 degrees. Pearson struggled above deck, clipped into a safety line, and lowered the jib. He spotted the Cape Wickham light on King Island. Encouraged, he went below to pump the bilge again. On his next watch, the light was farther away, and in the morning there was no land in sight. He was being blown toward the Furneaux Group.

From the log of the *Finegold*:

"Thursday, Jan. 10, 9:00 a.m.—Still storming. Giant rollers. Rain. Lost my rudder about noon yesterday. No engine, no rudder, no control. Turned on the EPIRB at 5:00 p.m. No response. Only good for 48 hours. Must pump bilge every few hours. Looks very bad as I am in a channel and could go on the rocks. Need help desperately."

As he clung to his bunk, gear clanging around the cabin, he stared out a porthole he had left uncovered. Deep green water rose halfway up the glass each time the boat rolled. He imagined the sickening crunch of rocks against the hull. Would it happen that night? In the next minute? Would Barbara mail the packages? Why hadn't they answered the EPIRB? He was certain of death, yet surprised that he was not terrified of dying. The one disturbing thought he kept returning to was that he had no one to blame but himself. For once in his life, there was no scapegoat for his failure. He was not prepared for that kind of loneliness.

Darkness fell. Pearson was in shock, instinctively pumping the bilge, taking a drink of water, eating a cracker. Suddenly, he heard a drone overhead—a plane. He rummaged through the cabin mess and found his flares. He could not get the hatch open fast enough. He fired two red ones, the international distress signal. The pilot circled. Pearson was waving frantically.

For the next seven hours, several planes spelled each other, keeping track of the *Finegold*. Pearson was out of the bunk only as much as he dared. At about 11:00 p.m. he spotted a glimmer of light out of the porthole. He fired his remaining red flare. The eerie crimson light illuminated a scene out of hell: mountainous black waves, undulating with a vertiginous rhythm. From off in the darkness, a white flare answered his. And then the whole ocean lit up like daylight. A helicopter far overhead dropped an intense white flare, and in the distance Pearson could see his salvation, the *M.S. Iron Prince*, an immense black freighter, moving slowly toward him.

Pearson clipped into his safety line, strung from bow to stern, and continually lit hand flares. He was waist-deep in water at times. When the freighter maneuvered alongside, using its bow thrusters, its floodlights were put on. The first mate bellowed down, "Are you the master?"

"Yes!" Pearson replied, almost eye to eye with the mate. The swells had lifted the *Finegold* level with the freighter's deck one second and dropped her 40 feet lower the next.

"How can we assist you?"

"I have no engine or rudder and am taking on water. Can you tow me?"

"We can try."

The only tow lines were at the stern of the freighter, and she inched forward, eventually putting the *Finegold* beneath the overhang above her stilled propeller. The swells there were just as bad. Pearson reached up at one point and felt cold steel. As his boat plunged, he dove to the deck. On the next swell the mizzenmast and shrouds crashed down around him. The heaving pounded the two vessels together, battening the *Finegold*'s hull.

Finally the M.S. *Iron Prince* inched away, and her crew tossed down a line knotted to a three-inch hawser. Pearson could barely pull the heavy towline across the expanse of water and aboard. Dehydrated and mostly sleepless for the past four days, he collapsed unconscious. When he came to, he managed to tie the hawser to a small stern cleat. Next over the rail of the M.S. *Iron Prince* came a rope ladder, but the swells were too heavy to use it. The crew then tossed him a single line. He stumbled back into the cabin, grabbed his log, a chart of the Bass Strait, and the hand harp. Then he tied the line around his waist and was pulled to safety.

The *Finegold* followed stern-first in the freighter's wake for a short distance and then slipped beneath the blackness. When the crew pulled in the hawser, the cleat was still attached to it.

Because he crossed the international dateline on the flight home, Warren Pearson was back at the San Francisco airport on the same day he was rescued. "It was as if the *whoooole* thing had never happened," he says in a listless falsetto, sounding like a mad old woman. "It was like I walked out of a theater and was walking across the parking lot to get in my car and go home."

At home, he mulled over the events for weeks. The storm had blown him 120 miles southeast of Kings Island, only halfway to the rocky coastline that had loomed so large in his imagination. If only he had ridden it out. If only he had made it to Kings Island. If only . . .

The expedition had cost him $80,000, $40,000 in the boat and gear and $40,000 in salary he forfeited by taking a year's leave. All he had left to show for his investment was a few mementos: the clothes he'd been wearing the night of the rescue, his log, the hand harp, the crumpled nautical chart, the deck cleat. But it was the loss of the Finegold that troubled him most. He felt as if he had abandoned a friend and a guardian. "I had a very deep connection with that boat. It cradled my life and what did I do? I jumped off and let it sink."

Some of his closest friends will not talk about the expedition with him. "A lot of people interpret it as a terrible, devastating thing for me materially," he says. "Others feel I must have paid a tremendous emotional price. Some people are indignant: Who the hell does he think he is that he can do something like that? They had me all figured out and then I did something like this. My mother and family think I am bitterly disappointed." Barbara, however, continues to view the expedition as a vision quest and is touched that he brought back the harp, a symbol of the heart.

Pearson prefers to look at the "other side of the balance sheet as well." He got some publicity for Antarctica—a piece in the local paper that made him out to be a naive chump, a big item in *The San Francisco Chronicle*, this article. "It was also a watershed in terms of my psychological development," he says. "I know I went for it; I did not rot away watching the television set. I followed my heart, took a shot at it, and got a lot back."

"And," he adds, toying with the deck cleat, "you have not heard the last about Warren Pearson and Antarctica."

December 1985

Richard Byrd (1888–1957) was one of Amer-
ica's great explorers in the Arctic as well as
Antarctica, where he spent most of one winter
alone at an underground station. He endured a
near-fatal bout of carbon monoxide poisoning
during his solo stay. Alone *recounts that scrape*
and others. But it is most interesting as a closely
observed rendering of one man's encounter with
his own human requirements—in a place that
feeds some of those needs and starves others.

The first days of May carried no hint of the calamities that would overtake me at the month's end. On the contrary, they were among the most wonderful days I had ever known. The blizzards departed, the cold moved down from the South Pole, and opposite the moon in a coal-black sky the cast-up light from the departed sun burned like a bonfire. During the first six days the temperature averaged −47.03°; much of the time it was deep in the minus forties and fifties. The winds scarcely blew. And a soundlessness fell over the Barrier. I have never known such utter quiet. Sometimes it lulled and hypnotized, like a waterfall or any other steady, familiar sound. At other times it struck into the consciousness as peremptorily as a sudden noise. It made me think of the fatal emptiness that comes when an airplane engine cuts out abruptly in flight. Up on the Barrier it was taut and immense; and, in spite of myself, I would be straining to listen—for nothing, really, nothing but the sheer excitement of silence. Underground, it became intense and concentrated. In the middle of a task or while reading a book, I was sometimes brought up hard with all my senses alert and suspicious, like a householder who imagines he hears a burglar in the house. Then, the small sounds of the hut—the hiss of the stove, the chatter of the instruments, the overlapping beats of the chronometers—would suddenly leap out against the soundlessness, all seeming self-conscious and hurried. And after a big wind I have been startled out of a sound sleep, without understanding why, until I realized that my subconscious self, which had become attuned to the rattling of the stovepipe and the surflike pounding of the blizzard overhead, had been unsettled by the abrupt calm.

It was a queer business. I felt as though I had been plumped upon another planet or into another geologic horizon of which man had no knowledge or memory. And yet, I thought at the time it was very good for me; I was learning what the philosophers have long been harping on—that a man can live profoundly without masses of things. For all my realism and skepticism there came over me, too powerfully to be denied, that exalted sense of identification—of oneness—with the outer world which is partly mystical but also certainty. I came to understand what Thoreau meant when he said, "My body is all sentient." There were moments when I felt more *alive* than at any other time in my life. Freed from materialistic distractions, my senses sharpened in new directions, and the random or commonplace affairs of the sky and the earth and the spirit, which ordinarily I would have ignored if I had noticed them at all, became exciting and portentous. Thus:

May 1. This afternoon, in the lee of the sastrugi formed by the last blow, I discovered some extraordinarily fluffy snow. It was so light that my breath alone was enough to send the crystals scurrying like tumbleweed; so fragile that, when I blew hard, they fell to pieces. I have named it "snow down." Although most of the crystals were not much bigger around than a quarter, some were as small as marbles and others as big as goose eggs. Apparently they were blown in on this morning's light westerly wind. I scooped up enough to fill a box—no easy task, for even so slight a disturbance as that created by my hands caused the crystals to fly away. The box was half again as big as a shoe box (approximately 600 cubic inches), but the contents, melted in the bucket, yielded barely half a cup of water. . . .

Later, during my walk, I saw a moon halo, the first since I've been here. I had remarked inwardly that the moon seemed almost unnaturally bright, but thought no more about it until something—perhaps a subtle change in the quality of moonlight—fetched my attention back to the sky. When I glanced up, a haze was spreading over the moon's face; and, as I watched, a system of luminous circles formed themselves gracefully around it. Almost instantly the moon was wholly surrounded by concentric bands of color, and the effect was as if a rainbow had been looped around a huge silver coin. Apple-green was the color of the wide outer band, whose diameter, I estimated, was nineteen times that of the moon itself. The effect lasted only five minutes or so. Then the colors drained from the moon, as they do from a rainbow; and almost simultaneously a dozen massive streamers of crimson-stained aurora, laced together with blackish stripes, seemed to leap straight out from the moon's brow. Then they, too, vanished.

May 3. . . . I again saw in the southeast, touching the horizon, a star so bright as to be startling. The first time I saw it several weeks ago I yielded for an instant to the fantastic notion that somebody was trying to signal me; that thought came to me again this afternoon. It's a queer sort of star, which appears and disappears irregularly, like the winking of a light.

The wind vane has been giving quite a bit of trouble lately. I've had to climb the pole once or twice every day to scrape the contact points. The temperature is holding pretty steadily between 50° and 60° below zero; and I must admit that the job is chillier than I bargained for. Freezing my hands, nose, and cheeks, separately or all together every time I mount the pole is an old story by now; today, for a change, I froze my chin. But all this is not as bad as it sounds. . . .

May 5. This has been a beautiful day. Although the sky was almost cloudless, an impalpable haze hung in the air, doubtless from falling crystals. In midafternoon it disappeared, and the Barrier to the north flooded with a rare pink light, pastel in its delicacy. The horizon line was a long slash of crimson, brighter than blood; and over this welled a straw-yellow ocean whose shores were the boundless blue of the night. I watched the sky a long time, concluding that such beauty was reserved for distant, dangerous places, and that nature has good reason for exacting her own special sacrifices from those determined to witness them. An intimation of my isolation seeped into my mood; this cold but lively afterglow was my compensation for the loss of the sun whose warmth and light were enriching the world beyond the horizon.

That afternoon, for variety's sake, I decided to direct my walk out along the radio antenna, which extended on a line about due east from the shack. The cold was not excessive—somewhere between 50° and 60°—below zero—but I was astonished to find how much rime had collected on the wire. It was swollen to many times its natural size; so much so, in fact, that I could just encircle it with my fingers; and the weight of the ice had caused it to sag in great loops between the poles.

A day or so before the sun had departed I had planted a bamboo stick about twenty yards beyond the last antenna pole. This was to serve as a beacon in case I ever happened to miss the pole in fog or storm. On this day I found the marker without difficulty.

I was standing there, thinking about something, when I suddenly remembered that I had left the stove going. So I turned back, making for the last antenna pole, whose shadowy pencil form I could just see. Head screwed down inside the windproof hood out of the wind, I paid no attention to where I was stepping. Then I had a horrible feeling of falling, and at the same time of being hurled sideways. Afterwards I could not remember hearing any sound. When my wits returned, I was sprawled out full length on the snow with one leg dangling over the side of an open crevasse.

I lay still, not daring to make a move lest I shake down the ledge supporting me. Then, an inch at a time, I crawled away. When I had gone about two yards, I came slowly to my feet, shivering from the closeness of the escape.

I had broken through the snow bridging of a blind crevasse—a roofed-over one which you cannot tell from solid surface. I edged back with my flashlight and took a look. The hole I had made was barely two feet across; and I could see that the roof was twelve inches or so thick. Stretched out on my belly, I pounded the roof in with the marker stick for a distance of several feet; then I turned the flashlight into the crevasse. I could see no bottom. My guess was that the crevasse was at least several hundred feet deep. At the surface it was not more than three feet across; but a little way down it bellied out, making a vast cave. The walls changed from blue to an emerald green, the color of sea ice. The usual crystals, created by the condensed exhalations from the warmer depths, did not festoon the walls; their absence indicated that the crevasse was of fairly recent origin.

I was glad to leave that place. Good luck had carried me across the crevasse at right angles to its length. Had I been walking in any other direction, I might well have gone to the bottom. Odd, I thought, that it hadn't let me through when I passed over it on the way out. Possibly I had hit the one weak spot. So as not to make a similar mistake, I fetched back two bamboo poles and planted them in front of the hole.

May 6. Today I broke the thermometer I keep in the hut. It is not important, really, as inside temperatures are not a part of my meteorological records; but I have been interested in finding out how cold it gets in the hut during the night when the fire is out.

Curiosity tempted me to ask Little America how the stock market was going. It was a ghastly mistake. I can in no earthly way alter the situation. Worry, therefore, is needless. Before leaving [home] I had invested my own funds—carefully, I thought—in the hope of making a little money and thus reducing the expedition's debt. This additional loss, on top of ever-mounting operating expenses, may be disastrous. Well, I don't need money here. The wisest course is to close off my mind to the bothersome details of the world.

It was one thing to instruct the mind; it was another to make the mind obey. The nature of the distinction was to be a fundamental part of my self-instruction at Advance Base, as is evidenced by a diary entry about this time: "Something—I don't know what—is getting me down," the entry goes. "I've been strangely irritable all day, and since supper have been depressed. . . . [This] would not seem important if I could only put my finger on the trouble, but I can't find any single thing to account for the mood. Yet, it has been there; and tonight, for the first time, I must admit that the problem of keeping my mind on an even keel is a serious one. . . ."

The entire entry, a longish one, is before me now. I have a clear recollection of how it came to be written. Supper was over, the dishes had been washed, the 8 p.m. "ob" was out of the way, and I had settled down to read. I picked up Veblen's Theory of the Leisure Class, which I was halfway through, but its concerns seemed fantastically remote to the monocracy of Advance Base. I went from that to Heloïse and Abélard, a story I have always loved; after a little while the words began to run together. Queerly, my eyes hurt, my head ached a little, though not enough to bother.

So I turned up the lamp a little, thinking that more light might help, and tried a few hands of solitaire. But this did no good. Nor did bathing my eyes in boric acid. I couldn't concentrate. My whole being was restive and unaccountably troubled. I got up and paced the room. My movements were almost automatic. Two strides—duck the light, sidestep the stove—another step—full turn at the bunk—back again— three strides from the door to the radio set—three back—and so on, tracing an endlessly repeated L. Months after I had left Advance Base, when the pain was ebbing into forgetfulness, I used to pace my room that way, my steps unconsciously regulated to the dimensions of the shack, and my head jerking away from an imaginary lantern.

That night the peace did not come that should have come. I was like a clock wound up to strike in an empty house. Everything I was doing seemed unfinished and crude, without relationship to the unfathomable desires in my mind. The futility and emptiness of my existence were symbolized by the simple act of jumping up from the chair. Nothing in the everyday habits of a man is ordinarily freighted with more purposefulness than the business of quitting a chair. The swift leverage may impel him on any one of a thousand different errands and opportunities. But with me it led only to blank walls.

I tried to be rational about it. The diary testifies to that. I took my mood apart and studied it as I might have studied the register. Had anything gone wrong during the day? No, it had been a very pleasant day. Though the temperature was in the minus fifties, I had worked hard on the Escape Tunnel; I had supped well on chicken soup, beans, dehydrated potatoes, spinach, and canned peaches. Had I reason to be worried about matters in the world to the north? On the contrary, the news over the last radio schedule had been reassuring. My family was well, and nothing was wrong at Little America. The debt was a problem, but I was used to debts; I could pay off this one as I had paid off the others. My physical condition? Except for the dull ache in my eyes and head, I felt fine; the ache came only at night, anyway, and was gone before I fell asleep. Maybe the fumes from the stove accounted for it. If this was the case, I had better crack the door when the stove was going during the day, and spend more time outside. The diet might also be a contributing cause, but I doubted it. I had been careful about vitamins.

"The most likely explanation," I concluded that night in the diary, "is that the trouble lies with myself. Manifestly, if I can harmonize the various things within me that may be in conflict and also fit myself more smoothly into this environment, I shall be at peace. It may be that the evenness and the darkness and the absence of life are too much for me to absorb in one chunk. I cannot accept that as a fact, if only because I have been here but forty-three days and many months must be lived out which will be no different from the first. . . . If I am to survive—or at least keep my mental balance—I must control and direct my thoughts. This should not be difficult. Any intelligent men should be able to find means of existence within himself. . . ."

Even from this distance I maintain that the attitude was a sensible one. The only fault was its glibness. The reasoning was too pat. I can see that now, but I lacked the prescience to see it then. It was true, as I reasoned that night in May, that the concerns and practices of the outer world had not intruded into my existence. That was proved by the weeks of utter tranquillity. It was also true, as I had concluded, that the way to keep them from intruding was through the censorship and control of the mind. But beyond these was a truth which that night I did not recognize; and this truth was that the whole complex nervous-muscular mechanism which is the body was waiting, as if with bated breath, for the intrusion of familiar stimuli from the outside world, and could not comprehend why they were denied.

A man can isolate himself from habits and conveniences—deliberately, as I have done; or accidentally, as a shipwrecked sailor might—and force his mind to forget. But the body is not so easily sidetracked. It keeps on remembering. Habit has set up in the core of the being a system of automatic physio-chemical actions and reactions which insist upon replenishment. That is where the conflict arises. I don't think that a man can do without sounds and smells and voices and touch, any more than he can do without phosphorus and calcium. This is, in general, what I meant by the vague term "evenness."

So I learned at Latitude 80° 08′ South. It was exhilarating to stand on the Barrier and contemplate the sky and luxuriate in a beauty I did not aspire to possess. In the presence of such beauty we are lifted above natural crassness. And it was a fine thing, too, to surrender to the illusion of intellectual disembodiment, to feel the mind go voyaging through space as smoothly and felicitously as it passes through the objects of its reflections. The body stood still, but the mind was free. It could travel the universe with the audacious mobility of a Wellsian time-space machine.

The senses were isolated in soundless dark; so, for that matter, was the mind; but one was stayed, while the other possessed the flight of a falcon; and the free choice and opportunity of the one everlastingly emphasized the poverty of the other. From the depth of my being would sometimes surge a fierce desire to be projected spectacularly into the living warmths and movements the mind revisited. Usually the desire had no special focus. It sought no single thing. Rather it darted and wavered over a panorama of human aspects—my family at dinner time, the sound of voices in a downstairs room, the cool feeling of rain.

Small matters, all of them; not realities but only the manifestations of reality. Yet, they and a thousand other remembrances of like substance assailed me at night. Not with the calm, revivifying strength of treasured memories; but bitterly and provokingly, as if they were fragments of something vast and not wholly recognizable which I had lost forever. This was the basis of my mood that night in May. Like fingers plucking at a counterpane, my thoughts moved through the days and nights of an existence that seemed to be irrevocably gone. In that mood I had walked before; I would walk like that again; and the glowing tranquillity built up in the afternoon would go out like a spent rocket.

Nevertheless, I practiced my preachments of a disciplined mind. Or perhaps discipline isn't exactly the right word; for what I did, or tried to do, was to focus my thinking on healthy, constructive images and concepts and thus crowd out the unhealthy ones. I built a wall between myself and the past in an effort to extract every ounce of diversion and creativeness inherent in my immediate surroundings. Every day I experimented with new schemes for increasing the content of the hours. "A grateful environment," according to Santayana, "is a substitute for happiness," for it can stimulate us from without just as good works can stimulate us from within. My environment was intrinsically treacherous and difficult, but I saw ways to make it agreeable. I tried to cook more rapidly, take weather and auroral observations more expertly, and do routine things systematically. Full mastery of the impinging moment was my goal. I lengthened my walks and did more reading, and kept my thoughts upon an impersonal plane. In other words, I tried resolutely to attend to my business.

All the while I experimented steadily with cold weather clothing. Inside the shack my usual outfit consisted of a thick woolen shirt, breeches, and underwear (medium weight); plus two pairs of woolen socks (one pair heavy, the other medium); plus a pair of homemade canvas boots, which were soled with thin strips of hairless sealskin, lined with a half-inch thickness of felt, and secured to the ankles by means of leather thongs fastened to the soles. The feet are most vulnerable to cold. They feel chilly sooner and stay that way longer than any other part of the body. This is partly because the circulation in the feet is not so good as in the rest of the body and because the cold from the snow gets to them from conduction and causes condensation. The permeability of canvas was a partial solution to the second difficulty. By making the boots two inches longer and half again as wide as ordinary shoes, I assisted the circulation. The boots were about as handsome as potato sacks, but they worked very well indeed. Whenever I had been a considerable time in the cold, I always changed my socks and inner liners and let the wet ones dry on the stove. The inner soles of my boots were coated with a layer of ice that never thawed. Cold was nothing new to me; and experience had taught me that the secret of protection is not so much the quantity or weight of the clothes as it is the size and quality and, above all, the way they are worn and cared for.

After I'd been at Advance Base a little while I could tell, from a glance at the thermograph, exactly what clothing I would need topside. If it were a matter of taking a quick observation, I'd just slip on a canvas windbreaker, mittens, and a woolen cap that pulled down over the ears. If I had shoveling to do, I'd substitute a helmet for the cap, and add windproof socks, pants, and parka. Walking, I'd wear a woolen parka under the windproofs, which are nothing more mysterious than fine-spun unbleached cotton blouses and pants, made of material no heavier than ordinary sheeting. I've felt wind cut through half an inch of wool as if it were nothing at all; whereas, paper-thin windproofs, closed at the ankles, chin, and waist with draw strings or elastics, were scarcely penetrated. The ideal material is not completely windproof, but lets enough air through to prevent moisture from collecting. At 65° below zero, I usually wore a mask. A simple thing, it consisted of a wire framework overlaid with windproof cloth. Two funnels led to the nose and mouth, and oval slits allowed me to see. I'd breathe in through the nose funnel, and out through the mouth funnel; and, when the latter clogged with ice from the breath's freezing, as it would in short order, I brushed it out with a mitten. On the very cold days, if I had to be out two hours or more, I usually wore my fur outfit (pants, parka, mittens, and mukluks), which was made of reindeer skin, the lightest and most flexible of the warm furs. Thus protected, I could walk through my own inhospitable medium as well insulated as a diver moving through his.

Thus in May, as in April, I never really lacked for something to do. For all the hush and evenness and the slow pulse of the night, my existence was anything but static. I was the inspector of snowstorms and the aurora, the night watchman, and father confessor to myself. Something was always happening, for better or worse. For example, the Tuesday radio schedule with Little America was eliminated, to save gasoline; while this left a blank spot in the hours, the remaining two schedules in turn became more animated. There was always a message from the family in our own private code, which Dyer read with a gracious and unflagging courtesy: "A as in Arthur, L as in laughter, C as in ceiling . . ." I can still hear him going on. Sometimes there were messages from friends. One message came from my old friend Franklin

D. Roosevelt in the White House, saying that he hoped that "the night was not too cold or the wind too strong for an occasional promenade in the dark." And almost always Poulter, or Rawson (now fully recovered), or Siple, or Noville, or Haines, or Innes-Taylor entered into the conversation to discuss an expedition problem or merely pass the time of day.

When I gained in one direction, I seemed to lose in another. Just when I was congratulating myself on having mastered the job of weather observer, the outside thermograph began to act up. A devilish contrivance, it occupied the instrument shelter topside, where hoarfrost settled on the trace, the pen, the drum, and even the workings. On the one occasion I brought the instrument into the shack to change the sheet and make an adjustment, the difference in temperature coated the metal with rime and stopped it dead. Thereafter I had no choice but to make the adjustments in the chill of the tunnel, with no protection for my hands except thin silk gloves; even these seemed infernally clumsy when I had to deal with the speed regulator, which must have been invented for the specific purpose of plaguing weather men.

Thus, even in the heart of the Ross Ice Barrier a solitary man had plenty to occupy him. Thus in the diary: ". . . I got Canfield twice tonight—extraordinary! The only games I played, too." And again: ". . . One of my favorite records is 'Home on the Range.' It's the second song I've ever learned to sing. (The other was 'Carry Me Back to Old Virginny,' and even that I never dared to sing except in the cockpit of an airplane, where nobody could hear me.) And tonight I sang while washing the dishes. Solitude hasn't mellowed my voice any, but I had great fun. A gala evening, in fact." The diary became more than a record; it became a means to think out loud. This was a pleasant way of filling the last hour; also, it helped to stabilize my philosophy. For example:

May 9. . . . I have been persistent in my effort to eliminate the after-supper periods of depression. Until tonight my mood has been progressively better; now I am despondent again. Reason tells me that I have no right to be depressed. My progress in eliminating the indefinable irritants has been better than I expected. I seem to be learning how to keep my thoughts and feelings on an even keel, for I have not been sensible of undue anxiety. Therefore, I suspect that my dark moods come from something affecting my physical being—possibly fumes from the stove, the lantern, or the gasoline generator. If that be the case, then my state of mind may possibly have helped to offset the depressing consequences of the poisoning—if that is what is affecting me.

It is really essential that I take careful stock of my situation because my enemy is subtle. This doesn't mean that I have become too introspective or that I am taking myself too seriously. My thoughts have been objective enough. But, if something is poisoning or otherwise afflicting my body, what effect will this have on my peace of mind? Certain types of physical ailments have a definitely depressing effect. The question is, how much can this effect be overcome by disregarding or even denying its existence? Suppose the disorder is organic and lies in a deep-seated complaint. Suppose it comes from bad food, from germs, or from the gases given off by the stove. How much resistance, then, can my mind impart to the body if the mind is properly directed?

Possibly something is harming me physically, and I am making things worse by some negative subconscious emotion. Then my mind and body are both sick, and I have a vicious circle to break. Do the mind and the body exist separately, along parallel lines? Is the physical part mostly mental, or the mind mostly physical? How much does the mental control the physical? Indeed, how much division is there between mind and body? The body can take charge of the mind, but isn't it natural and best for the mind to take charge of the body? The brain is part of the body, but I am not conscious of my brain. The mind seems to be the real "I". . . .

Which is it, then? My mind or my body or both? It is of vital importance that I find the truth. Aside from the slight trouble with my eyes and the fact that my lungs are still sensitive to cold, I am not conscious of any physical deterioration. Diet, I am sure, has nothing to do with my moodiness. The fumes are the one question mark. The pain in my eyes and the headachy feeling come in the early evening, after the stove has been on a long time. And sometimes the air in the tunnel is thick after the gasoline engine has been running during a radio schedule. But it is hard to believe that the exhaust gases from either the stove or the engine are really damaging. The ventilation seems to be adequate, so long as I keep the vents clear of ice. . . .

I remember that after finishing the foregoing entry I got up and inspected the stove. I walked all around, covertly scrutinizing the simple structure as I might a friend whose motives I had come to suspect. But my expression must have been anything but grave. The stove was more ludicrous than sinister. At that moment it was performing the humble duty of warming the water bucket in which my underwear was soaking. Even the gentle hiss of the burner seemed ineffectual; and the contrast between the tiny stove, which came just above my knees, and the grotesquely attenuated length of pipe was as ridiculous as anything of the sort could be. The only faults I could find with it were two. One was the burner's tendency to splutter and smoke from the water dripping down from the bucket when I melted snow. The other was the tendency of the pipe to fill with ice, and then, as it thawed, to let the water pour down into the stove. I had already made a hole in a right-angle joint to catch the water before it reached the burner; if that didn't work I could bend the joint into a V, making an easily drained trap.

Beyond this I could not think of anything important to do; for that matter, nothing more seemed necessary. The ventilating pipes were drawing well, considering the conditions under which they were operating. Certainly I had plenty of air. Every now and then during the day I'd crack the door an inch or two; when the room turned so cold that my nose hurt, I'd shut it again. To make the relatively distant reaches more attractive, I named one corner Palm Beach and the other Malibu; but with the door open I seldom felt very comfortable in either place without fur pants on. This is the honest truth. Indeed, on more than one occasion the glass of water which I put down beside the key at the start of a radio schedule was skimmed over with ice before I had time to drink it.

As the diary testifies, my mind was satisfied that the diet was providing the proper amount of vitamins. True, I had already pulled in my belt two notches, and would take in a third notch before the month was out. But that was to be expected. Although I had made an exhaustive study of dietetics, especially vitamins, in connection with provisioning my expeditions, just to be on the safe side, I decided to consult an excellent authority, called *New Dietetics*, a present from my friend John H. Kellogg. At first, though I hunted high and low, I couldn't find the book; finally I asked Dyer, on a radio schedule, please to send somebody after Siple and find out from him where it had been stowed. Ten minutes later Siple sent word back that he had last seen the book in a box on the veranda. And there I found it.

A quick reading of the book confirmed what I knew already: namely, that so far as choice of foods went, my diet was thoroughly balanced. But, as a double check, I asked Little America to consult a nationally known food laboratory in Rochester, New York. The experts there promptly reported back that my diet was adequate in every respect.

May 11. 12:15 a.m. It is late, but I've just had an experience which I wish to record. At midnight I went topside to have a last look at the aurora, but found only a spotty glow on the horizon extending from north to northeast. I had been playing the Victrola while I waited for the midnight hour. I was using my homemade repeater and was playing one of the records of Beethoven's Fifth Symphony. The night was calm and clear. I left the door to my shack open and also my trapdoor. I stood there in the darkness to look around at some of my favorite constellations, which were as bright as I had ever seen them.

Presently I began to have the illusion that what I was seeing was also what I was hearing, so perfectly did the music seem to blend with what was happening in the sky. As the notes swelled, the dull aurora on the horizon pulsed and quickened and draped itself into arches and fanning beams which reached across the sky until at my zenith the display attained its crescendo. The music and the night became one; and I told myself that all beauty was akin and sprang from the same substance. I recalled a gallant, unselfish act that was of the same essence as the music and the aurora.

10 p.m. Solitude is an excellent laboratory in which to observe the extent to which manners and habits are conditioned by others. My table manners are atrocious—in this respect I've dipped back hundreds of years; in fact, I have no manners whatsoever. If I feel like it, I eat with

my fingers, or out of a can, or standing up—in other words, whichever is easiest. What's left over, I just heave into the slop pail, close to my feet. Come to think of it, no reason why I shouldn't. It's rather a convenient way to eat; I seem to remember reading in Epicurus that a man living alone lives the life of a wolf.

A life alone makes the need for external demonstration almost disappear. Now I seldom cuss, although at first I was quick to open fire at everything that tried my patience. Attending to the electrical circuit on the anemometer pole is no less cold than it was in the beginning; but I work in soundless torment, knowing that the night is vast and profanity can shock no one but myself.

My sense of humor remains, but the only sources of it are my books and myself, and, after all, my time to read is limited. Earlier today, when I came into the hut with my water bucket in one hand and the lantern in the other, I put the lantern on the stove and hung up the bucket. I laughed at this; but, now when I laugh, I laugh inside; for I seem to have forgotten how to do it out loud. This leads me to think that audible laughter is principally a mechanism for sharing pleasure.

I find, too, that absence of conversation makes it harder for me to think in words. Sometimes, while walking, I talk to myself and listen to the words, but they sound hollow and unfamiliar. Today, for instance, I was thinking of the extraordinary effect of the lack of diversions upon my existence; but describing it is beyond my power. I could feel the difference between this life and a normal life; I could see the difference in my mind's eye, but I couldn't satisfactorily express the subtleties in words. That may be because I have already come to live more deeply within myself; what I feel needs no further definition, since the senses are intuitive and exact. . . .

My hair hasn't been cut in months. I've let it grow because it comes down around my neck and keeps it warm. I still shave once a week—and that only because I have found that a beard is an infernal nuisance outside on account of its tendency to ice up from the breath and freeze the face. Looking in the mirror this morning, I decided that a man without women around him is a man without vanity; my cheeks are blistered and my nose is red and bulbous from a hundred frostbites. How I look is no longer of the least importance: all that matters is how

I feel. However, I have kept clean, as clean as I would keep myself at home. But cleanliness has nothing to do with etiquette or coquetry. It is comfort. My senses enjoy the evening bath and are uncomfortable at the touch of underwear that is too dirty.

I've been trying to analyze the effect of isolation on a man. As I said, it is difficult for me to put this into words. I can only feel the absence of certain things, the exaggeration of others. In civilization my necessarily gregarious life with its countless distractions and diversions had blinded me to how vitally important a role they really did play. I find that their sudden removal has been much more of a wrench than I had anticipated. As much as anything, I miss being insulted every now and then, which is probably the Virginian in me.

May 12. . . . The silence of this place is as real and solid as sound. More real, in fact, than the occasional creaks of the Barrier and the heavier concussions of snow quakes. . . . It seems to merge in and become part of the indescribable *evenness*, as do the cold and the dark and the relentless ticking of the clocks. This evenness fills the air with its mood of unchangeableness; it sits across from me at the table, and gets into the bunk with me at night. And no thought will wander so far as not eventually to be brought up hard by it. This is timelessness in its ultimate meaning. Very often my mood soars above it; but, when this mood goes, I find myself craving change—a look at trees, a rock, a handful of earth, the sound of foghorns, anything belonging to the world of movement and living things.

But I refuse to be disconcerted. This is a great experience. The despondency which used to come after supper—probably because that is the hour when we expect companionship—seems to have disappeared. Incidentally, I have mastered the business of waking myself in the morning; it has returned as mysteriously as it disappeared. Every morning for the last fortnight I've awakened within five minutes of the time I set in my mind.

I'm getting absent-minded. Last night I put sugar in the soup, and tonight I plunked a spoonful of cornmeal mush on the table where the plate should have been. I've been reading stories from several old English magazines. I got started on a murder serial, but I'll be damned if I can find two crucial installments. So I've had no choice but to try the love stories, and it is queer to reflect that beyond the horizon the joyful aspects of life go on. Well, this is the one continent where no woman has ever set foot; I can't say that it is any better on that account. In fact, the stampede to the altar that took place after the return of my previous expedition would seem to offer strong corroboration of that. Of the forty-one men with me at Little America, thirty were bachelors. Several married the first girls they met in New Zealand; most of the rest got married immediately upon their return to the United States. Two of the bachelors were around fifty years old, and both were married shortly after reaching home. There are only a few left, and I suspect their lonesome state is not entirely their fault.

May 16. It's just a week since the last after-supper depression. I don't want to be overconfident, but I believe I have it licked. . . .

May 17. . . . I have more leisure than I shall probably ever have again. Thanks to the routine way I do things, my opportunities for intellectual exercise are virtually unlimited. I can, if I choose, spend hours over a single page in a book. I thought tonight what a very full and simple life it is—indeed, all I really lack is temptation.

Partly as an amusement I have been speculating on thought harmony. If man is, as I believe, an integral part of the universe and since grace and smoothness mark the movements of most things in it— such as the electrons and protons within the atom and the planets within the solar system and the stars within the galaxies—then a normal mind should function with something of the same harmoniousness.

Anyhow, my thoughts seem to come together more smoothly than ever before. . . .

This was a grand period; I was conscious only of a mind utterly at peace, a mind adrift upon the smooth, romantic tides of imagination, like a ship responding to the strength and purpose in the enveloping medium. A man's moments of serenity are few, but a few will sustain him a lifetime. I found my measure of inward peace then; the stately echoes lasted a long time. For the world then was like poetry—that poetry which is "emotion remembered in tranquillity."

Perhaps this period was just the repeated pattern of my youth. I sometimes think so. When I was growing up, I used to steal out of the house at night, and go walking in Glass's woods, which were a little way up the road from our place. In the heavy shadows of the Shenandoah Valley hills, the darkness was a little terrifying, as it always is to small boys; but, when I would pause and look up into the sky, a feeling that was midway between peace and exhilaration would seize me. I never quite succeeded, as a boy, in analyzing that feeling, any more than I did when it used to come to me as a naval officer, in the night watches at sea, and later when, as an explorer, I first looked upon mountains and lands which no one before me had ever seen. No doubt it was partly animal: the sheer expanding discovery of being alive, of growing, of no longer being afraid. But there was more to it than just that. There was the sense of identification with vast movements: the premonition of destiny that is implicit in every man; and the sense of waiting for the momentary revelation.

from The Voyage of the Jeannette
by George W. DeLong

Lieutenant George W. DeLong (1844–1881) of the U.S. Navy set out for the North Pole in 1879, hoping to get there via an innovative route between Alaska and Siberia. His ship, the Jeannette, spent two winters frozen in place 750 miles from the Pole, and sank on June 12, 1881. The crew of 20 men made for land. One boat and its seven occupants were lost. The 14 survivors landed in the Siberian wilderness in September.

O*ctober 1st, Saturday.*—One hundred and eleventh day, and a new month. Called all hands as soon as the cook announced boiling water, and at 6.45 had our breakfast; one half pound of deer meat and tea. Sent Nindemann and Alexey to examine main river, other men to collect wood. The doctor resumed the cutting away of poor Ericksen's toes this morning. No doubt it will have to continue until half his feet are gone, unless death ensues, or we get to some settlement. Only one toe left now. Temperature 18°.

At 7.30 Nindemann and Alexey were seen to have crossed, and I immediately sent men to carry one load over.

Left the following record:—

Saturday, October 1, 1881.
Fourteen of the officers and men of the U.S. Arctic Steamer *Jeannette* reached this hut on Wednesday, September 28th, and having been forced to wait for the river to freeze over, are proceeding to cross to the west side this a.m. on their journey to reach some settlement on the Lena River. We have two days'

provisions, but having been fortunate enough thus far to get game in our pressing needs, we have no fear for the future.

Our party are all well, except one man, Ericksen, whose toes have been amputated in consequence of frost-bite. Other records will be found in several huts on the east side of this river, along which we have come from the northward.

[List of party.]

GEORGE W. DELONG,
Lieutenant U. S. Navy, Commanding Expedition.

At 8.30 we made the final trip, and got our sick man over in safety. From there we proceeded until 11.20, dragging our man on the sled. Halted for dinner; one half pound meat and tea each. At one went ahead again until 5.05.

Actually under way: 8.30 to 9:15, 9.30 to 10.20, 10:30 to 11.20, 1.00 to 1.40, 1.50 to 2.10, 2.20 to 2.40, 3.00 to 3.25, 3.35 to 4.00, 4.15 to 4.35, 4.45 to 5:05. Total, 5h. 15m. At least two miles an hour. Distance made good ten to twelve miles.

And where are we? I think at the beginning of the Lena River at last. "Sagastyr" has been to us a myth. We saw two old huts at a distance, and that was all, but they were out of our reach, and the day not half gone. Kept on ice all the way, and therefore I think we were over water, but the stream was so narrow and so crooked that it never could have been a navigable water. My chart is simply useless. I must go on plodding to the southward, trusting in God to guide me to a settlement, for I have long since realized that we are powerless to help ourselves.

A bright, calm, beautiful day. Bright sunshine to cheer us up, an icy road, and one day's rations yet. Boots frozen, of course, and balled up. No hut in sight, and we halt on a bluff to spend a cold and comfortless night. Supper one half pound meat and tea. Made a rousing fire, built a log bed, set a watch (two hours each) to keep the fire going, and at eight p.m. crawled into our blankets.

October 2nd, Sunday.—I think we all slept fairly well until midnight; but from that time it was so cold and uncomfortable that sleep was out of the question. At 4.30 we were all out and in front of the fire, daylight just appearing. Ericksen kept talking in his sleep all night, and effectually kept those awake who were not already awakened by the cold.

Breakfast five a.m. One half pound meat and tea. Bright, cloudless morning. Light N. airs. At seven went ahead, following frozen water wherever we could find it, and at 9.20 I feel quite sure we have gone some distance on the main river. I think our gait was at least two miles an hour, and our time under way two hours four minutes. I call our forenoon work at least six miles: 7.00 to 7.35, 7.45 to 8.05, 8.15 to 8.30, 8.40 to 8.50, 9.20 to 9.40, 9.50 to 10.12, 10.22 to 10.40, 10.55 to 11.15. Dinner camp. 1.00 to 1.30, 1.40 to 2.00, 2.15 to 2.35, 2.45 to 3.00, 3.20 to 3.40, 3.50 to 4.05, 4.15 to 4.20.

Divine service before dinner. Dinner one half pound meat and tea. Started ahead at one p.m., and by 4.15 had completed two marching hours and made four miles. I was much bewildered by the frequent narrowing of the river to a small vein of ice, and the irregular rambling way in which it ran. Frequently it led us into sand bank or deep snow, and our floundering around was both exhaustive of energy and consumptive of time. There is no use denying it, we are pretty weak. Our food is not enough to keep up our strength, and when we lose a night's sleep we feel it keenly. I had several bad falls on the ice this afternoon which shook me up pretty badly. A freshening N. E. wind had blown the efflorescence off the ice, and left smooth, clear spots as clear as glass. Frozen boots are but poor foot gear, and besides cramping the feet, are like boots of iron in walking. Slip, slide, and down you are on your back.

At 4.05 p.m. I saw more wood than we had sighted since our dinner camp, and but little ahead. I therefore called a halt and "camped," *i.e.*, sat down, made a fire and got supper. Then we stood by for a second cold and wretched night. There was so much wind that we had to put our tent halves up for a screen, and sit shivering in our half blankets.

October 3rd, Monday.—One hundred and thirteenth day. At midnight it was so fearfully cold and wretched that I served out tea to all hands, and on that we managed to struggle along until five a.m., when we ate our last deer meat and had more tea. Our remaining food now consists of four fourteenths pounds pemmican each, and a half-starved dog. May God again incline unto our aid. How much farther we have to go before reaching a shelter or a settlement, He alone knows.

Brisk wind. Ericksen seems failing. He is weak and tremulous, and the moment he closes his eyes talks incessantly in Danish, German, and English. No one could sleep even if our other surroundings permitted.

For some cause my watch stopped at 10.45 last night while one of the men on watch had it. I set it as near as I could come to the time by guessing, and we must run by that until I can do better. Sun rose yesterday morning at 6.40 by the watch when running all right: 7.05 to 7.40 (35 m.), 7.50 to 8.20 (30 m.), 8.30 to 9.00 (30 m.), 9.15 to 9.35 (20m.), 9.50 to 10.10 (20 m.), 10.25 to 10.40 (15 m.), 11.00 to 11.20, 11.30 to 11.50, 11.50 dinner—1 h. 55 m.—2 h. 35 m., say five miles.

Our forenoon's walk I put as above at five miles. Some time and distance was lost by crossing the river upon seeing numerous fox-traps. A man's track was also seen in the snow, bound south, and we followed it until it crossed the river to the west bank again. Here we were obliged to go back in our tracks, for the river was open in places, and we could not follow the man's track direct. Another of the dozen shoals which infest the river swung us off to the eastward, too, and I hastened to get on the west bank again, reaching there at 11.50 for dinner. Our last four fourteenths pound pemmican.

At 1.40 got under way again and made a long fleet until 2.20. While at the other side of the river Alexey said he saw a hut, and during our dinner camp he again saw it. Under our circumstances my desire was to get to it as speedily as possible. As Alexey pointed out it was on the left bank of the river of which we were now on the right side looking south. But a sand bank gave us excellent walking for a mile, until we took to the river ice and got across it diagonally. Here, at 2.20, I called a rest, and Alexey mounted the bluff to take a look again. He now announced that he saw a second hut about one and a quarter miles back from the coast, the first hut being about the same distance south and on the edge of the bluff. The heavy dragging across country of a sick man on a sled made me incline to the hut on the shore, since, as the distance was about the same, we could get over the ice in one third of the time.

Nindemann, who climbed the bluff, while he saw that the object inland was a hut, was not so confident about the one on the shore. Alexey, however, was quite positive, and not seeing very well myself I unfortunately took his eyes as best and ordered an advance along the river to the southward. Away we went, Nindemann and Alexey leading, and had progressed about a mile when, splash! in I went through the ice up to my shoulders before my knapsack brought me up. While I was crawling out, in went Görtz to his neck about fifty yards behind me, and behind him in went Mr. Collins to his waist. Here was a time. The moment we came out of the water we were one sheet of ice, and danger of frost-bite was imminent. Along we hobbled, however, until we came, at 3.45, abreast the point on which the hut was seen. Here Nindemann climbed the bluff, followed by the doctor. At first the cry was, "All right, come ahead," but no sooner were we all up than Nindemann shouted, "There is no hut here." To my dismay and alarm nothing but a large mound of earth was to be seen, which, from its regular shape and singular position would seem to have been built artificially for a beacon; so sure was Nindemann that it was a hut that he went all around it looking for a door, and then climbed on top to look for a hole in the roof. But of no avail. It was nothing but a mound of earth. Sick at heart I ordered a camp to be made in a hole in the bluff face, and soon before a roaring fire we were drying (and burning) our clothes, while the cold wind ate into our backs.

And now for supper! Nothing remained but the dog. I therefore ordered him killed and dressed by Iversen, and soon after a kind of stew was made of such parts as could not be carried, of which everybody except the doctor and myself eagerly partook. To us two it was a nauseating mess and—but why go on with such a disagreeable subject. I had the remainder weighed, and I am quite sure we had twenty-seven pounds. The animal was fat and—as he had been fed on pemmican— presumably clean, but—

Immediately upon halting I had sent off Alexey with his gun toward the hut inland, to determine whether that was a myth like our present one. He returned about dark, certain that it was a large hut, for he had been inside of it, and had found some deer meat, scraps, and bones. For a moment I was tempted to start everybody for it, but Alexey was by no means sure he could find it in the dark, and if we lost our way we should be worse off than before. We accordingly prepared to make the best of it where we were.

We three wet people were burning and steaming before the fire. Collins and Görtz had taken some alcohol, but I could not get it down. Cold, wet, with a raw N. W. wind impossible to avoid or screen, our future was a wretched, dreary night. Ericksen soon became delirious, and his talking was a horrible accompaniment to the wretchedness of our surroundings. Warm we could not get, and getting dry seemed out of the question. Nearly everybody seemed dazed and stupefied, and I feared that some of us would perish during the night. How cold it was I do not know, for my last thermometer was broken in my many falls on the ice, but I think it must have been below zero. A watch was set to keep the fire going and we huddled around it, and thus our third night without sleep was passed. If Alexey had not wrapped his sealskin around me and sat down alongside of me to keep me warm by the heat of his body, I think I should have frozen to death. As it was I steamed, and shivered, and shook. Ericksen's groans and rambling talk rang out on the night air, and such a dreary, wretched night I hope I shall never see again.

October 4th, Tuesday.—One hundred and fourteenth day. At the first approach of daylight we all began to move around, and the cook was set to work making tea. The doctor now made the unpleasant discovery that during the night Ericksen had got his gloves off and that now his hands were frozen. Men were at once set to work rubbing them, and by six a.m. we had so far restored circulation as to risk moving the man. Each one had hastily swallowed a cup of tea, and got his load in readiness. Ericksen was quite unconscious, and we lashed him on the sled. A S. W. gale was blowing, and the sensation of cold was intense; but at six a.m. we started, made a forced fleet of it, and at eight a.m. had got the man and ourselves, thank God, under the cover of a hut large enough to hold us. Here we at once made a fire, and for the first time since Saturday morning last got warm.

The doctor at once examined Ericksen and found him very low indeed. His pulse was very feeble, he was quite unconscious, and under the shock of the exposure of the past night he was sinking very fast.

Fears were entertained that he might not last many hours, and I therefore called upon every one to join with me in reading the prayers for a sick person before we sought any rest for ourselves. This was done in a quiet and reverent manner, though I fear my broken utterances made but little of the service audible. Then setting a watch we all, except Alexey, laid down to sleep at ten a.m. Alexey went off to hunt, but returned at noon wet, having broken through the ice and fallen in the river.

At six p.m. all roused up, and I considered it necessary to think of some food for my party. Half a pound of dog was fried for each one and a cup of tea given, and that constituted our day's food. But we were so grateful that we were not exposed to the merciless S. W. gale that tore around us that we did not mind short rations.

October 5th, Wednesday.—One hundred and fifteenth day. The cook commenced at 7.30 to get tea, made from yesterday's tea leaves. Nothing can be served out to eat until evening. One half pound dog per day is our food until some relief is afforded us. Alexey went off hunting again at nine, and I set the men to work collecting light sticks enough to make a flooring for the house, for the frozen ground thawing under everybody has kept them damp and wet and robbed them of much sleep.

S. W. gale continues. Mortification has set in in Ericksen's leg and he is sinking. Amputation would be of no use, for he would probably die under the operation. He is partially conscious. At twelve Alexey came back, having seen nothing. He crossed the river this time, but unable longer to face the cold gale was obliged to return.

I am of the opinion that we are on Tit Ary Island, on its eastern side, and about twenty-five miles from Ku Mark Surka, which I take to be a settlement. This is a last hope, for our Sagastyr has long since faded away. The hut in which we are is quite new, and clearly not the astronomical station marked on my chart. In fact this hut is not finished, having no door and no porch. It may be intended for a summer hut, though the numerous set fox-traps would lead me to suppose that it would occasionally be visited at other times. Upon this last chance and one other seem to rest all our hopes of escape, for I can see nothing more to be done. As soon as this gale abates I shall send

Nindemann and one other man to make a forced march to Ku Mark Surka for relief. At six p.m. served out one half pound of dog meat and second-hand tea, and then went to sleep.

October 6th, Thursday.—One hundred and sixteenth day. Called all hands at 7.30. Had a cup of third-hand tea with one half ounce of alcohol in it. Everybody very weak. Gale moderating somewhat. Sent Alexey out to hunt. Shall start Nindemann and Noros at noon to make the forced march to Ku Mark Surka. At 8.45 a.m. our messmate Ericksen departed this life. Addressed a few words of cheer and comfort to the men. Alexey came back empty-handed. Too much drifting snow. What in God's name is going to become of us,—fourteen pounds dog meat left, and twenty-five miles to a possible settlement? As to burying Ericksen, I cannot dig a grave, for the ground is frozen and we have nothing to dig with. There is nothing to do but to bury him in the river. Sewed him up in the flaps of the tent, and covered him with my flag. Got tea ready, and with one half ounce alcohol we will try to make out to bury him. But we are all so weak that I do not see how we are going to move.

At 12.40 p.m. read the burial service and carried our departed shipmate's body down to the river, where, a hole having been cut in the ice, he was buried; three volleys from our two Remingtons being fired over him as a funeral honor.

A board was prepared with this cut on it:—

● ● ●

IN MEMORY

H. H. ERICKSEN,

OCT. 6, 1881.

U.S.S. Jeannette.

and this will be stuck in the river bank abreast his grave.

His clothing was divided up among his messmates. Iversen has his Bible and a lock of his hair. Kaack has a lock of his hair.

Supper at five p.m.—one half pound dog meat and tea.

October 7th, Friday.—One hundred and seventeenth day. Breakfast, consisting of our last one half pound dog meat and tea. Our last grain of tea was put in the kettle this morning, and we are now about to undertake our journey of twenty-five miles with some old tea-leaves and two quarts alcohol. However, I trust in God, and I believe that He who has fed us thus far will not suffer us to die of want now.

Commenced preparations for departure at 7.10. Our Winchester rifle being out of order is, with one hundred and sixty-one rounds ammunition, left behind. We have with us two Remingtons and two hundred and forty-three rounds ammunition. Left the following record in the hut:—

Friday, October 7, 1881.

The undermentioned officers and men of the late U. S. Steamer *Jeannette* are leaving here this morning to make a forced march to Ku Mark Surka, or some other settlement on the Lena River. We reached here on Tuesday, October 4th, with a disabled comrade, H. H. Ericksen (seaman), who died yesterday morning, and was buried in the river at noon. His death resulted from frost-bite and exhaustion, due to consequent exposure. The rest of us are well, but have no provisions left—having eaten our last this morning.

Under way at 8.30 and proceeded until 11.20, by which time we had made about three miles. Here we were all pretty well done up, and, moreover, seemed to be wandering in a labyrinth. A large lump of wood swept in by an eddy seemed to be a likely place to get hot water, and I halted the party. For dinner we had one ounce alcohol in a pot of tea. Then went ahead, and soon struck what seemed like the river again. Here four of us broke through the ice in trying to cross, and fearing frost-bite I had a fire built on the west bank to dry us. Sent Alexey off meanwhile to look for food, directing him not to go far nor to stay long; but at 3.30 he had not returned, nor was he in sight. Light S. W. breeze, hazy; mountains in sight to southward.

At 5.30 Alexey returned with one ptarmigan, of which we made soup, and with one half ounce alcohol had our supper. Then crawled under our blankets for a sleep. Light W. breeze; full moon; starlight. Not very cold. Alexey saw river a mile wide with no ice in it.

October 8th, Saturday.—One hundred and eighteenth day. Called all hands at 5.30. Breakfast, one ounce alcohol in a pint of hot water.

Doctor's note: Alcohol proves of great advantage; keeps off craving for food, preventing gnawing at stomach, and has kept up the strength of the men, as given,—three ounces per day as estimated, and in accordance with Dr. Anstie's experiments.

Went ahead until 10.30; one ounce alcohol 6.30 to 10.30; five miles; struck big river; 11.30 ahead again; sand bank. Meet small river. Have to turn back. Halt at five. Only made advance one mile more. Hard luck. Snow; S. S. E. wind. Cold camp; but little wood; one half ounce alcohol.

October 9th, Sunday.—One hundred and nineteenth day. All hands at 4.30 one ounce alcohol. Read divine service. Send Nindemann and Noros ahead for relief; they carry their blankets, one rifle, forty rounds ammunition, two ounces alcohol. Orders to keep west bank of river until they reach settlement; They started at seven; cheered them. Under way at eight. Crossed creek. Broke through ice. All wet up to knees. Stopped and built fires. Dried clothes. Under way again at 10.30. Lee breaking down. At one strike river bank. Halt for dinner,—one ounce alcohol. Alexey shot three ptarmigans. Made soup. We are following Nindemann's track, though he is long since out of sight. Under way at 3.30. High bluff. Ice running rapidly to northward in river. Halt at 4.40 upon coming to wood. Find canoe. Lay our heads on it and go to sleep; one half ounce alcohol for supper.

October 10th, Monday.—One hundred and twentieth day. Last half ounce alcohol at 5.30; at 6.30 send Alexey off to look for ptarmigan. Eat deerskin scraps. Yesterday morning ate my deerskin foot-nips. Light S. S. E. airs. Not very cold. Under way at eight. In crossing creek three of us got wet. Built fire and dried out. Ahead again until eleven. Used up. Built fire. Made a drink out of the tea-leaves from alcohol bottle. On again at noon. Fresh S. S. W. wind, drifting snow, very hard going. Lee begging to be left. Some little beach, and then long stretches of high bank. Ptarmigan tracks plentiful. Following Nindemann's tracks. At three halted, used up; crawled into a hole in the bank, collected wood and built fire. Alexey away in quest of game. Nothing for supper except a spoonful of glycerine. All hands weak and feeble, but cheerful. God help us.

October 11th, Tuesday.—One hundred and twenty-first day. S. W. gale with snow. Unable to move. No game. One spoonful glycerine and hot water for food. No more wood in our vicinity.

October 12th, Wednesday.—One hundred and twenty-second day. Breakfast; last spoonful glycerine and hot water. For dinner we tried a couple of handfuls of Arctic willow in a pot of water and drank the infusion. Everybody getting weaker and weaker. Hardly strength to get fire-wood. S. W. gale with snow.

October 13th, Thursday.—One hundred and twenty-third day. Willow tea. Strong S.W. wind. No news from Nindemann. We are in the hands of God, and unless He intervenes we are lost. We cannot move against the wind, and staying here means starvation. Afternoon went ahead for a mile, crossing either another river or a bend in the big one. After crossing, missed Lee. Went down in a hole in the bank and camped. Sent back for Lee. He had turned back, lain down, and was waiting to die. All united in saying Lord's Prayer and Creed after supper. Living gale of wind. Horrible night.

October 14th, Friday.—One hundred and twenty-fourth day. Breakfast, willow tea. Dinner, one half teaspoonful sweet oil and willow tea. Alexey shot one ptarmigan. Had soup. S. W. wind, moderating.

October 15th, Saturday.—One hundred and twenty-fifth day. Breakfast, willow tea and two old boots. Conclude to move on at sunrise. Alexey breaks down, also Lee. Come to empty grain raft. Halt and camp. Signs of smoke at twilight to southward.

October 16th, Sunday.—One hundred and twenty-sixth day. Alexey broken down. Divine service.

October 17th, Monday.—One hundred and twenty-seventh day. Alexey dying. Doctor baptized him. Read prayers for sick. Mr. Collins' birthday—forty years old. About sunset Alexey died. Exhaustion from starvation. Covered him with ensign and laid him in the crib.

October 18th, Tuesday.—One hundred and twenty-eighth day. Calm and mild, snow falling. Buried Alexey in the afternoon. Laid him on the ice of the river, and covered him over with slabs of ice.

October 19th, Wednesday.—One hundred and twenty-ninth day. Cutting up tent to make foot gear. Doctor went ahead to find new camp. Shifted by dark.

October 20th, Thursday.—One hundred and thirtieth day. Bright and sunny, but very cold. Lee and Kaack done up.

October 21st, Friday.—One hundred and thirty-first day. Kaack was found dead about midnight between the doctor and myself. Lee died about noon. Read prayers for sick when we found he was going.

October 22d, Saturday.—One hundred and thirty-second day. Too weak to carry the bodies of Lee and Kaack out on the ice. The doctor, Collins, and I carried them around the corner out of sight. Then my eye closed up.

October 23d, Sunday.—One hundred and thirty-third day. Everybody pretty weak. Slept or rested all day, and then managed to get enough wood in before dark. Read part of divine service. Suffering in our feet. No foot gear.

October 24th, Monday.—One hundred and thirty-fourth day. A hard night.

October 25th, Tuesday.—One hundred and thirty-fifth day.

October 26th, Wednesday.—One hundred and thirty-sixth day.

October 27th, Thursday.—One hundred and thirty-seventh day. Iversen broken down.

October 28th, Friday.—One hundred and thirty-eighth day. Iversen died during early morning.

October 29th, Saturday.—One hundred and thirty-ninth day. Dressler died during night.

October 30th, Sunday.—One hundred and fortieth day. Boyd and Görtz died during night. Mr. Collins dying.

from Arctic Dreams
by Barry Lopez

Barry Lopez (born 1945) writes dreamlike prose; revelations arrive in shapes you cannot forecast. His work is informed by compassion for the men who visit the arctic landscape, for the animals who live there, and for the landscape itself. Lopez addresses all three in this passage from his 1986 book Arctic Dreams, *an extended rumination on his travels in the North.*

n the 7th of April 1909, Robert Peary departed the vicinity of the Geographic North Pole, bound for Cape Columbia, Ellesmere Island, and his ship, the Roosevelt, which lay beyond at Cape Sheridan. He had arrived the day before, with five men, five sledges, and thirty-eight dogs. In the cross-examination he was subjected to later, Peary was criticized for having no man with him who could vouch for his solar observations, confirming the latitude. Peary's answer was that he wasn't about to share the glory with someone who had not earned the right to be there as he had—and there was no one, in his view.

The men who were with him on that day he regarded as no threat to his prestige. In a photograph, five of them stand on a hummock before a piece of sea ice, on which Peary has planted the American flag. Ooqueah holds the flag of the Navy League. Ootah has the colors of Peary's college fraternity in his hands. Egingwah holds a flag of the Daughters of the American Revolution, and Seegloo a Red Cross flag. Matthew Henson, Peary's black manservant, holds the flag that probably meant the most to Peary—a homemade polar flag, pieces of which he had left at four other of his "farthest norths" in the previous nine years.

The blue-eyed, auburn-haired man with the walrus mustache was fifty-three and in robust health at the Pole. Close up, the squinting eyes and weather-polished face showed the wear of twenty-three years in the North. He had wished all of his life to secure some accomplishment that would make him stand out from other men, one awesome, untoppable deed. Now he had it. But this man who so enjoyed the trappings of importance, who wished to be envied, also wished to be liked. He wrote to a woman he loved, after he graduated from Bowdoin, "I should like to gain that attractive personality that when I was with a person, they would always have to like me, whether they wanted to or not." But this was not to be.

As Peary grew older, as the misfortune with bad weather that always seemed to befall his journeys continued, he grew more rigid and less congenial. He exhibited that edge of irritation that emanates from self-important people who think, privately, they may have failed. Toward the end of his life, wounded no one will ever know how deeply by Frederick Cook's claim to have been at the Pole twelve months before him, Peary became recklessly arrogant and despotic.

The few excerpts from Peary's private journals that have been published reveal a man beyond the one who grasped for fame, someone beyond the hauteur, a man with tender regard for his wife and, early on, a certain sensitivity and compassion. He knew that by constantly abandoning his family and pursuing his quest for the Pole, in abandoning certain human duties and obligations, he might be thought "criminally foolish," as he put it. He was troubled by self-doubt and on at least one occasion seems to have toyed with suicide, so bleak did his prospects of making a name for himself seem.

Like all great men, Peary was importuned by oddballs and hounded by dissatisfied people. He grew to hate the parody of himself that grew out of endless public speeches and interviews. For all his disregard and unapproachability, his conniving and maneuvering, a pervading loneliness clung to him. And one is moved to see his life in a less critical way. Something went on inside him that no one else but perhaps his wife understood. After 1902, missing joints from each of his ten toes from frostbite, he walked down Senate corridors and across the streets of Washington, D.C., with a peculiar gliding shuffle. His determination to succeed, the depth and power of this man's obsession, absolutely stills the imagination of anyone who has looked upon the landscape he traversed.

In some ways Peary and Vilhjalmur Stefansson, the most visible twentieth-century arctic explorer, were alike. Both were individualists who built life-long reputations around their arctic exploits. Both were avid, sometimes unscrupulous promoters of their own enterprises and accomplishments. Both were heedless of the slaughter of animals it took to maintain their arctic endeavors. Both were dogged by petty detractors. As they settled into their reputations, they became men who preferred talking to listening, who forgot or denied the others whose lives and toil made their reputations. And, like many explorers, what was in fact nothing more than good luck they came to promote as the result of their own sagacity and careful planning.

Stefansson had a flawed understanding of arctic biology and climate, but he was insistent and dogmatic in his misconceptions. They are most clearly set forth in his book *The Friendly Arctic*, in which he maintains that men, particularly white men, can travel anywhere in the Arctic and the land will provide. Stefansson became so infatuated with this idea, after the book vaulted him to popular acclaim, that he could never see the land as a refutation of it. To prove to people who doubted him that he was right, he killed animals everywhere he went, and left behind what was inconvenient to transport.

Stefansson was also a social Darwinist; he believed in racial superiority and economic destiny. En route to the Arctic in 1908, he was captivated by the sight of natural gas flare-offs burning along the Athabasca River. "It is the torch of Science," wrote Stefansson, "lighting the way of civilization and economic development to the realm of the unknown North." The tundra was for him an extension of the American prairies, and he lamented the fact that "billions of tons of edible vegetation" that could be feeding cattle were going to waste yearly on the northern prairies. He felt that certain wild animals, like the caribou, "cumbered the land" and had to go, because they forestalled the development of ranching and agriculture. Like Theodore Roosevelt, who fought only to save prey species and who reviled predators, Stefansson wanted to make nature over to suit his beliefs about human destiny. His knowledge of the land, despite his great popularity, was selective and self-serving.

Stefansson was an explorer of prodigious determination but not an inspiring leader. He was a poor judge of character, he freely admitted; he could not get some of the people he employed to believe in his work; and he ignored important details in his plans. He was, however, a true visionary. He succeeded between 1913 and 1918 in accomplishing the expeditionary tasks he set for himself despite serious illness, appalling loneliness (he received but a single personal letter in the mailbag one year) and physical hardship, and the rudeness and contempt of some of his companions. (In those years he discovered Brock and Borden islands in the western high Arctic, Meighen Island in the north, defined the previously confused geography of King Christian Island and the Findlay Group, and made extensive pioneering soundings in the Beaufort Sea.)

Stefansson returned from the Arctic in 1919 more convinced than ever that Canada's economic future lay in the North and that the Arctic Ocean was destined to become a "Polar Mediterranean," with large coastal ports, submarine traffic beneath the ice, and a network of transpolar air routes. To convince skeptics, he embarked upon a scheme to raise reindeer on southern Baffin Island, a poorly thought-out project that ended disastrously and showed more than anything how illusionary Stefansson's understanding of the Arctic was.

He nearly wore himself out during this period of his life with lecture tours and commitments to write books and articles, and he made a serious miscalculation in insisting that Canada claim Wrangel Island, a Russian possession, for a future base of operations for arctic transport. Canada's handling of the affair eventually held it up to international embarrassment, and the debacle ended in a tragedy that reminded too many people of the *Karluk*: Stefansson sent his own expedition to Wrangel Island to establish occupation—four young college men and an Eskimo woman (to prepare and mend their skin clothing). The four men, following Stefansson's directions for living off the land, died. The woman survived.

In Ottawa, before he found himself no longer welcome in Canada,

Stefansson was called "Windjammer" behind his back, for the loquacious and headlong way in which he promoted his ideas. Stefansson's impetuous insistence on arctic development was based on a distorted view of the land, ironic in the light of his extensive travels. He became an anachronism and then, finally, something of a hero to men promoting oil development, mineral extraction, muskox ranching, and other projects for northern economic development.

Despite his overbearing nature, Stefansson was an approachable and thoughtful man. He willingly shared his moments of geographic discovery. He praised others' skills. And he readily acknowledged his own failures of tact and planning. His compassion toward sled dogs is singular among arctic explorers. (He despised Nansen's and Peary's habit of feeding sled dogs to each other to save weight on long journeys. And in a moving and poignant passage in *The Friendly Arctic*, so revealing of his loneliness, Stefansson assesses the character of a dog named Lindy with great generosity and empathy, concluding, "When he came to die I lost my best friend in the world, whom I shall never forget.")

In his later years, Stefansson became an idol to young men because he irritated self-important and pompous people and because he stood resolutely by his theories. He was pleased to share what he knew and to recommend books from his enormous library; as a friend put it, he had "an unabashed philosophy of eternal youth, complete with revolt and optimism." Stefansson liked young men for the same reason Peary did—they believed in his goals and they threw themselves unquestion-ingly and energetically into the work at hand. And they were loyal.

Stefansson lived a long life. His energy and independence were an inspiration to many. Peary's life ended in bitterness in 1920. His claim to the Pole was disputed by powerful enemies whom he had publicly ridiculed—Greely in the United States and the Norwegians Sverdrup and Nansen. The confused public image of him is due, in part, to his dedication to achieving a goal that many could not quite catch the importance of. In a speech on the floor of the House of Representatives in 1910, the Honorable J. Hampton Moore of Pennsylvania spoke in support of Peary's claim to have been first at the Pole, and caused to be introduced into the record a number of congratulatory telegrams sent to Peary. They range from President Taft's somewhat quizzical pat on the back to Theodore Roosevelt's cable, sent from his safari camp in Africa and bursting with American pride and hyperbole.

Peary and Stefansson both wrung fame from the Arctic. The distance between the real land and Stefansson's notions about it, or between the unpossessable land and Peary's appropriation of it (both gaps effectively bridged by astute public relations campaigns), is a generic source of trouble in our own time. The landscape can be labeled and then manipulated. It is possible, with insistent and impersonal technology, to deny any innate order or dignity in it.

Peary and Stefansson, too, were public figures, admired for their energy and vision. The personal insecurity and loneliness that besieged them, and that they sought a way around in the Arctic, however, provokes consideration of several dilemmas. What is the point at which the "tragic" loneliness of an individual, which drives him toward accomplishment, no longer effectively leads but confounds the well-being of the larger society? And what will be the disposition of the landscape? Will it be used, always, in whatever way we will, or will it one day be accorded some dignity of its own? And, finally, what does the nature of the heroic become, once the landscape is threatened?

In 1918 the American artist and illustrator Rockwell Kent arrived at Fox Island off Alaska's Kenai Peninsula with his nine-year-old son, young Rockwell. "We came to this new land, a man and a boy, entirely on a dreamer's search," he wrote. "Having had a vision of Northern Paradise, we came to find it." He meant to heal himself somehow and to get to know his son. He believed the land would help him to do that, and that it would care for them both.

Kent was a remarkable twentieth-century American. A socialist, he professed himself to the Strenuous Life of Theodore Roosevelt. He delighted in thumbing his nose at social conventions. He identified himself with the drama and characters of the Icelandic sagas, and was fascinated by cold, harsh, testing environments. He was abrasive, self-righteous, and occasionally cruel to people he felt superior to, but he was also a romantic and a man of idealistic visions. And, in spite of the apparent contradiction between his socialist beliefs and his success as an artist and businessman, he was a person of integrity. He argued in his art and in heroic prose for the essential dignity of human beings and for the existence of man's Godlike qualities. His enthusiasm for life was genuine and unbounded, and he was completely dedicated to the work that reflected his beliefs.

On Fox Island, Kent exulted in clearing the land and creating a parklike setting. He was glad to be away from the "confusing intricacy of modern society." His illusions about wilderness were always somewhat at odds with the requirements of daily life on the island, which caused him to reflect that "the romance of [this] adventure hangs on slender threads." Kent realized that what invigorated him in this northern landscape was not so much the land but what he made of the land—what his imagination made of the color, the contours, the shading. His attachment to the landscape was passionate; he responded ecstatically to beauty in the land, in Alaska and on trips to Greenland as well. But his attachment was almost entirely metaphorical; and it was sustained by all the attachments to civilization Kent would not forgo— his mail, trips into the village of Seward for the staples of his vegetarian diet, the neighborly assistance of the island's owner, who lived in a house a few yards from Kent's cabin.

When he and his son left after six months, his neighbor said, "You might as well have spent a couple of months back in the mountains of New York for all you've seen of Alaska." But Kent felt no need to travel further. The invigoration he felt, the renewed sense of wilderness that now compelled his art, made it possible to return to the marital and professional difficulties that he faced in New York.

Kent's metaphorical experience with the land, the way his imagination worked against it, differs markedly from Stefansson's and Peary's manifestly arduous encounters. But it was no less real. And the experience that Kent had—to find oneself in the land, to feel some intrinsic, overwhelmingly sane order in it, to participate in that order— is the aim of many twentieth-century people who travel to such remote regions. Relationships with the land that are intensely metaphorical, like Kent's, are a lofty achievement of the human mind. They are a sophisticated response, like the creation of maps, or the development of a language that grows out of a certain landscape. The mind can imagine beauty and conjure intimacy. It can find solace where literal analysis finds only trees and rocks and grass.

In July 1929, eleven years after the sojourn on Fox Island, Kent and two companions shipwrecked at Karajak Fiord on the mountainous west coast of Greenland. Walking inland, they came to a lake "round as the moon." The gale that had wrecked them was still blowing. Kent wrote that the lake's

> pebbly shore shows smooth and clean and bright against the deep green water. [We] descend to it and, standing there, look over at the mountain wall that bounds it. The dark cliffs rise sheer from lake to sky. From its high edge pours a torrent. And the gale, lifting that torrent in mid-air, disperses it in smoke.
>
> [We] stand there looking at it all: at the mountains, at the smoking waterfall, at the dark green lake with wind puffs silvering its plain, at the flowers that fringe the pebbly shore and star the banks.

One of them says, "Maybe we have lived only to be here now."

A salient element emerges in Peary's recounting of his arctic journeys, which reminds me of this scene of tranquil beauty after a violent shipwreck. As far as I know, it is consistent with the experience and feelings of most other arctic explorers. The initial trip into that far northern landscape is perceived by the explorer as something from which one might derive prestige, money, social advantage, or notable awards and adulation. Although these intentions are not lost sight of on subsequent trips, they are never so purely held or so highly regarded as they are before the first journey begins. They are tempered by a mounting sense of consternation and awe. It is as though the land slowly works its way into the man and by virtue of its character eclipses these motives. The land becomes large, alive like an animal; it humbles him in a way he cannot pronounce. It is not that the land is simply beautiful but that it is powerful. Its power derives from the tension between its obvious beauty and its capacity to take life. Its power flows into the mind from a realization of how darkness and light are bound together within it, and the feeling that this is the floor of creation.

Three of us were driving north on the trans-Alaska pipeline haul road, pulling a boat behind a pickup. For miles at a time we were the only vehicle, then a tractor-trailer truck—pugnacious and hell-bent—would shoulder past, flailing us with gravel. From Fairbanks to Prudhoe Bay the road parallels the elevated, gleaming pipeline. Both pathways in the corridor have a manicured, unnatural stillness about them, like white-board fences running over the hills of a summer pasture. One evening we passed a lone seed-and-fertilizing operation, spraying grass seed and nutrients on the slopes and berms of the road, to prevent erosion. There would be no unruly tundra here. These were the seeds of neat Kentucky grasses.

One day we had a flat tire. Two of us changed it while the third stood by with a loaded .308 and a close eye on a female grizzly and her yearling cub, rooting in a willow swale 30 yards away. We saw a single wolf—a few biologists in Fairbanks had asked us to watch for them. The truckers, they said, had shot most of the wolves along the road; perhaps a few were drifting back in, with the traffic so light now. Short-eared owls flew up as we drove along. Single caribou bulls trotted off in their light-footed way, like shy waterfowl. Moose standing along the Sagavanirktok River were nodding in the willow browse. And red foxes, with their long black legs, pranced down the road ahead of us, heads thrown back over their shoulders. That night I thought about the animals, and how the road had come up amidst them.

We arrived at the oil fields at Prudhoe Bay on an afternoon when light blazed on the tundra and swans were gliding serenely in rectangles of water between the road dikes. But this landscape was more austere than any I had ever seen in the Arctic. Small buildings, one or two together at a time, stood on the horizon. It reminded me of West Texas, land throttled for water and oil. Muscular equipment sitting idle like slouched fists in oil-stained yards. It was no business of mine. I was only here to stay overnight. In the morning we would put the boat in the water and head west to the Jones Islands.

The bungalow camp we stayed in was wretched with the hopes of cheap wealth, with the pallid, worn-out flesh and swollen bellies of supervisors in ball caps, and full of the desire of young men for women with impossible shapes; for a winning poker hand; a night with a bottle gone undetected. The older men, mumbling of their debts, picking through the sweepings of their despair alone in the cafeteria, might well not have lived through the misery, to hear the young men talk of wealth only a fool would miss out on.

We left in the morning, bound for another world entirely, the world of science, a gathering of data for calculations and consultations that would send these men to yet some other site, the deceit intact.

Months later, on a cold March morning, I came to Prudhoe Bay for an official visit. I was met at the airport by a young and courteous public relations officer, who shook hands earnestly and gave me the first of several badges to wear as we drove around the complex. The police at road checkpoints and at building entrances examined these credentials and then smiled without meaning to be cordial. Here was the familiar chill of one's dignity resting for a moment in the hand of an authority of artificial size, knowing it might be set aside like a small stone for further scrutiny if you revealed impatience or bemusement. Industrial spying, it was apologetically explained—disgruntled former employees; the possibility of drug traffic; or environmental saboteurs.

We drove out along the edge of the sea ice and examined a near-shore drill rig from a distance—too chilly to walk over, said my host, as though our distant view met the letter of his and my responsibilities.

We ate lunch in the cafeteria of the oil company's headquarters building, a sky-lit atrium of patrician silences, of slacks and perfume and well-mannered people, of plants in deferential attendance. The food was perfectly prepared. (I recalled the low-ceilinged cafeterias with their thread-bare, food-stained carpets, the cigarette-burned tables, the sluggish food and clatter of Melmac where the others ate.)

On the way to Gathering Station #1 we pull over, to be passed by the largest truckload of anything I have ever seen: a building on a trailer headed for the Kuparuk River. In the ditch by the road lies a freshly fallen crane, the wheels of the cab still turning in the sunshine. The man with me smiles. It is −28°F.

At Gathering Station #1 the oil from four well areas is cooled. Water is removed. Gas is separated off. Above ground for the first time, the primal fluid moves quickly through pipes at military angles and sits under pressure in tanks with gleaming, spartan dials. The painted concrete floors are spotless. There is no stray tool or wipe rag. Anything that threatens harm or only to fray clothing is padded, covered. The brightly lit pastel rooms carry heat from deep in the earth and lead to each other like a series of airlocks, or boiler rooms in the bowels of an enormous ship. I see no one. The human presence is in the logic of the machinery, the control of the unrefined oil, the wild liquid in the grid of pipes. There is nothing here for the oil but to follow instructions.

Tempered, it flows to Pump Station #1.

The pavilion outside the fence at the pump station is drifted in with snow. No one comes here, not in this season. I climb over the drifts and wipe wind-crusted snow from Plexiglas-covered panels that enumerate the local plants and animals. The sentences are pleasant, meant to offend no one. Everything—animals, oil, destiny—is made to seem to fit somewhat naturally together. People are not mentioned. I look up at Pump Station #1, past the cyclone fencing and barbed wire. The slogging pumps sequestered within insulated buildings on the tundra, the fields of pipe, the roughshod trucks, all the muscular engineering, the Viking bellows that draws and gathers and directs— that it all runs to the head of this seemingly innocent pipe, lined out like a stainless-steel thread toward the indifferent Brooks Range, that it is all reduced to the southward journey of this 48-inch pipe, seems impossible.

No toil, no wildness shows. It could not seem to the chaperoned visitor more composed, inoffensive, or civilized.

None of the proportions are familiar. I stand in the windblown pavilion looking at the near and distant buildings. I remember a similar view of the launch complexes at Cape Canaveral. It is not just the outsize equipment lumbering down the roads here but the exaggerated presence of threat, hidden enemies. My face is beginning to freeze. The man in the blue Chevrolet van with the heaters blasting is smiling. No guide could be more pleasant. It is time to eat again—I think that is what he is saying. I look back at the pipeline, this final polished extrusion of all the engineering. There are so few people here, I keep thinking. Deep in the holds of those impersonal buildings, the only biology is the dark Devonian fluid in the pipes.

On the way back to the cafeteria the man asks me what I think of the oil industry. He has tried not to seem prying, but this is the third time he has asked. I speak slowly. "I do not know anything about the oil industry. I am interested mostly in the landscape, why we come here and what we see. I am not a business analyst, an economist, a social planner. The engineering is astounding. The true cost, I think, must be unknown."

During dinner he tells me a story. A few years ago there were three birch trees in an atrium in the building's lobby. In September their leaves turned yellow and curled over. Then they just hung there, because the air in the enclosure was too still. No wind. Fall came when a man from building maintenance went in and shook the trees.

Before we drove the few miles over to Deadhorse, the Prudhoe Bay airport, my host said he wanted me to see the rest of the Base Operations Building. A movie theater with tiered rows of plush red velour seats. Electronic game rooms. Wide-screen television alcoves. Pool tables. Weight-lifting room. Swimming pool. Squash courts. Running track. More television alcoves. Whirlpool treatment and massage. The temperatures in the different rooms are different perfectly. Everything is cushioned, carpeted, padded. There are no unpleasant sounds. No blemishes. You do not have to pay for anything. He shows me his rooms.

Later we are standing at a railing, looking out through insulated glass at the blue evening on the tundra. I thank him for the tour. We have enjoyed each other. I marvel at the expense, at all the amenities that are offered. He is looking at the snow. "Golden handcuffs." That is all he says with his wry smile.

It is hard to travel in the Arctic and not encounter industrial development. Too many lines of logistic support, transportation, and communication pass through these sites. I passed through Prudhoe Bay four or five times in the course of several years, and visited both lead-zinc mines in the Canadian Archipelago, the Nanisivik Mine on Strathcona Sound on Baffin Island, and the Polaris Mine on Little Cornwallis

Island. And one winter I toured Panarctic's facilities at Rae Point on Melville Island, and their drill rigs on the sea ice off Mackenzie King and Lougheed islands.

I was drawn to all these places for reasons I cannot fully articulate. For the most part, my feelings were what they had been at Prudhoe Bay—a mixture of fascination at the sophistication of the technology; sadness born out of the dismalness of life for many of the men employed here, which no amount of red velour, free arcade games, and open snack bars can erase; and misgiving at the sullen, dismissive attitude taken toward the land, the violent way in which it is addressed. At pretensions to a knowledge of the Arctic, drawn from the perusal of a public relations pamphlet and from the pages of pulp novels. A supervisor at an isolated drill rig smiled sardonically when I asked him if men ever walked away from the buildings on their off-hours. "You can count the people who care about what's out there on the fingers of one hand." The remark represents fairly the situation at most military and industrial sites in the Arctic.

Away from the carefully tended environment of a corporate showcase base of operations, the industrial scene is much bleaker. In the most distant camps, to my sensibilities at least, were some of the saddest human lives I have ever known. The society is all male. The tedium of schedules is unrelieved. Drugs and alcohol are smuggled in. Pornographic magazines abound, which seems neither here nor there until one realizes that they are nearly inescapable, and that they are part of a resentful attitude toward the responsibilities of family life. There is a distrust, a cursing of women, that is unsettling. Woman and machinery and the land are all spoken of in the same way—seduction, domestication, domination, control. This observation represents no new insight, of course, into the psychology of development in Western culture; but it is not academic. It is as real as the scars on the faces of flight attendants I interviewed in Alaska who were physically and sexually abused by frustrated workmen flying to and from Prudhoe Bay.

The atmosphere in some of the camps is little different from the environment of a small state prison, down to the existence of racial cliques. This is part of factory life in America, an ugly way the country has arranged itself, a predicament from which economic and political visionaries would extricate us. There is a lurking suspicion among the workers I spoke to that in spite of their good wages they were somehow being cheated, that any chance for advancement from their menial situation was, for most of them, an illusion. And they were convinced that someone, somewhere, was to blame. Their frustration was predictably directed at their employers, at overeducated engineers or petroleum geologists, and at vague political and ethnic groups whom they saw as confused and impractical critics of growth, of progress. Some of these men felt that the Arctic was really a great wasteland "with a few stupid birds," too vast to be hurt. Whatever strong men could accomplish against the elements in such a place, they insisted, was inherently right. The last words of many of these discussions, whether they were delivered quizzically or cynically or in disbelief, were summary—what else is it good for?

Many arctic oil and mine workers are hard-pressed to explain—and mostly not interested in—what it is good for, beyond what is in the ground; or in what its future will be; or in the fate of its people and animals. "Technology is inevitable," a drilling supervisor told me with finality one day. "People just got to get that through their heads." The sensibility of many of the foremen and crew chiefs, to characterize the extreme, is colonial. The tone of voice is impatient and the vocabulary is economic. The mentality is largely innocent of history and arctic ecology, cavalier about human psychological requirements, and manipulative. And the attitude of the extremist, at least in this regard, filters down. These thoughts are parroted by other workers who feel defensive, or embattled by critics. Men who make such extreme statements often give the impression of not having thought through what they are saying. They only mean to keep their jobs, or talk themselves out of doubt.

In the mines and oil fields, of course, were other, different men, who criticized in private conversation what was being done "for the money." As a group, they felt a responsibility for what they were doing. They did not see their jobs solely as a source of income. Many told me they wanted to return to the Arctic after making enough money to go back to school. They wanted to travel in the Arctic and read more about it. They meant no harm, and were uneasy themselves about the damage they were capable of doing. In Canada they feared the collusive force that government and industry were capable of bringing to bear—that the restraints against it were too weak. These were mostly younger men; and the sentiments were not rare among them.

More memorable somehow, and ultimately more gratifying, were the thoughts of several older men who spoke to me on different occasions about the conditions under which they worked. (It was one of them who had suggested the parallel with prison life.) These were seasoned men of dignified bearing in their forties and fifties, the sort of people you have regard for instantly, regardless of the circumstances. They were neither insistent nor opinionated in offering their observations, which made it easier to speculate in their presence; and they gave an impression of deliberation and self-knowledge.

They shook their heads over industrial mismanagement, that humorless, deskbound ignorance that brings people and land together in such a way that both the land and the people suffer. They said, without any condescension, that the companies that employed them sometimes clearly erred, and that they acted in high-handed and sometimes illegal ways. But these were more acknowledgments of a state of affairs than criticism. They spoke as much of their families, of their wives and children. They spoke of them with indulgence and unconscious admiration. You could build anything on the decency of such men.

In the wake of these latter conversations the world seemed on balance to me, or at least well intentioned. Part of what was attractive about these men was that their concern for the health of the land and their concern for the fate of people were not separate issues. They were not for me, either. And one evening, lying in my bunk, it became clear that the fate of each was hinged on the same thing, on the source of their dignity, on whether it was innate or not.

The source of their dignity—not among themselves, but in a larger social context—was the approval of their superiors, an assessment made by people who were not their peers. (Largely unfamiliar with modern Eskimo life, these men nevertheless had an intuitive and sympathetic response to the predicament of Eskimos constantly being scrutinized and judged by outsiders.) Their dignity as workmen, and therefore their self-respect, was not whole. To an outside viewer they, like the land, were subject to manipulation. Their dignity was received. It grew out of how well they responded to directions.

In my experience, most people in the Arctic who direct the activities of employees or who seek to streamline the process of resource extraction without regard to what harm might be done to the land, do so with the idea that their goals are desirable and admirable, and that they are shared by everyone. Their own source of dignity, in fact, derives from a belief that they are working in this way "for the common good." In their view the working man must provide cheerful labor, be punctual, and demonstrate allegiance to a concept of a greater good orchestrated from above. The Eskimo, for his part, must conduct himself either as a sober and aspiring middle-class wage earner or, alternately, as an "authentic, traditional Eskimo," that is, according to an idealized and unrealistic caricature created by the outsider. The land, the very ground itself, the plants and the animals, must also produce something—petroleum, medicines, food, the setting for a movie—if it is to achieve any measure of dignity. If it does not, it is waste. Tundra wasteland. A waste of time.

Without dignity, of course, people are powerless. Strip a person or the land of dignity and you can direct any scheme you wish against them or it, with impunity and with the best of motives. To some this kind of efficiency is a modern technique, lamentable but not evil. For others it is a debilitating degradation, a loss of integrity and spirit that no kind of economic well-being can ever justify.

The solution to this very old and disconcerting situation among the men I spoke to, when I asked, was utopian. They believed in the will of good people. They thought some way could be found to take life-affecting decisions away from ignorant, venal, and unimaginative persons. Yes, they said, an innate not a tendered dignity put individuals in the best position to act, to think through the difficult problems of what to do about technologies that mangled people and mangled the land. But they did not know where you started, where the first, hard changes had to be made.

I was traveling with a friend once, in northern Baffin Island. We were in a hunting camp at the edge of the sea ice with about thirty Eskimos. It was damp and windy—raw weather. Out of the sky one morning—

we had been in this atmosphere long enough to make the event seem slightly confusing at first—came a helicopter, which landed at the camp. A man got out and walked over to the tent where we were staying. He was the president of a shipping company. He was concerned that an icebreaking ore ship that had recently been in Admiralty Inlet might have adversely affected hunting for the Eskimos or made travel over the sea ice more difficult for them. (The ship's track had relieved pressure in the ice, which would cause it to break up in an unusual pattern as spring progressed. The track might possibly lure narwhals into a fatal savssat. Or the noise of the ship's engines might frighten narwhals away from the floe edge, where the Eskimos were hunting.)

There were several unusual aspects to this man's visit. First, Eskimos virtually never get to talk directly with "the head man," the person whose decisions vitally affect the direction of their lives. They are usually held at bay by dozens of intermediaries. Second, important men more often have pressing schedules and retinues with them, which preclude protracted or serious conversation. Third, it is unusual for anyone at all to show a concern this pointed, this knowledgeable. The man offered to fly several hunters out along the 40 miles of ship track in the helicopter so they could inspect it. He would land wherever they wanted. The hunters went with him, and were glad for the opportunity to see the situation from the air.

That accomplished, the man could have left, feeling a wave of genuine gratitude from the Eskimos for his thoughtfulness. But he stayed. He sat in a tent in the hunting camp and ate the "country food" that was offered, along with bannock and tea. He did not try to summarize or explain anything. He did not ask a lot of questions to demonstrate his interest. He just sat quietly and ate. He handed a gawking child a piece of bannock and said a few things about the weather. By his simple appreciation of the company, by his acceptance of these unfamiliar circumstances, he made everyone in the tent feel comfortable. The dignity of the occasion arose from an atmosphere of courtesy that he alone could have established.

He sat for more than an hour. And then he said good-bye and left. One incident in the vastness. But it was a fine moment, a gesture you could carry away with you.

One brilliant July morning I flew out of Resolute on Cornwallis Island for the Canadian weather station at Eureka, on northern Ellesmere Island. I traveled with a flight map in my lap. From this height, and with the map, I found a corroboration of what I knew of the land— from history books, from walking around in it, from talking to people long resident here, from eating food the land produced, from traveling over it with people who felt defined by it. There were walrus in the upper part of Wellington Channel. We passed over Grinnell Peninsula, long thought an island, named for the generous Henry Grinnell. Far to the west I could see the dark waters of a perennial polynya in the ice in Penny Strait, and to the east country I wanted one day, if ever there was a chance, to see from the ground, at the head of Jones Sound and the southern end of Simmons Peninsula. In winter.

We drew up on the southeast corner of Axel Heiberg Island, which Otto Sverdrup had explored. Good Friday Bay. Surprise Fiord. Wolf Fiord. At the head of these fiords were glaciers that did not reach tidewater—huge hesitations on the brown earth of the valleys. In the east light I was reminded of the mountain ranges of Arizona, of the colors of canyons on the Colorado Plateau—ocherous browns, washed tans, flat yellows. I was mesmerized by the view of Axel Heiberg: distant mountains in a sky of clear air; steep slopes of gray scree tumbled out onto the backs of white glaciers, the lime-green tongues of vegetation etched so sharply against the darker mountains it seemed in the morning light that the scene occurred behind polished glass. I realized this island was as remote as anything I could imagine, and for the first time in all the months I had spent North, I felt myself crossing a line into the Far North. It was as though I had passed through one of those walls of pressure one feels descending from mountains. I had a clarity of mind that made the map in my lap seem both wondrous and strange in its approximations. I looked west into Mokka Fiord, to a chain of lakes between two whitish gypsum domes. Beyond was the patterned ground of the mesic tundra. The browns and blacks and whites were so rich I could feel them. The beauty here is a beauty you feel in your flesh. You feel it physically, and that is why it is sometimes terrifying to approach. Other beauty takes only the heart, or the mind.

I lost for long moments my sense of time and purpose as a human being. In the walls of Axel Heiberg I found what I had known of mountains as a child; that from them came a knowledge that was received, for which there were no words, only, vaguely, prayers. What I loved as a man, the love for parents and wife and children and friends, I felt suffused with in that moment, flushed in the face. The fierce testament of life in abeyance on the winter tundra, the sharp taste of irok on evening walks on Baffin Island, the haunting sound of old-squaw in the ice, *ahaalik, ahaalik*. At the sudden whiteness of a snow-bank on the brown earth at Mokka Fiord, I remembered vividly arctic hares, three feet tall and running on their hind legs, hundreds of them, across Seward Peninsula. In the stillness of Axel Heiberg I felt for the first time the edges of an unentered landscape.

That intense reverie came because of the light, the clearness of the air, and certainly the desire to comprehend, which, however I might try to suspend it, was always there. I found in adumbrations of the land, in suggestions of the landscape and all that it contained, the ways human life sorts through itself and survives. To look at the land was never to forget the people it contained.

For a relationship with landscape to be lasting, it must be reciprocal. At the level at which the land supplies our food, this is not difficult to comprehend, and the mutuality is often recalled in a grace at meals. At the level at which landscape seems beautiful or frightening to us and leaves us affected, or at the level at which it furnishes us with the metaphors and symbols with which we pry into mystery, the nature of reciprocity is harder to define. In approaching the land with an attitude of obligation, willing to observe courtesies difficult to articulate—perhaps only a gesture of the hands—one establishes a regard from which dignity can emerge. From that dignified relationship with the land, it is possible to imagine an extension of dignified relationships throughout one's life. Each relationship is formed of the same integrity, which initially makes the mind say: the things in the land fit together perfectly, even though they are always changing. I wish the order of my life to be arranged in the same way I find the light, the slight movement of the wind, the voice of a bird, the heading of a seed pod I see before me. This impeccable and indisputable integrity I want in myself.

One of the oldest dreams of mankind is to find a dignity that might include all living things. And one of the greatest of human longings must be to bring such dignity to one's own dreams, for each to find his or her own life exemplary in some way. The struggle to do this is a struggle because an adult sensibility must find some way to include all the dark threads of life. A way to do this is to pay attention to what occurs in a land not touched by human schemes, where an original order prevails.

The dignity we seek is one beyond that articulated by Enlightenment philosophers. A more radical Enlightenment is necessary, in which dignity is understood as an innate quality, not as something tendered by someone outside. And that common dignity must include the land and its plants and creatures. Otherwise it is only an invention, and not, as it should be, a perception about the nature of living matter.

The plane, that so well designed, dependable, and ubiquitous workhorse of the Canadian Arctic, the Twin Otter, swung out over Fosheim Peninsula, a rolling upland, far northern oasis, on its approach to the Eureka airstrip. I could see muskoxen feeding to the north.

There is a peninsula at the southern end of Baffin Island called *Meta Incognita*, named by Queen Elizabeth. The words are often translated as the "Unknown Edge" or the "Mysterious Land." (Frobisher thought this the shore of North America.) It is possible, however, that Elizabeth had another meaning in mind. The word *meta*, strictly speaking, means "cone." In classical Rome the towers at either end of the race course in the Colosseum, around which the chariots turned, were called *metae*. It may have been that Elizabeth meant to suggest a similar course, with London the *meta cognita*, the known entity, and the land Frobisher found the unknown entity, the *meta incognita*. North America, then, was the turn at the far end of the course, something England felt herself reaching toward, and around which she would eventually make a turn of unknown meaning before coming home.

The European culture from which the ancestors of many of us came has yet to make this turn, I think. It has yet to understand the wisdom, preserved in North America, that lies in the richness and sanctity of a wild landscape, what it can mean in the unfolding of human life, the staying of a troubled human spirit.

The other phrase that comes to mind is more obscure. It is the Latin motto from the title banner of *The North Georgia Gazette: per freta hactenus negata,* meaning to have negotiated a strait the very existence of which has been denied. But it also suggests a continuing movement through unknown waters. It is, simultaneously, an expression of fear and of accomplishment, the cusp on which human life finds its richest expression.

The plane landed. Light was lambent on the waters of Slidre Fiord. From the weather station six dogs came toward us, lumbering like wolves, a movement that suggested they could drop buffalo. I reached out and patted one of them tentatively on the head.

The Last Pork Chop
by Edward Abbey

Edward Abbey (1927–1989) wrote about many landscapes. This 1984 piece for Outside *magazine is about an arctic rafting trip: He wanted to see a grizzly bear. Abbey inhabits his best writing: Read it and you know that he was an observer and an admirer of the world; a passionate critic; a crank who had a good time, who let the world's mystery uplift him, who was angry at us, who loved us.*

In Medias Res, Alaska; June 24

W e watch the little Cessna roar down the gravel bar toward the river, going away. At full throttle, into the wind, pilot and airplane are fully committed—they must take off or die. Once again the miracle takes place, the fragile craft lifts itself from the ground and rises into the air, noisy as a bumblebee, delicate as a butterfly. Function of the airfoil, pulled forward by a whirling screw. And I am delighted, one more time, by the daring of my species and the audacity of our flying machines. There is poetry and music in our technology, a beauty as touching as that of eagle, moss campion, raven, or yonder limestone boulder shining under the Arctic sun.

The airplane diminishes downriver, banks, and turns through a pass in the hills and is gone, out of sight, suddenly silent, ephemeral and lovely as a dream.

I notice now that we have been left behind. Two of us, myself and Dana Van Burgh the Third, a handsome, hearty river guide who looks a bit like Paul McCartney or maybe one of Elvis Presley's possible sons. The Cessna is bound for an Eskimo village called Kaktovik ("fish-seining place") about a hundred miles away on the most dismal, desperate, degraded rat hole in the world—Barter Island. If all goes well the plane will return in two hours with more of our equipment and two or three more members of our party. Our expedition. Mark Jensen's Alaska River Expeditions, Haines, Alaska.

The river at our side, more crystalline than golden, is called the Kongakut, and the plan, if all goes right, is to float down this river in two rubber rafts to another straight gravel bar eighty miles away. There, ten days from now, the airplane will pick us up and ferry us back—to Kaktovik, and Barter Island. Something to look forward to. But the river is alive with Arctic char and grayling, first-rate primeval fishing waters, and in the valley and among the treeless mountains around us roam the caribou, the wolf, the Dall sheep (close cousin to the bighorn), the moose, and of course the hypothetical grizzly bear. Himself, *Ursus arctos horribilis*. So they say.

If I seem skeptical about the bear it is because after several efforts I have yet to see with my own eyes a grizzly in the wild. I spent a summer as a fire lookout in Glacier National Park in Montana, and I saw a few black bears but not one grizzly. Even hiking alone, after dark, through alder thickets on a mountain trail, I failed to attract the GRIZ (the plural form of which is GRIZZ). I sweated up another mountain trail behind Douglas Peacock, himself half-grizzly, to a secret place he calls the Grizzly Hilton, where he has filmed, encountered, and *talked with* many grizzlies, but we saw nothing except flies, mosquitoes, and the devil's club, a mean, ugly plant with hairy leaves, thorny stems, a fist of inedible yellow berries on its top. Ten days on the Tatshenshini River in the wilderness of the Yukon and southeast Alaska again failed to produce an authentic grizzly bear. I even tried the Tucson Zoo one time, but the alleged grizzly (if such there be) refused to emerge from its den in the rear of the cage. I could see a single dark paw with ragged claws, a host of loitering flies, nothing more.

The grizzly bear is an inferential beast.

Of course I've seen the inferential evidence—the photographs and movies, the broad tracks in the sand, the deep claw marks on a spruce tree higher than I could reach, the fresh bear shit steaming like hot caviar on the trail. And I've heard and read the testimony of many others. What does it come to? Inference. If "p" then "q." It could all be a practical joke, a hoax, even a conspiracy. Which is more likely? asked Mark Twain (I paraphrase): that the unicorn exists or that men tell lies?

The grizzly bear is a myth.

The high peaks of the Brooks Range stand behind us, to the south, barren of trees, dappled with snowfields and a few small glaciers. To the east is Canada, perhaps a hundred miles away. The nearest city in that direction would be Murmansk. Murmansk, Russia. The nearest city to the west is also Murmansk. The nearest city in any direction is Fairbanks, about 600 miles to the southwest. (If you are willing to allow Fairbanks a place in the category of city. And why not? We are a generous people.) The nearest permanently inhabited or reinhabited town, after Kaktovik up there in the Beaufort Sea, is an Athabascan Indian settlement called Arctic Village, a couple of hundred miles away on the other side, the southern, wetter side, of the Brooks Range.

After the Australian outback, this is the most remote spot on which I've managed to install myself, on this particular planet, so far. But it seems benign here, especially, the river flowing nearby, its water clean enough to drink, directly, without boiling or purifying. Imagine the rare, almost-forgotten pleasure of dipping a cup into a river—not a stream but a river—and drinking the water at once, without hesitation, without fear. There are no beaver in the Brooks, no domestic cattle, no permanent humans, and extremely few transient humans, and therefore no coliform bacteria. So far.

And the sun keeps shining, circling, shining, not so intensely as in the desert or at high elevations (we're only 2,500 feet above sea level here), but more persistently. With a doughty, dogged persistence—that midsummer sun will never go down.

We gather firewood. Timberline begins at sea level on the north side of the Brooks Range divide, but there is a scrubby growth of willow, shoulder high, along the crystal river, and little groves of small, slender cottonwoods—like baby aspens—tucked in sheltered corners here and there. We garner driftwood, enough for a couple of days, from the gravel bar.

Dana stops, hearing a noise in the willow thicket downstream. A noise like the thump and thud of heavy feet. He faces that way, watching intently. The noise stops. I look the other way, upstream and to both sides, afraid of something *fierce* creeping up on us from behind.

"It ain't wilderness," says my friend Doug Peacock, "unless there's a critter out there that can kill you and eat you."

Two pump-action short-barreled shotguns lie on our duffel a hundred feet away, loaded with 12-gauge slugs. Back at the Barter Island airstrip Dana had explained the shotguns in the following way to one of our passengers:

"You fire the first shot in front of the GRIZ, into the ground, to scare him away. If he don't scare but keeps advancing you wait until you can't stand it anymore, then shoot to kill. First a shot to knock him down, next a shot to finish him off."

I like Dana's phrase, *Until you can't stand it anymore* . . . Thoroughly subjective but admirably rational.

The noise we heard is not repeated; Dana and I surmise that the sound came from a lone caribou browsing on willow leaves. We finish our work. Erecting my own tent out on the gravel bar close to the river, where the breeze is breezier and the mosquitoes scattered, I happen to glance up and see a file of caribou—twelve or fifteen of them, moving rapidly down the open mountainside on the other side of the Kongakut Valley. They appear to be heading for an acre field of overflow ice, the white *Aufeis*, as the Germans call it, which covers much of the bottom land a half-mile to our north. I watch them for a while through my binoculars. Pale brown or yellowish in color, as big as elk, each animal carries an impressive rack of antlers (not horns) on its head, the cow and yearling as well as the bull. They look to me like storybook reindeer, exactly the kind that Santa Claus once harnessed to his sleigh. The caribou gather on the ice and linger there, perhaps to escape for a time the flying swarms of devils that infest the grass, flowers, shrubs, heather, and bracken of the tundra-upholstered hillsides.

The Cessna returns, circles once, floats down upon the rough shingle of the gravel bar, bounces to another hair-raising stop in an aura of dust. A door is opened from within, disgorging our trip leader, Mark Jensen; another half-ton of baggage; the pilot; and a lawyer. A lawyer on the Kongakut River? Everybody has to be somewhere, said the philosopher Parmenides, explaining his theory of the plenum. Her name is Ginger

Fletcher, and she comes from Salt Lake City, where she works as a public defender. She's that kind of lawyer, public-spirited, and a smart, lively, good-looking young woman to boot. (I list her more conspicuous attributes in random order of importance.) Later, when she opens a bottle of schnapps from her bag, we name her Ginger Schnapps.

Mark Jensen, like so many professional outdoors people, is one of those depressingly youngish types (thirty-four years old) with the body of a trained athlete, hands like Vise-Grips, and a keen mind bright with ideas and full of enthusiasm for any project that promises the rewards of difficulty. He has the usual array of primary skills, being a first-class boatman, fisherman, hunter, camp cook, mountain climber, and so on and so forth. He has hair like Robert Redford and a sort of Robert Mitchum high-bridged nose that gives him, in profile, the classical heroic Homeric look. Life is not fair. In compensation he addresses everyone as "mate" or "partner," which fools no one. Enough of these *Übermenschen*. I wish that Fran Lebowitz or Nora Ephron were here. My sort of people.

Jensen smiles, opens a big thermos jug, and pours each of us a cupful of hot, smoking coffee. Our pilot, young Gil Zemansky, Ph.D. (biology), gulps his quickly; we pivot his aircraft around by hand, nose into the wind, and off he roars in all-out effort, racketing over the stones and gravel at fifty miles an hour, heading toward the willow thicket, the boulders, the river, departing Earth as before at the last plausible moment. He has one more trip to make, three more passengers to bring us, before his work is done and the day ends. But of course, I remind myself, it's late June in the Arctic; this day will not end, not for us. For us that sun will never go down.

We carry the baggage off the landing strip, build up the fire, start a two-gallon pot of coffee, eat a snack before supper. Or is it lunch? Ginger puts up her tent back in the caribou-cropped willows. We watch more caribou trickle over the mountain to join their friends on the ice field. A golden eagle sails overhead and the gulls come and go, hoping for someone to catch and gut a fish.

I realize that I have described all of these people, including the pilot, as young. Compared to me they are. Everywhere I go these days I seem to find myself surrounded by younger and younger humans. If one keeps hanging about, as I do, then the temporal horizon expands, the pursuing generations extend toward infinity. But why should I care? Sagging into my late middle age, I have discovered one clear consolation for my stiffening back (I never could touch my toes anyway, and why should I want to?), my mildewed pancreas, my missing gallbladder, my *panza de cerveza*, my cranky and arthritic Anglo-Saxon attitudes. And the consolation is this, that I am content with my limitations.

Unsuspecting, the caribou come to meet us, a herd of twenty-five or so. Anxious and bug-harassed creatures, they usually keep on the move. They pass us, their big ungulate feet clicking, then stop, turn, go the other way, as finely attuned to one another's movements and emotions as a school of minnows. Watching them at close range, I can see the velvet on their antlers, the large glowing eyeballs, the supple muscles, the spring and tension in their step. Each animal moves within its personalized cloud of gnats, flies, mosquitoes, every insect probing for entrance into an eye, nostril, ear, mouth, vagina, pizzle, rectum, or wound. I do not envy the caribou. North of here on the calving grounds, the bear and wolves are attacking their newborn at this very hour. The natives hound them on snowmobiles (or snow machines, as Alaskans say), shooting them down by the thousands with high-powered, scope-sighted rifles ("subsistence hunting"). Even the golden eagle, according to some Alaska Fish and Game officials, will attack and kill a caribou calf. Nobody envies the caribou. But like fruit flies, rabbits, alley cats, street rats, and the human race, caribou possess one great talent for survival: not intelligence or the power of reasoning, but fertility—a high rate of reproduction.

Once more our aerial taxicab returns, unloading the balance of the 1983 Kongakut expedition: John Feeley, a schoolteacher from a little town called Whittier in southern Alaska; Maurine Bachman, a legal secretary from Anchorage; and Mike Bladyka, an anesthesiologist from Los Angeles. Good people, happy to be here. All of us but John have been on a river trip with Mark Jensen before. Obeying the territorial, nesting instinct, each man sets up his tent first thing. Maurine moves in with Ginger. John uncases his rod and goes fishing. Mike joins the crowd in the cook tent, out of the wind, to manufacture the salad for our first wilderness dinner. I too do my part: I sit on my ammo can and activate my word processor. It's a good one. User-friendly, cheap, silent, no vibrations or radiation, no moving parts, no maintenance, no power source needed, easily replaceable, fully portable, it consists of a notebook and a ballpoint pen from desert trees, 9559 n. camino del plata, tucson, ariz. The necessary software must be supplied by the operator, but as friendly critics have pointed out, an author's head is full of that.

For dinner we get by on soup, salad, spaghetti and sauce with meatballs. We drink no beer on this trip. When air freight costs one dollar a pound beer is not cost-effective; we subsist on wine, whiskey, schnapps, and, best of all, the 40-degree, immaculately conceived waters of the Kongakut River.

The sun angles sidewise behind some western peaks. But there is no sunset, no evening. Not even a twilight. The bald, unmediated light continues to shine on the mountainsides east of the river. There are a couple of wristwatches in our group, but no one refers to them. There seems no point to it. At last, and reluctantly, one by one, we let the wind or the mosquitoes or fatigue—it's been a long day—worry us into our tents.

The light inside my translucent nylon dome is bright enough to read a book by. The mosquitoes gather outside the netting of my doorway, poking their Pinocchio noses through the interstices, sniffing at me like bloodhounds. A few have followed me inside. I hunt them down, one at a time, and pinch their little heads off. For such resolute, persistent, vicious, bloodthirsty animalcules, they are surprisingly fragile. As individuals. One slap on the snout and they crumple. Collectively, they can drive a bull moose insane. I feel no remorse in extinguishing their miserable lives. I'm a cold-hearted bleeding heart. Yet I know that even the mosquito has a function, you might say a purpose, in the great web of life. Their larvae help feed fingerlings, for example. Certain of their women help spread the viruses and parasitic protozoa that give us dengue, yellow fever, and malaria, for example, keeping in control the human population of places like Borneo, Angola, and Italy. No organism can be condemned as totally useless.

Nevertheless, one does not wish them well. I would not kill them all, but I will certainly kill every one I can catch. Send them back where they came from.

We sleep. I dream that I hear robins, 300 miles north of the Arctic Circle. Dreaming of Home, Pennsylvania.

June 25

Today we climb a mountain. We follow a brook up a deep ravine, over the rocks and a deep-pile carpet of tundra, lupine, buttercups, forget-me-nots, campion, mountain avens, bayrose, eight-petal dryas, kinnikinick, saxifrage ("stonebreakers"), woolly lousewort (a favorite of mine), Labrador tea, drunken bumblebees, piles of caribou droppings like chocolate-covered almonds, pictographic lichen on the limestone, and many little yellow composites. What are these? asks Ginger. Don't know, says Mark. Water gurgles under the rocks. Call it a virus, says Dana; that's what doctors do when they don't know. Ain't that right, Doc? Doctor Mike smiles, chuffing along with me in the rear guard of the party. Aside from myself, he is the only person here over the age of thirty-five.

We scramble up a pile of scree and eat lunch on the summit, 2,500 feet above the river, 5,000 feet above sea level. Snowy peaks lift hoary heads (as John Muir would say) in most—not all—directions. We are in that part of the Brooks Range called the Romanzof Mountains, which recalls the former colonizers of the Alaskan territory. To the Russians Alaska must have seemed like merely a two-bit extension of Siberia. Extreme East Slobbovia. No wonder they parted with it so cheaply.

Americans think Alaska is big. The Northwest Territories of Canada are bigger. Siberia is one and a half times bigger than both combined. So much for surface extension. If the state of Utah—which consists mostly of mountains, plateaus, mesas, buttes, pinnacles, synclines, anticlines, folds, reefs, canyons, and vertical canyon walls—were ironed out flat it would take up more room on a map than Texas. What does that prove? It's what is there, or here, now, that matters.

So much for chauvinism. Most of the mountains around us, so far as we know, have never been climbed by anybody but the Dall bighorns. The majority have not even been named, except for the most prominent, like Michelson (9,239 feet) and Chamberlin (9,020).

We return to camp by a different route, finding fresh bear sign on the way: torn-up sod, where the bear was rooting for marmots and ground squirrels; a well-trod bear trail; a messy pile of bear dung. Dana carries his shotgun slung on shoulder, but we stay alert as we march along. There is an animal out here that is bigger than we are.

We tramp through a mile of muskeg at the foot of the hills. Muskeg consists of tussocks of balled-up grass, each tussock the size of a human head, all rooted in a bog. It is difficult to walk among them in the soft muck, even more difficult to walk upon or over them. We lurch and stumble through the mire, and as we advance great shimmering hosts of mosquitoes rise eagerly from the weeds to greet us. Alaska is not only the biggest of the fifty states, it is also the boggiest and buggiest. Dripping in sweat and the greasy oil of insect repellent, we stagger on. Takes guts to live in Alaska, no doubt about it. I am favorably impressed, once again, by the pluck and hardihood of these people, both native and white. I wonder though, sometimes, about their native intelligence.

We reach camp, the fresh breeze, the welcome hard ground of the gravel beach, and wade into the icy river for a drink, then a shampoo, a bath—ladies upstream, men downstream.

Shivering in the wind, I dry myself with my cleanest dirty shirt. Forgot to bring a towel. The wind is coming up the river, as usual, from the north and the frozen Arctic Sea; I can feel that chill malignancy penetrate the marrow of my bones. Hurriedly I dress, layering on a shirt, a hooded sweatshirt, and a parka. When I feel warm the wind stops.

And *they* come out again. I wait. One slap on the arm kills nine. Forgot to bring cigars. I reach for the repellent.

We have Mexican food for supper, preceded by a pitcher of margaritas iced with snow carried down from the mountain in a daypack by Mike, a thoughtful and foresighted man. We drink to his health. Life is rough on the Last Frontier. Don't feel quite right myself, but it's only a matter of acclimatizing: When I left Tucson three days ago the temperature was 106 in the shade; at Salt Lake City, where we paused for a day and a night, it was 65 degrees and stormy; at Fairbanks (elevation 448 feet), where I stayed for two nights, the air was humid, muggy, and close to 90 degrees—and hotter than that in my little cell at the El Sleazo Hotel on the banks of the Chena River. From Fairbanks by DC-3 to Barter Island, on the edge of the Arctic ice pack, we found ourselves in the heart of the wind-chill factory—even the Eskimos were wearing their parkas; and now on the river, where the wind comes and goes, the temperature seems to fluctuate from subfreezing to 80 and back again. No one complains about the weather except me, and I do it inwardly only; can't let the others know that the most sissified rugged outdoorsman in the West is now squatting among them on his ammo can, huddled in thermal long johns, wool pants, wool shirt, flannel sweatshirt, wool ski cap, and a flannel-lined hooded parka.

Before turning in for the sun-bright night I requisition a handful of aspirin from the expedition infirmary; Mark also doses me with 10,000 milligrams of vitamin C and other huge jellied capsules, spansules, and suppositories, each about horse-size. "Can't get sick on us, mate," he says. "You know there are no germs north of the Arctic Circle."

"Of course not," I agree. "But one could always show up." Crawling into my geodesic tent, sliding into my antique, greasy, duct-tape-mended mummy bag, I say to myself, No germs, eh? Well, if I were a germ I wouldn't want to live here either.

The sun shines all night long.

June 26

I awaken by degrees to the sound of robins chirping in the cherry trees of Home, Pennsylvania. Impossible. But when I emerge from my cocoon the first thing I see is a fat robin redbreast bouncing along on the gravel bar. How could such a small, harmless, innocent bird travel so far? Or as Jensen says, how many fpm (wing flaps per minute) to cover 3,000 miles?

Mark has caught an 18-inch char for breakfast. Six or seven pounds. He packs it with lemon, paprika, and butter; wraps it in aluminum foil; and bakes it on a grill over the low driftwood fire. The flesh is firm, sweet, pink, something like fresh salmon but better, not so oily, much like the Dolly Varden we used to eat, years ago, from that little lake—Akakola—below the Numa Ridge fire lookout in Glacier Park. The Dolly Varden, in fact, is a type of char.

Today we set out on the Kongakut. We inflate, rig, and load the two neoprene rafts; strike tents; police the site. Like all good professional outfitters, Mark Jensen practices no-trace camping. Everything noncombustible is hammered flat with a stone and packed out. The ashes from the fire, collected on the metal fire pan, are dumped into the river, where they will end their chemic lives blended with the Arctic Ocean. Even our footprints—since we've made camp on the flood plain—will be obliterated by the next rise in the river.

We launch forth. Check the time by Maurine's quartz crystal wristwatch: 2:00 p.m. in Fairbanks. We have again failed to crack the noon barrier. But here, where high noon lasts for hours, it does not matter.

We float downstream through the treeless hills, among the golden tundra mountains. It's something like boating through Colorado at 13,000 feet. We see golden plovers out on the flats, another golden eagle overhead. And the gulls. And the robins. And a raven.

"My favorite bird," says Mark. "Smart, talented, handsome—"

"Like you," says Ginger.

"Like me. When I—" He points to the high mountainside on our left. "Sheep."

A herd of Dall bighorns is grazing up there, a dozen of them, ewes, lambs, rams with curling horns. Placid, motionless, they watch us—phantom beings out of nowhere—drifting through their world.

"When I come back," continues Mark, "I want to come back as a raven."

"Crawling with lice," Ginger points out. "Smelling like a dead fish."

"With a beak even bigger than the beak you've got now," says Maurine. "Proportionately speaking."

Smiling, Mark stands up between the oars to survey the channel ahead. Like most Alaskan rivers the Kongakut is shallow, broad, and braided, hard to read, forcing the boatman to search constantly for the one navigable channel among many false options. Following us in the second boat, Dana watches carefully. Only Mark has seen this river before.

All goes well today. In the evening we make camp on another bar, a pleasant site with limestone cliffs overlooking the river, a grove of little ten-foot cottonwoods on the other shore, a vista upriver of the valley we have come through and the splendid craggy snowy mountains beyond. The classic alpine-Arctic scene—photogenic, fundamental, perfect.

Why are there almost no trees on the North Slope of the Brooks? The reason is the permafrost two feet below the surface, a substratum of rocklike ice that prevents trees from sinking roots. Only close to the river, where the ground is warmer, can the dwarf willows and midget cottonwoods take hold.

Years ago I was employed briefly as a technical writer for the Western Electric Company in New York City. The company had a contract with the War Department to prepare training manuals for the workers building the Arctic radar stations and air bases of the Distant Early Warning System. One hundred of us sat at desks in one huge office ten floors above Barclay Street in lower Manhattan. Fluorescent lights glared down upon our bent, white-shirted backs. (All technical writers were required to wear white shirts. With tie.) Since my security clearance had not yet come through, I was assigned the menial task of editing the manual called *How to Dispose of Human Sewage in Permafrost*. I told the boss I wanted to be sent to the Arctic in order to conduct firsthand field studies. He told me that my job was spelling, grammar, and punctuation, not shit research. I returned to my desk among the other stuffed, bent white shirts—we all faced in the same direction—and stared moodily out the window for two weeks, watching the sun go down over Hoboken, New Jersey.

The boss came to me. "Abbey," he said, "do you really want to work for Western Electric?" "No sir," I said, "not really." "I thought not," he said. "We're letting you go as of 1700 hours today." I could have kissed him—and knowing New York, I probably should have. "That's all right, sir," I said. "I'm leaving right now, as of 1330 hours." And I did. Spent the afternoon at the White Horse Tavern on Hudson Street, then with cronies at Minsky's Burlesque in Newark. Reported to my wife, drunk and happy, at 2200 hours with what was left of my first and final Western Electric paycheck. Pointed the old Chevy pickup south and west at 2300 hours and headed for Arizona. Never did learn how to dispose of human sewage (is there any other kind?) in permafrost.

But I know now. What they do on Barter Island, at least, is dump it into a sewage lagoon two feet deep, chlorinate the water, and drink it. And how do they dispose of general garbage on the North Slope? They don't; they leave it on the surface, where it becomes the highest and most scenic feature of the landscape.

Beef Stroganoff for supper. The Russian influence lingers on in nostalgia-loving Alaska.

Loaded with aspirin and more of Jensen's horse medicine, I retire early to my tent, still feeling lousy. Forgot the towel, forgot the cigars, forgot to bring a book. So I borrow a paperback from Maurine, something called *Still Life With Woodpecker*. Yes, that appears to be the title. I glance at the blurbs, the summary on the back cover. "You didn't bring anything for grown-ups?" She has not. "Did anybody?" I ask the group.

Dana offers me a book called *The Dancing Wu Li Masters*, by a Mr. Gary Zukav. "How about a Gideon's Bible? Or a dictionary?" Mark offers his ammo-can edition of Merriam-Webster. "Already read that one," I say. I borrow the first two, ungrateful bastard, and sulk off. The wind has died; a number of dancing Wu Li masters follow me into my tent. I slaughter them and bed down with Tom Robbins and Mr. Gary Zukav. *Ménage à trois . . . de poupée . . . entente . . .*

June 27

Breakfast goes by in a blur. We load the boats, shove off, glide down the current between walls of turquoise-colored *Aufeis*. Horned white sheep crawl upon the distant hillsides like woolly maggots. Clouds cover the sun; the Arctic wind comes sweeping up the river. Dana strains at the oars, sweating hard to keep up with Mark while I sit huddled in the bow swaddled in layers of Pendleton and polyester and self-pity. "Let me know if you see a GRIZZ," I growl, nodding off. He nods.

Hours pass, along with some gravel bars, a few willow thickets, more walls of ice. This is the kind of thing, I say to myself, that no one actually wants to do. And afterward you're not even glad you did it. Unlike the infantry, or suicide, or exploratory surgery. I become aware of danger ahead. Trouble: I look up hopefully.

Mark has beached his rubber raft on a most unlikely, rough, difficult spot. Emphatically, he signals Dana to bring his boat alongside. "Ready for a fast landing," Dana says, pulling hard toward shore. I pick the coiled bowline from under my rubber boots. We grate onto the ice and gravel. I stagger out with the rope and hold the boat against the violent tug of the current. Dana jumps out, and we heave the boat higher onto the gravel. There is nothing here to tie up to: All hands are summoned to drag both boats out of the river.

Mark talks quietly to Dana. Followed by John, they go off to investigate something ahead. All that I can see, from where we have landed, is the river funneling into a narrow channel between vertical walls of blue ice six to ten feet high. Fifty yards ahead the river swerves around a bend, going out of view within the icy walls. We have stopped at the last possible takeout point short of a full commitment to the ice canyon.

"What seems to be the trouble here?" I ask, holding out my GI canteen cup. Ginger is pouring hot coffee from the thermos jug. My hands shake with cold; I need both hands to hold my cup steady.

"Don't know," she says. "Mark said he doesn't like the looks of the river here."

"Looks like the same old Styx to me," Mike says from deep within his parka hood. I'm glad to see that he, too, is feeling the cold. Los Angeles. He and I, the only southwesterners in the party, are equally thin-blooded.

Mark, Dana, John come back. Mark looks somber, an unusual expression for his habitually cheerful face. "We'll camp here, mates."

"Here? On the ice?"

He points to the left bank, beyond the ice. "Over there." We unload the boats and carry our gear and baggage to dry land, then come back for the boats. By then we've seen what the problem is. Not far beyond the bend the river goes *under* the ice, emerging a hundred feet beyond. If we had gone on in the boats we would have been trapped and drowned beneath the ice, or, if flushed through, we would probably have died of hypothermia before we found dry matches and sufficient wood to get a big fire going.

"I had this feeling," Mark says.

June 28

I totter down the hill from my tent and join the jolly bunch around the breakfast fire. Mutely, sadly, I hold out my tin cup; someone pours coffee into it. "How's it going, partner?" our leader says.

"Great," I mumble, "great."

I swallow my coffee and watch Ginger and Mike squabbling politely over Mark's last blueberry pancake. You take it, she says. Naw, you take it, Mike says. They remind me, in my fluish delirium, of my friend Kevin Briggs, another river rat, and his

Parable of the Last Pork Chop

My friend Kevin is a stout, husky fellow, and, being a graduate student of philosophy and literature, he is always hungry. One day he and five classmates were invited to lunch by their teacher, Ms. Doctor Professor H. A kind, well-meaning, but frugal woman, Professor H. seated her six guests at the dining table in her home and set a platter holding exactly seven pork chops at the head of the table. Kevin, seated on her right, too hungry to waste time counting the pork chops, helped himself to two from the top and passed the platter on. Professor H. meanwhile had gone back to her kitchen. She returned with the mashed potatoes and gravy just as the platter had nearly completed its round of the table. One pork chop remained. She sat down. The young man on her left, who had not yet served himself, looked at the last pork chop, then at his hostess. She looked at him. Both laughed awkwardly. You take it, he said. Oh no, she said, you take it. I'm really not hungry, he said. I'm not either, really, she said. Kevin, by this time, had gobbled down everything on his plate; he reached across the table with his fork and stabbed the last pork chop. I'll eat it, he said. And he did.

Moral? He who hesitates is second? No, Kevin explained to me, not at all. Remember the words of our Lord and Savior: "To him that hath much, much shall be given. But verily, from him that hath little, that little shall be taken away" (Matt. 13:12).

Mark Jensen, looking at me, says, "We'll stay here a couple of days. Who wants to climb another mountain?"

I creep back to my tent. I read the borrowed books.

Hours later I am roused from a deep stupor by Mark, bringing me with his own hands a bowl of hot celery soup and a plate containing chunks of fish with noodles and mashed potatoes. It looks good, and I am hungry.

"How's it going, partner?"

"Fine, Mark, fine. Say, this is damn good fish. You catch another char?"

"That's turkey. Out of a can."

"Damn good. See any GRIZZ?"

"Had a glimpse of one going over the next ridge. Only for a minute. A true silvertip—we could see the fur shining on the shoulder hump. You should've been there, mate."

"I know. What else?"

"Lots of sheep. A wolf. A lone bull caribou."

"Sure sorry I missed that bear."

"We thought of you, mate. If I'd had a good rope with me I'd have lassoed the son of a bitch and drug him back here. Better take some more of these pharmaceuticals."

June 30

Another gay, sunny, brisk, breezy Arctic morning. We carry the boats to the river, since the river will not come to us, and proceed as before, downstream. My flu has entered its terminal phase and I am ready to meet my Maker, eyeball to eyeball, way up here on top of the world, as we say in these parts.

The top of the world. But of course the giddy, dizzying truth is that the words *top* and *bottom*, from a planetary point of view, have no meaning. From out here in deep space, where I am orbiting, there is no top, there is no bottom, no floor, no ceiling, to anything. We spin through an infinite void, following our curving path around the sun, which is as bewildered as we are. True, the infinite is incomprehensible—but the finite is absurd. Einstein claimed otherwise, I know, but Einstein was only a mortal like us. No ceiling, no floor, no walls. . . . We are 350 miles north of the Arctic Circle, and we flow as we go, like spindrift, like bits of Styrofoam, through the outliers of what Mark says is the northernmost mountain range in the world, i.e., on Earth. Will we ever get back to downtown Kaktovik?

I think of the Eskimos there, holed up all day inside their $250,000 air-freighted prefab modular houses (paid for with oil royalties), watching *Mr. Rogers' Neighborhood* on their brand-new color-TV sets. A few grinning kids race up and down the dirt street, among the melting snowbanks, on their Honda ATCs. What we call "road lice" back in the Southwest. (Girls love horses. Little boys love machines. Grown-up men and women like to walk.) The kids seem to have nothing else to do. A dead bowhead whale—rare species—lies rotting on the waterfront, partially dismembered. Slabs of whale blubber—*muktuk*—are stacked in the yard of each house, along with the empty plywood crates, the diesel spills, the oil drums, the Skiddoo parts, the caribou antlers, the musk-ox bones, the wolf pelts, the moose heads, the worn-out rubber boots, the tin cans and liquor bottles and loose papers and plastic potsherds. In each yard lies one howling arthritic Husky dog, token souvenir of former days, short-chained to a stake out of reach of the muktuk. The dogs are never released from the chain.

And the wind blows day and night, forever, out of the north, from beyond the dead whale on the beach, from beyond the mangled ice floes, out of the infinite wastes of the most awesome sight in the North: that pale, cold, no-man's-land, that endless frozen *whiteness* leading as far as eye can perceive out over the Beaufort Sea and into the Arctic Ocean. Toward the Pole.

What will happen to these people when the North Slope oil gives out? The Eskimos and other Alaskan natives still enjoy the hunt, as much or more than ever, and when they do go hunting, on their screaming packs of snow machines, they kill everything that moves, or so I was told. But this kind of hunting, whether of land or sea animals, depends upon technology and access to the cash nexus—money. (The musk ox, for example, had to be reintroduced from Canada into the Arctic National Wildlife Refuge because the natives, equipped with white man's machines and armed with white man's weapons, had exterminated the local herds.) Impossible to imagine, I was told, that the new generations would or could return to the traditional nomadic way, using primitive weapons, following the game in its seasonal migrations from Alaska to Canada and back, surviving in hide tents and sod huts under the snow as their ancestors—their still-living grandparents—had done. Unimaginable. When the oil money is gone, they'll all move to the slums of Fairbanks, Anchorage, and Seattle, join the public welfare culture, before consenting to such romantic humiliation. Can't blame them: until the coming of the white man the natives spent half their lives on the edge of starvation. Famine was common. Now, despite alcoholism, violence, suicide, their population is growing—and fast.

What happens to these people when they migrate to the city? I think of "Two Street" (Second Avenue), Fairbanks, which resembles the center of Flagstaff or Gallup on a Saturday night. There is even a "Navajo Taco Stand" on one corner, selling genuine Athabascan tacos (fry bread, shredded lettuce, and hamburger), and the street is lined with grim little bars jam-packed with brawling Indians and Eskimos. Just like down home: the Club 66 in Flag, the Eagle in Gallup, or the Silver Dollar in Bluff on the edge of the Navajo reservation.

We camp today at a broad open place that Mark has named Velvet Valley. Under a spiny, purple, crenellated mountain that looks like Mordor, like the Hall of the Mountain King, like Darth Vader's childhood playpen, like the home of the Wicked Witch of the North, extends a lovely valley clothed in golden tundra, a million bloody blooming flowers, the lambent light of the midnight sun. (I dislike that word *lambent*, but it must be employed.) A soft, benevolent radiance, you might say, playing upon the emerald green, the virgin swales of grass and moss and heather and Swede-heads.

The Arctic wind blows merrily: it takes four of us to get the cook tent up, our only communal shelter. I scrounge for firewood with the others, and soon we've got a good fire burning near the entrance to the tent, a big meal under way inside.

More time slippage. We'd eaten lunch at five in the afternoon, we're having dinner at eleven. Time, says Einstein, is a function of space. Or, said another philosopher, time is but the mind of space. How true. And is everything finally only relative? It is not. The light is fixed and absolute. Especially the Arctic light. We'll eat dinner at eleven and have a midnight snack in Seward's Icebox at four in the morning if we bloody well feel like it. Who's to stop us?

The sun shines all night long.

July 3

John and Mark catch a big char and a small grayling for breakfast. A fine kettle of fish.

We go for a walk up the Velvet Valley, through the willows, through the muskeg, up onto the tundra, deep into the valley. Flowers everywhere, each flower concealing a knot of mosquitoes, but we're accustomed to the little shitheads by now; they don't bother us; we rub on the bug juice and let the insects dance and hover—patterns of organic energy made visible—in futile molecular orbits one inch from the skin. Like the flies in Australia the mosquitoes here become simply part of the atmosphere, the decor, the ambience. We ignore them.

A ram watches us from a high point of rock; his flock grazes above. Mark kneels by a mountain stream trying to photograph the cross-hatched ripples of converging currents. Dana glasses the high ridges for bear, shotgun at his side. John is fishing back at the river. Mike, Maurine, and Ginger are eating cheese and crackers and identifying the many flowers, with the help of a guidebook, that I have not mentioned. I sit on the grass scribbling these notes, with a clump of Siberian asters fluttering at my elbow.

This is what I am writing:

Alaska is not, as the state license plate asserts, the Last Frontier. Alaska is the final big bite on the American table, where there is never quite enough to go around. "We're here for the megabucks," said a construction worker in the Bunkhouse at Kaktovik, "and nothing else." At the Bunkhouse the room and board cost $150 a day, on the monthly rate, but a cook can earn $10,000 a month. Others much more. Alaska is where a man feels free to destroy an entire valley by placer mining, as I could see from the air over Fairbanks, in order to extract one peanut butter jar full of gold dust. Flying from Barter Island to the Kongakut, Gil Zemansky showed me the vast spread of unspoiled coastal plain where Arco, Chevron, and others plan oil and gas exploration in the near future, using D-7 bulldozers pulling sledges, thus invading the caribou calving grounds and tearing up the tundra and foothills of the Arctic National Wildlife Refuge, last great genuine wilderness area left in the fifty United States. In southeast Alaska the U.S. Forest Service is allowing the logging companies to clear-cut and decimate vast areas of the Tongass National Forest, home of our national bird and officially, ostensibly, the legal property of the American public—all of us.

Last Frontier? Not exactly: Anchorage, Fairbanks, and outposts like

Barter Island, with their glass-and-aluminum office buildings, their airlift prefab fiberboard hovels for the natives and the workers, their compounds of elaborate and destructive machinery, exhibit merely the latest development in the planetary expansion of space-age sleaze—not a frontier but only one more high-tech slum. For Americans, another colony. Alaska is the last pork chop.

Down the river, through the portal of the mountains into the foothills, approaching the coastal plain, we float northward in our little air-filled boats. Seeing that I have come back to life, the literary natives on shipboard badger me with bookish questions. I am happy to oblige.

What's the best book about Alaska? The best book about the North, I say, is *The Call of the Wild*. In the language of critics, Jack London captures there the essence of the mythos of the wilderness. No, my companions say, the best book about Alaska. *Winter News*, I say, by John Haines—pure poetry; and by pure I mean poetry about ordinary things, about the great weather, about daily living experience, as opposed to technical poetry, which is concerned mainly with prosody—with technique. (One of my favorite lectures.) Don't lecture, they say; what about prose—books in prose. (I sense a trap about to snap.) I pause for a moment, pretending to reflect, and say *Going to Extremes*, by Joe McGinnis. A brilliant book. Mandatory for anyone who wants a sense of what contemporary life in Alaska is like. My opinion does not sit well with the locals. No! they say; McGinnis writes only about the sensational. Alaska is a sensational place, I reply. He's a scandalmonger, they say. Alaska is a scandalous place, I say; McGinnis tells the truth. How much time have you spent in Alaska? they want to know. About four weeks, all told, I answer. They smile in scorn. Four weeks of observation, I explain, is better than a lifetime of daydreaming. What about *Coming Into the Country?* someone asks. I had to admit that I had started on that book but never finished it. McPhee, I explain, is a first-rate reporter, but too mild, too nice, too cautious—no point of view. More questions. You like Robert Service? I love him. But, says one inquisitor, I don't think you really love Alaska, do you? The most attractive feature of Alaska, I say, is its tiny, insignificant human population—thanks to its miserable climate. I like the mountains, the

glaciers, the wildlife, and the roominess, I hasten to add—or I would if
the bugs would stop crowding me. I think you are a geographical chauv-
inist, she says, a spatial bigot. Special? Spatial. Well, I confess, I'll admit
I've lived too long in the Southwest; I should have saved that for last.
Then what are you doing in Alaska? she says.

Me?

You.

Slumming, I explain.

Quiet, whispers Mark, resting on the oars. Look over there.

We look where he points. Three wolves are watching us from another
bar beside the river, less than a hundred feet away. Three great gray
shaggy wolves, backlighted by the low sun, staring at us. Silently we
drift closer. Gently, Mark pulls the boat onto the gravel, where it stops.
Don't get out, Mark whispers. The wolves watch, the cameras come out,
the wolves start to move away into the willow thicket and toward the
open tundra. A whistle stops the last one as it climbs the bank. I stare
at the wolf through my binoculars, the wolf stares at me; for one still,
frozen, sacred moment I see the wild green fire in its eyes. Then it
shrugs, moves, vanishes.

We drift on, silently, down the clear gray waters. After a while my
friend says to me: When's the last time you saw something like that in
Arizona? In your whole crowded, polluted, stinking Southwest?

Me?

You.

Moi?

Vous.

Another pause. Never did, I say.

You ought to be ashamed of yourself.

I am.

You ought to take back everything you've said.

I take it all back. (*But*, I think, all the same . . .)

Now the river tangles itself into a dozen different channels, all
shallow. The main channel runs straight into a jungle of willow. We
unload the boats, portage them and our gear around the obstruction. As
I'm lugging two ten-gallon ammo cans across the damp silt I see a pair
of tracks coming toward me. Big feet with claw marks longer than my

fingers. The feet are not so long as mine, but they are twice as wide. Double wides, size 10-EEEE. I stop and look around through the silence and the emptiness.

Old Ephraim, where are you?

He does not appear.

We go on. We camp for the day and the daytime night at what Mark calls Buena Vista—a grand view upriver of the Portal, Wicked Witch Mountain, the hanging glaciers of the high peaks beyond. Char-broiled char for supper.

John and I go for a long walk into the hills, over the spongy tundra, taking one of the shotguns with us. Peacock can face his bear with only a camera; I want firepower. As we walk uphill toward the sun we see the mosquitoes waiting for us, about two and a half billion of them hovering in place above the field, the little wings and bodies glowing in the sunlight. "It looks like a zone defense," John says. But they part before us, lackadaisical atoms unable to make up their pinpoint minds, yielding before our scent and our more concentrated nodules of organic energy, as Alan Watts would say. John is a quiet fellow, likable, attractive despite his Yasser Arafat-type beard. He tells me a little about life in Whittier, Alaska. To get to his classroom in winter he walks from his bachelor apartment in a dormitory through an underground tunnel to the adjacent but separate school building. The wind outside, he says, would knock you down; when there is no wind the snow comes up to your armpits. Yet Whittier is in the far south of central Alaska—the balmy part. (You have to be balmy to live there.) When the one road out of town is closed he buckles on touring skis and glides five miles over the pass to the railway station for a ride to the heart of Anchorage. He likes his life in Whittier. (He says.) Likes his students, the bright and lively Indian kids. Doesn't mind the isolation—he's a reader of books. Is fond of snow, ice, wind, mountains, the soft summer—bugs and icicles both. How long do you plan to stay there? I ask him. Oh, another year, maybe two. Then where? Oh . . . back to the other world.

July 4

Mark celebrates with four blasts of the shotgun, shattering the morning air. Thinking a GRIZ is raiding the camp, I go running back only to see our leader and the others drinking coffee around the fire. Mark is always drinking coffee, and he makes strong coffee, stout, vigorous, and powerful. "Listen, mate," he says, explaining his secret formula, "you don't need *near* as much water to make coffee as some people think."

John stands by the river with his camera, photographing another dead fish. He lost most of his rod to the Kongakut days ago but didn't let that stop him; he attached his reel and a new line to his rod case and went on fishing. We've had char and grayling coming out our ears for a week. We're up to our asses in fish. But good—beats bacon and beans by a country mile. And I *like* bacon and beans.

Last stop on the river. We're encamped at the place known as Caribou Pass, near another straight gravel bar on which Gil Zemansky will land to pick us up for the last flight to Barter Island, where we then will catch the Air North DC-3 for the journey over the Brooks Range to Fairbanks and points south.

Caribou Pass—but where are the caribou? They're supposed to be massing out on the coast 100,000 strong. So far the biggest bunch we've seen was 25 head. But here is where they should pass, through these low hills, on their annual trip into the Yukon and south from there to the edge of the forest, where they spend—where they endure, somehow—the dark, six-month Yukon winter.

On the hill above us, a mile away, stands a white wall-tent and a little below it four small bivouac tents: Bear Camp. A squad of wildlife students from the University of Alaska is living up there, trapping (alive) and identifying the rodents in the tundra, watching for the caribou herds, the wolves, the GRIZZ. Mark has told them about my grizzly problem, and when a young, blond-haired, brown-skinned man named Mike Phillips comes rushing down the hillside I climb up the hill to meet him. A male grizzly, he reports, one mile east of Bear Camp. He rushes up the hill; I trudge after him. When I get there, on the high point, the bear has disappeared. Down in that willow thicket along the creek, says Mike, pointing. We glass the area for an hour, but the bear is gone. Probably took off behind the ridge, Mike explains, and crossed over the divide. Of course it would, I think, knowing that I was coming. The grizzly bear, I explain to Mike, is apocryphal, like the griffin, the centaur, and the yeti. You wouldn't think so, he replies, if you'd been with me two days ago. And he tells me about the scene at the caribou birthing grounds, the leisurely, arrogant GRIZZ he'd observed circling the great herd, chasing the cows and devouring some of the newborn young.

We watch for another hour, but the grizzly does not show. I return to the river. There I find my own party staring at a spectacle two miles away on the hillside west of the river. A big herd of caribou, 2,000, 3,000 of them, a compact animal mass, is advancing steadily to the south. If they go up the side valley over there they'll be blocked by the mountains; if they come our way they'll have to pass within a quarter-mile of where we stand, waiting and hoping.

But something, we can't see what, spooks the herd, and after milling in confusion for a few minutes the caribou reach consensus and reverse direction, returning north the way they had come, jogging along at a smart pace. Within ten minutes the entire herd is out of sight. The caribou, like the grizzly, is an unpredictable animal. It refuses to be guided by precedent, or reason, or common sense, or the wishes of a delegation of tourists.

An albino mosquito lands on my forearm. She walks nervously back and forth on my naked skin, searching for the ideal pore to probe for blood. I wait. She selects a spot she likes; the needle nose, like the drooping snout of a supersonic jet, comes down and enters. Slight prickling sensation. I hear an audible snorkeling sound—but no, I must be imagining that. I am about to slap the little thing into eternity, into its next cycle on the meat-wheel of life, when something stays my hand. Let this little one live, a voice says in my inner ear. Just once, be merciful. I hesitate. Another voice says, Don't let that Buddhist karma run over your Darwinian dogma: Mash the brute. But still I hesitate, and as I do the tiny albino withdraws her dildo, waggles her wings, and floats off into the mob. God only knows what ghastly plague I may have loosed upon humanity and the caribou by letting that one go. But I feel good about it.

We deflate and unrig the rafts, roll them up into snug bundles, stack boats, oars, rowing frames, ammo boxes, rubber bags, icebox, tents, and other dunnage at the downwind end of the imaginary airstrip.

The Cessna comes, and the ferry operation to Barter Island begins.

Mark assigns me the third and final flight, giving me four extra hours on the shore of the Kongakut. Last chance. Last chance for what? I know what but dare not bait the gods by even thinking of it. Last chance for an understanding with the Spirit of the Arctic, that's what.

We wait. The plane comes and goes again with most of the cargo and all passengers but Maurine, John, and me. Two more hours.

John sleeps. Maurine is reading a book and watching the hills and meditating. I go for a walk beside the river, over the gravel bars and through the willow, heading north. The cold green waters rush past at my side, breaking over the rocks with a surflike turbulence, bound for the northern sea. A mile beyond the airstrip I am cut off by a headland. I stop and look back. The shining river races toward me. The velvet-covered hills rise on either side; the great jagged wall of the Brooks extends across the southern horizon—700 miles of largely unknown mountains, reaching across Alaska from the Yukon to the Bering Sea. The end of the Rockies. The final American wilderness.

Where is he?

The willow leaves flash their silvery undersides in the wind; McCone poppies and the purple lupine and red bayrose and yellow composites dance on the hillsides. Wordsworth would enjoy the spectacle. I think. But he might not care much for what I'm waiting for. Expecting. Both shotguns lean on the last pile of duffel where John lies sleeping, out of sight, out of hearing. I am unarmed,ready, open. Let it come.

Two shrikes watch me from the willows. Three screaming gulls pursue a golden eagle high above the river, diving and pecking at its head, trying to turn it into a bald eagle. I long to see that eagle flip on its back in midair, snatch one of those gulls in its deadly talons, and— *rip its head off!* But the eagle sails on in a straight, steady airline toward the hills, and the gulls drop away, bored.

My bear does not come.

As the plane takes off Gil Zemansky says, "I'm going to show you something." He banks and turns off course and enters a pass through the foothills west of the river. We fly a thousand feet above the lion-colored tundra. Little ponds and bog holes wink, sparkle, glitter in the light.

We cross another ridge. And there below, suddenly, the hills appear to be in motion, alive, as if the skin of the earth had begun to crawl over its rockbound bones. A broad river of caribou streams in waves west-southwesterly up the ridges and through the valleys, all its elements in rapid, parallel advance. It takes me a moment to realize that I am looking down on the greatest mass movement of untamed four-hoofed animals I may ever see. It's like the stampede of the wildebeest on the Serengeti Plain.

"My God," I say, "how many?"

Gil banks and circles, looking down. "Hard to tell. It's only a part of the Porcupine River herd. Maybe 40,000, maybe 50,000."

John and Maurine are busy taking pictures. I'm too excited to get out my binoculars. "Any GRIZZ down there?"

Gil looks again. "Bound to be a few," he says. "But they blend in so well we'd never see them."

He circles one more time, then takes a bearing northwest for Barter Island and Kaktovik, over the last foothills and 2,000 feet above the coastal plain. Well, I'm thinking, now I'm satisfied. Now I've seen it, the secret of the essence of the riddle of the Spirit of the Arctic—the flowering of life, of life wild, free, and abundant, in the midst of the hardest, cruelest land on the northern half of Earth.

And then as we approach the coast and the flat, small island at its edge, the frozen sea appears again, that curving rim of bland, silent *whiteness* stretching on and on and on, unbroken, toward the stillness of the polar climax—and beyond. And I know at last that I have seen but little of the real North, and of that little, understood less.

We don't know what it means.

from Six Came Back
by David L. Brainard

U.S. Army Lieutenant Adolphus Greeley and 24 men steamed north in 1881 to man a weather station on the shores of Ellesmere Island. After two winters at their post, the group made their way south by boat and sledge to a camp where they awaited a long overdue relief ship. Food ran short, and the men's situation became desperate. Sergeant David L. Brainard (1856–1946) was among the six survivors.

A clear, beautiful day. At noon a thermometer exposed in the sun indicated 40°. Every bright day we lie on a pile of old clothing and sleeping bags outside and bask in the sunlight.

I caught sixteen pounds of shrimps and four pounds of vegetation. Extremely tired and weak afterward. The hunters and myself receive a double ration of the thin shrimp stew.

A portion of a can of lard, which had been used as ointment for Elison's wounds, was today issued in equal portions to all. The remainder of the diluted alcohol was also issued. The green buds of saxifrage have been introduced by some in their stews. It has not upset their stomachs and appears to be nutritive.

Sunday, May 18th.

Long shot a large raven at 5 a.m. I had attempted it only two hours earlier, but the bird escaped me. He will be used for shrimp bait. I fished in a storm all forenoon, but caught only ten pounds and about two of vegetation.

A vessel could have sailed in Smith Sound today. It was iceless.

To the joy of all, three more issues of alcohol were found in a rubber bag in the boat.

May 19th.

Fredericks went out at 4 a.m. to cut ice for breakfast. In a moment he returned greatly excited, with the welcome information, "Bear outside." He and Long immediately started in pursuit with their rifles. I followed more leisurely with the shotgun. After an hour's tramp, I turned back, not wishing to break down my strength and compromise the source of our only support—the shrimps.

Fredericks returned at 10 a.m. and Long came in about an hour later. Neither had been able to get within range of the animal. They were thoroughly exhausted by their arduous journey, and had turned back while they had strength enough to reach Camp Clay. When first seen this morning, the bear was standing a few feet from the hut.

The large English sledge was cut up for fuel today. Ellis quietly breathed his last at 10:30 a.m. No symptoms of scurvy were apparent. Death was due solely to starvation.

The last issue of diluted alcohol was made today.

May 20th.

Ellis was buried at noon on Cemetery Ridge. We could scarcely find enough men with strength sufficient to haul his remains.

If our government does not send a vessel with the whalers when they pass Melville Bay in the early days of June, it will be an act of criminal negligence, or else inexcusable ignorance.

Today I caught only twelve pounds of shrimps and two of kelp. Another bear or a large seal would save us all from a fate similar to that which overtook the party under Franklin.

May 21st.

I had a long conversation with Lieut. Greely this morning. He is not at all hopeful. He desires me to take charge of some of his papers and, in the event of his death, I am to place them in the hands of the Chief Signal Officer.

Dr. Pavy circulated a paper written by himself, certifying to his medical skill and his devotion to his professional duties, and asked for signers. He did this, of course, to offset the fact of his arrest last autumn when he refused to re-enlist. About fourteen of the men signed the paper, but Lieut. Greely either would not, or was not asked.

May 22nd.

The tent was placed in position near Cemetery Ridge. Five of the party will sleep in it tonight.

Ralston is most likely dying now (4 p.m.). He drank some rum two hours ago and during the forenoon ate large quantities of the saxifrage and sang a song. Less than an hour ago, Lieut. Greely fed him with a portion of his shrimp stew. Now he is delirious.

The meagre amount of food consumed does not require our bowels to function oftener than from twelve to eighteen days. This act is always attended with great pain and followed by extreme exhaustion.

May 23rd.

With the exception of the five strongest, the party has moved to the hill. The tent with a small shelter in front accommodates them all. Elison was moved on his mattress—a wearing task.

Israel is so weak that he had to be hauled on a sledge. Lieut. Kisling-bury and Whisler are about as bad. They cannot long survive.

I caught only ten pounds of shrimps. My strength was not equal to managing the kelp rake. Fredericks has worked faithfully today in erecting the shelter in front of the tent and making the sick comfortable.

Ralston died at 1 a.m. His end appeared painless. His remains were not buried owing to the excessive weakness of our strongest men.

May 24th.

Dr. Pavy, Salor, Long and myself slept in the shanty which had been our winter abode. It is damp and without a roof and pretty well dismantled.

Ralston was buried before breakfast. Whisler died at noon. The Doctor says his death was caused by fright. With nutritious food he would have had no cause to feel frightened. He died begging forgiveness for having stolen some bacon several weeks ago.

I overhauled the effects of our dead comrades and placed them in shape for transportation home.

Schneider's face is quite badly swollen, probably from the effects of eating saxifrage, now used in place of sea vegetation which I am no longer able to obtain.

Caterpillars are getting quite numerous now on the bare spots on Cemetery Ridge. Bender saw one crawling near the tent yesterday and hastily transferred it to his mouth, remarking, "This is too much meat to lose."

Sunday, May 25th.

Southeasterly wind began blowing at 10 a.m. and continued all day. In the evening it blew a moderate gale. In the heavy drift I was unable to make the customary trip to the shrimping grounds, although the demand for them is great.

We buried Whisler after dinner when the storm was at its height.

Four of us still sleep in the old shanty and are but poorly protected against the storms. But there is no remedy for the matter. Our strength is not equal to the task of getting out the canvas necessary to build a shelter.

My God! This life is horrible; will it never change?

Seal skin thongs cut into small pieces were used in the stew this evening to eke out the scanty supply of shrimps. Small quantities of the skin were burned to a cinder on the fire and then ravenously devoured.

May 26th.

Schneider was detected stealing food (shrimps and tea) and was also accused of making unfair divisions in the issue of these articles. He was relieved from the duties of cook and Bender has volunteered to do the cooking for both messes.

For the first time this year, sufficient water for preparing supper was collected from pools among the rocks. With the exception of a few drifting fragments, Smith Sound is free of ice and a vessel can navigate any portion of it with perfect impunity.

I caught eight pounds of shrimps and two of vegetation before breakfast. I could have obtained more under ordinary physical conditions, but owing to excessive weakness and a dull throbbing in my head, I was compelled to desist. In the evening, I went down again and returned at eleven o'clock with 12 pounds more. I will try to extend the few inferior shrimp baits until June 1st. After that date unless we get game, we will have to depend on sea vegetation, saxifrage and a small black lichen (tripe de roche) which grows here on the rocks in abundance.

A few garments of seal skin and boots of the same material, together with our oil-tanned sleeping bag covers, will have to be used as a substitute for meat. The soles from an old pair of seal skin boots furnished us, in addition to a few shrimps, with a scanty breakfast and supper.

May 27th.

Israel, the youngest member of our party, passed away just after midnight. He died very easily and after losing consciousness which was about eleven hours before his death, he talked of food, restaurants, etc. His frankness, honesty and generosity had won the hearts of all. For lack of strength, we could not bury him today.

We worked nearly all day to erect a shelter in front of the tent, and tonight we will all sleep together. I was too exhausted to fish.

A heated discussion about the medicines took place between Lieut. Greely and Dr. Pavy, the details of which I have neither the interest, the inclination nor the strength to record.

May 28th.

I caught nine pounds of shrimps and Long returned from open water with a dovekie. The dovekie was divided between Long and myself by general acclamation.

The sound is now open and as free of ice as in August, 1881, when we steamed northward to Lady Franklin Bay. If there is a rescue party somewhere near, why do they not come while there is yet time to save a few lives?

Israel was buried at noon on Cemetery Ridge.

The invalids are about the same as yesterday.

I shall never forget the delicacy of flavor of the dovekie stew which I ate this evening.

May 29th.

Clear, calm weather in the forenoon, but at 1 p.m. the sky clouded and almost immediately after a southeast gale burst upon us. The drift penetrated our rude shelter, defying all efforts to keep it out. The shelter was first blown full of snow and gravel and then blown down. The poles which supported the canvas are now lying across our bodies. In the tent they are better protected, but still their lot is far from pleasant.

Long was driven from the edge of the ice by the approach of the storm and joining me at the fishery, we returned together; but only after a struggle in the gale. I had caught eight pounds of shrimps and Long had one dovekie. I went to the old hut for wood and while there the storm increased, confining me to its walls for two weary hours. On returning to the tent, the Doctor and Salor refused to admit me to the bag in which I occupied a place and in which they were lying. I had to crawl into one of the abandoned bags outside. This was frozen and drifted full of snow. The gale prevented cooking our scanty supper of shrimps and in consequence we ate nothing.

Although I gave directions yesterday that all scraps and pieces of seal skin were to be considered public property, Bender was detected eating some. He confessed and in explanation said that he could not resist the temptation. I told Fredericks to collect everything eatable in the way of seal skin and I would lock it in the storehouse.

May 30th.

The gale did not abate until after midnight. I passed a wretched night outdoors in the wild fury of the storm. A large snow drift accumulated inside and about my sleeping bag and my hands, feet and face were swollen from exposure. Rheumatic pains seized hold of me and, smarting under the wrong done me by my sleeping companions, mental agony was added to physical torture.

Our breakfast of shrimps was eaten at 10 a.m. We had fasted twenty-six hours. Today I caught six pounds of shrimps. The last piece of bait was placed in the nets. It will last a few days more.

How we manage to live on from six to ten pounds of shrimps per day I have no idea.

A gale from the northwest began at 6 p.m. This is the most uninviting region. It reminds us of the Boat Camp on Newman Bay, Greenland.

May 31st.

The gale continued all day and was accompanied by a heavy snow-storm. We were not only held close prisoners in our shelter, but also in our bags, as drift over a foot deep covered us. We were unable to cook and consequently had nothing to eat during the day, not even a swallow of water.

Of all the days of suffering, none can compare with this. If I knew I had another month of this existence, I would stop the engine this moment.

In my daily journeys across Cemetery Ridge to the fishery, it was but natural at first that my reflections should be sad and gloomy. There lie my departed comrades and to their left is the vacant space where, in a few days, my remains will be deposited if sufficient strength remains to those who may survive me. The brass buttons on Lieut. Lockwood's blouse, worn bright by the flying gravel, protrude through the scanty covering of earth which our depleted strength barely enabled us to place over him. At first, these dazzling buttons would awaken thoughts of those bright days at Fort Conger and the half-forgotten scene of his death, and the universal sorrow that was felt at his departure. But later, my own wretched circumstances have served to counteract these feelings, and I can pass and repass this place without emotion and almost with indifference.

Sunday, June 1st.

The gale subsiding at 1 a.m., we immediately turned out of our com-fortable quarters to remove the snow which had accumulated over us. The snow had also penetrated our sleeping bags.

Breakfast consisted of three ounces of shrimps and a cup of weak tea to each man. We were without food for thirty-six hours.

Lieut. Kislingbury became unconscious at 8 a.m. and breathed his last at 3 p.m. Before he lost consciousness he begged piteously for a drink of water, but this the Doctor denied him. He then sang the

Doxology in a clear but weak voice and, falling back in his sleeping bag, was soon in the embrace of Death.

The sky cleared at 8 a.m. and the sun came out bright and clear. At 3 p.m. the sky again clouded and light snow began falling. Temperature at 10 a.m. 35°.

Pools of water are forming everywhere in the rocks and in depressions about our tent. Water sufficient for two days was collected by the cooks. It is very fortunate as our fuel is fast disappearing.

Long shot a dovekie. One of his eyes was injured by the recoil of his gun and I had to lead him home.

I caught eight pounds of shrimps. The snow is very deep and soft. Long and I were gone from the house over seven hours. Less than two hours were spent at the fishery, the remainder of the time being consumed in walking. We felt ready to drop from fatigue on returning.

June 2nd.

After an absence of over seven hours, I returned with only five pounds of shrimps. My baits are almost useless.

We buried Lieut. Kislingbury this morning.

Schneider is no longer able to work. Bender is little better. Lieut. Greely and Gardiner are very weak. Salor became delirious at 7 p.m.

Long shot a dovekie.

Vast fields of ice are moving down the sound. If it would choke in the narrow part, this might drive the seals and birds to this side.

• • •

June 3rd.

Fair weather. A light wind blew steadily from the southeast all day and thawing advanced considerably. Water is trickling down the hillside, forming in pools near the tent and thus providing all the water required.

Long did not go out today owing to windy weather.

I caught only six pounds of shrimps.

Salor died at 3 a.m. I was lying by his side in the same bag at the time. Not having the necessary strength to remove him and not feeling inclined to get up, I went to sleep in the same bag with the remains and did not awake until breakfast was announced at 9 a.m.

Doctor Pavy was making some rather absurd prescriptions this evening and talking incoherently.

For weeks I have noticed Linn's feet protruding from the gravel heaped over his body. Day by day the elements have reduced the scanty covering until Linn's feet are fully exposed to the gales sweeping over Cemetery Ridge. I have often thought that I would replace that which had blown away, but my waning strength has caused me to defer this for so long that I cannot think of attempting it now.

June 4th.

A beautiful day. The wind which was blowing last evening abated at 6 a.m., but again sprang up this evening. High, blustering wind storms appear to be normal weather here.

I caught seven pounds of shrimps and Long shot a dovekie.

Fredericks, occasionally assisted by Henry, is doing all the work about camp—cooking, gathering saxifrage for fuel, and cutting wood from the boat. Schneider manages to bring in salt water for the cook, but can do nothing more. Bender and Connell can do but very little.

During the last few days, I have eaten a great many of the dark-colored rock lichens, finding them quite palatable and not at all injurious to the stomach, the experiences of Franklin and Hayes notwithstanding.

Smith Sound is a beautiful sheet of water today, not a piece of ice in sight and the surface as smooth as a mirror. How easily we could be reached by a relief vessel or a party from Littleton Island!

We buried Salor in the tidal crack. We did not feel strong enough to dig a grave on Cemetery Ridge.

June 5th.

Dr. Pavy is very weak. He refuses to partake of the shrimp stew and is kept up by weak tea alone.

I caught five pounds of shrimps.

Reindeer moss in small quantities has been found at this point. The vegetation—poppies, saxifrage, grasses, etc.—is becoming green. The mosses growing in damp ground are looking quite beautiful.

Owing to the thievish propensity of Henry which has again broken out, it became necessary in order to insure the safety of the party for Lieut. Greely to issue an order to Long, Fredericks and myself to shoot him without delay, if detected in appropriating to his own use any articles of public property. I insert a copy of the order.

Near Cape Sabine,
June 5th, 1884.

To Sergeants Brainard, Fredericks and Long:

Private Henry having been repeatedly guilty of stealing the provisions of this party which is now perishing slowly by starvation, has so far been condoned and pardoned. It is, *however, imperatively ordered* that if this man be detected either eating food of any kind not issued him regularly, or making caches, or appropriating any article of provisions, you will at once shoot him and report the matter to me. Any other course would be a fatal leniency, the man being able to overpower any two of our present force.

(signed) A. W. Greely,
Lt. 5th Cav. A. S. O. & Asst.
Comdg. Lady Franklin Bay Ex.

Henry has twice stolen the greater portion of dovekie intended for the hunter and the shrimper. He was also detected eating seal skin lashing and seal skin boots stolen from the public stock. The stealing of old seal skin boots etc. may seem to some a very insignificant affair, but to us such articles mean life.

June 6th.

I fished over seven hours for the tantalizing little shrimps and caught only two and a half pounds. My baits are almost worthless. What are we to do? I have tried everything at hand, but with no favorable results. I would again drag for sea vegetation, but my failing strength is not equal to the task. I can do nothing more than stagger down to the shrimping grounds and return.

Bender died at 5:45 p.m. and Dr. Pavy, who had been weakening rapidly for the last few days, passed away at 6 p.m.

A further confession on the part of Henry to Lieut. Greely of stealing and the fact of his having been caught stealing shrimps this morning, caused the issuing of the following order:

Near Cape Sabine,
June 6th, 1884.

To Sergeants Brainard, Long and Fredericks:

Notwithstanding promises given by Private C. B. Henry yesterday he has since acknowledged to me having tampered with seal thongs, if not other food at the old camp. This pertinacity and audacity is the destruction of this party if not at once ended. Private Henry will be shot today, all care being taken to prevent his injuring anyone as his physical strength is greater than that of any two men. Decide the manner of death by two ball and one blank cartridge.

This order is *imperative and absolutely necessary* for *any chance* of life.

(signed) A. W. Greely,
1st Lt. 5th Cav. A. S. O. & Asst.
Comdg. L. F. B. Ex.

No further explanation in the matter is necessary. The order was duly executed at 2 p.m. and later it was read aloud to the assembled party. Although deploring the necessity for such severe measures, all were unanimous in the opinion that no other course could have been pursued.

In Henry's effects were found the following articles stolen from the public stores: Several strips of seal skin, one pair of seal boots, a coil of seal skin thongs, knives, etc.

Flies, very large and numerous, are to be observed every warm day about the tent in numbers sufficient to frighten a model housewife.

June 7th.

Fredericks is now doing all that he can for the sick, in addition to the cooking. He is certainly a wonderful fellow.

Long shot nothing today. I caught only two pounds of shrimps.

I gathered together all the seal skin which is intended for food. Oil-tanned skins from which the hair was removed will be eaten in stews. I do not find as much of this article as I had expected.

Schneider now confesses that Henry and Bender whose bag he shared ate large quantities of seal skin clothing in their bags at night after the others retired. Since our hut was quite dark, even after the holes had been cut through, they were practically safe from detection.

Biederbick and Connell gathered a few lichens and a little reindeer moss. This evening we dined on a stew composed of a pair of boot soles, a handful of reindeer moss and a few rock lichens. The small quantity of shrimps which I furnish daily is sufficient only for the morning meal.

We dressed the bodies of Dr. Pavy and Bender for their graves, but were unable to bury them.

Sunday, June 8th.

This has been the clearest, brightest and most enjoyable day on these inhospitable shores. Temperature at 11 a.m. 38°. Nothing but a wretched stew of shrimps for breakfast this morning (less than three ounces per man) and a thin unpalatable stew of seal thongs for dinner.

Schneider worked for a long time burning the hair from seal skin clothing which was divided at dinner time. Lieut. Greely worked for five hours today and collected about two quarts of lichens. Connell gathered a small quantity of saxifrage in full flower blossom. These blossoms are sweet and palatable. Biederbick collected about the same quantity of lichens. He also made a discovery which increases the perfidy of Henry—a small cache of bear meat in the rocks near the tent.

Long and myself went down to the winter house and brought up a quantity of wood for fuel. Our strength is nearly gone. If we should get game, we are too weak to bring it in. If we are saved at all, the vessel which is to find us will have to make haste. Very few days remain to us.

June 9th.

Our breakfast consisted of a few shrimps and the usual cup of tea. At dinner we had no stew, but only a cup of tea and a piece of burned seal skin. A few lichens eaten raw were also used.

Connell appears quite strong, but doubtless has incipient scurvy. He gathered a quantity of saxifrage for fuel. Schneider burned the hair from a few seal skin garments which were eaten this evening. Long shot a dovekie.

Bender was buried in the tidal crack this morning and during the evening, Dr. Pavy was plunged into the same crystal grave.

Long's thirty-second birthday. He received a spoonful of rum in honor of the occasion.

June 10th.

Gardiner is much worse.

Long and myself felt greatly strengthened by the portion of dovekie stew. We had a stew of black rock lichens for dinner and found it of a gelatinous consistency, not unpalatable and evidently possessing some nutriment.

Disappointment Berg is now connected with the open water by wide lanes. Disintegration of the floe is likely to occur at any moment. The snow has entirely disappeared from the rocks and exposed places.

Saxifrage is now in blossom and ready for pressing. The grass is growing green. I saw a bumble bee today flitting about among the flowers.

After fishing for a long time, I gave up in despair having caught only two pounds.

June 11th.

Long returned from the open water at 1:30 a.m. having killed two guillemots. One was used by the party in a stew and the other will be divided amongst those who are doing the heavy work.

A great misfortune befell me today. The spring tides have broken out the ice at the shrimping ground and my nets are lost. My baits, miserable as they were, are gone also. We will have no breakfast tomorrow morning, except a cup of tea.

It was late when I returned from fishing and everyone had retired. I did not have the heart to wake up the poor fellows, but let them sleep on quietly under the delusion that breakfast awaits them on awakening. How I pity them!

I made a flag for a distress signal.

June 12th.

We had only a cup of tea for breakfast. I found a new shrimping place this morning near the tent. After several hours' work I returned with two pounds. Our evening meal—a few boiled lichens and a cup of tea.

Connell's face appears full and healthy, but it is only swollen. He expressed a wish to work, cook and live by himself. This request Lieut. Greely would not grant.

Gardiner died at 5 p.m. Patience and fortitude have characterized his sufferings. He clung to life with a wonderful pertinacity and only succumbed when physical weakness had crushed his will. At 2 a.m. he became unconscious. For hours previous he held a portrait of his wife and his mother in his hand, gazing fondly on their faces, and when his spirit had passed into another world, the skeleton fingers still clutched the picture of those he had loved.

From this date I shall expect a relief vessel to arrive at any moment. Water has broken into the rocky point nearest our winter hut. I placed the signal flag in position on the rocky point facing the sea. It can be seen for a long distance.

June 13th.

A southeast wind, brisk and damp, prevailed all day preventing the lichen gatherers from venturing out. Our supper, it follows, was simple—seal skin *temiak* (coat) roasted over a saxifrage fire. We breakfasted off the results of last evening's shrimping.

The physical condition of the party appears unchanged. Mental vigor is fast ebbing. Biederbick was discharged from the army today, in consequence of the expiration of his term of service.

I caught about one pound of shrimps. I have nothing but the two guillemot skins for bait and they are nearly gone.

Owing to the weather Gardiner was not buried.

My signal flag has been blown down.

June 14th.

Gale subsided at 4 a.m., the weather remaining cloudy all day. Temperature at 11 a.m. 41°.

We were all very weak when we turned out for the day's labor of procuring food. Lieut. Greely, Connell and Biederbick gathered lichens for supper and breakfast tomorrow. Fredericks performed the usual camp work, and Long and myself buried Gardiner in the tidal crack. After dinner I went to the shrimping grounds, but caught only one pound.

The floe ice is breaking from shore. Disappointment Berg is now free.

I replaced the signal flag in position.

We have named the rock lichens Arctic mushrooms.

Sunday, June 15th.

Cloudy, stormy disagreeable weather. Indications of high wind on the sound. Light snow fell during the forenoon.

The oil-tanned seal skin cover to Lieut. Greely's sleeping bag has been removed and divided between Connell, Schneider, Biederbick and Elison. The remainder of the party will use the cover to Long's sleeping bag.

Schneider was begging hard this evening for opium pills that he might die easily and quickly.

The sense of hunger appears to have disappeared. We eat simply to preserve life. Crumbs of bread at our winter quarter which are occasionally exposed through the melting of the snow are picked from heaps of the vilest filth and eaten with relish. Henry ate ptarmigan droppings; Bender ate caterpillars, worms, etc. Saxifrage, lichens and other vegetation together with the intestines of animals would now be luxuries.

I worked several hours in the raw, chilling winds and caught little more than a pound of shrimps.

June 16th.

The lichen gatherers were again kept from their labors by a high wind. Consequently our morning stew was very meagre. For supper we had nothing at all. We are calmly awaiting relief or death. One or the other must visit us soon.

The shrimps, our last resource except the lichens, have failed us. For full five hours I worked as persistently as my strength would permit. At the end of that time, I had caught only two or three ounces. Even these I did not carry home. I was barely able to crawl there myself.

Sometime during the day Disappointment Berg moved silently out from the position which it has occupied for so long.

The last of our tea was used this morning.

June 17th.

Saxifrage tea was served this morning as a substitute for English tea. It was very bitter and unpalatable. Despite all my efforts to swallow this fluid, I was compelled to give up in disgust. This was all that we had for breakfast, except a few mouthfuls of roasted seal skin which had been left from better days. For dinner a lichen stew was prepared, but did not go far toward satisfying our starving party.

I brought up an armful of fuel from the old camp. I was too weak to cut it. Fredericks is also about broken down. Schneider is almost entirely helpless.

The sleeping bags of Long and myself were stripped of their seal skin covering and the pieces divided to be eaten. This is the last material in camp that we can use for food. We are badly broken down and all will go together. Who will be left to bury us with our departed comrades?

The channel was perfectly free of ice this evening and its surface like glass.

June 18th.

We had saxifrage tea again for breakfast, together with a portion of the sleeping bag cover boiled. There has been a perceptible diminution of strength in the party today. I was unable to go out until 4 p.m. when I crawled and staggered, I scarcely know how, to the rocks a few yards away and scraped off a small quantity of lichens.

As we have nothing to cook and the saxifrage tea was voted a nuisance, no fire was made this evening. Besides this, Fredericks says that he is not able to cook more than one meal a day. A few mouthfuls of the boiled seal skin sufficed for supper. What would seem remarkable is that we long for certain articles of food, but at the same time the sense of hunger is absent. The fearful gnawing at our stomachs, experienced last fall and winter, has left us.

Long shot two dovekies last night, but they drifted out with the tide and he secured neither. He will now do his hunting in the daytime. Probably the tide will be more favorable.

Soon after eating his breakfast, Schneider became unconscious and at 6 p.m. breathed his last.

Connell complained of dimness of vision this evening on his return from gathering lichens. Biederbick, very inconsiderately, changed underclothing throughout today. It now occurs to us that we have neither changed clothing nor bathed since we left Fort Conger last August— nearly eleven months!

Schneider died just three years from the day when he was detailed for duty with the expedition.

June 19th.

During the morning the weather was clear and westerly winds prevailed. During the afternoon the wind changed to southeast and attained a high velocity.

Long went out during the night, not returning until a late hour this morning. He had killed two dovekies and two eider ducks, but the ebbing tide had carried them seaward before they could be reached with the long pole which he carried.

I found a small piece of driftwood in the rocks about thirty feet above the level of the sea. It bears marks of rough usage in the ice and the appearance would indicate great antiquity. I found a similar piece a few days ago about fifteen feet lower than this. This fact is indisputable evidence of the gradual rise of the land from the sea.

The party is weaker. The lichens are scarce. Had my recommendations been adopted, others of the party might be alive now. Several weeks ago I ate a quantity of lichens and, finding them palatable and not at all injurious, I urged Lieut. Greely to use them for food. He probably would have done so except for the emphatic medical opinion of Dr. Pavy, who pronounced them extremely dangerous to the system and recommended that they should not be resorted to except in the last extremity.

Connell has symptoms of scurvy. I attribute my swollen face and limbs to the same insidious disease.

I found and gathered a fine bed of reindeer moss. While removing Schneider's remains from the tent, we noticed an offensive odor from the mouth, perhaps caused by scurvy.

June 21st.

Our summer solstice! The wind is still blowing a gale from the south. Temperature 7 a.m. 31°; minimum recorded 28°.

Tent in dilapidated condition. Shelter scarcely habitable for Long and myself. It will most likely be blown down if the storm does not abate. Snow squalls at intervals. Ice has broken for a long distance into Buchanan Strait.

A lichen stew for breakfast and a few pieces of boiled seal skin for supper. Connell worse. He says that his legs are useless below the knees.

Since the day before yesterday, Elison has eaten his stew by having a spoon tied to the stump of his frozen arm.

from South

by Sir Ernest Shackleton

The reputation of Sir Ernest Shackleton (1874–1922) has enjoyed a surprising revival. Companion and rival of Scott, Sir Ernest was an admirable figure—another heroic failure from Antarctica's annals. In 1912, he attempted to cross the southern continent, but ice crushed his ship, the Endurance. Here, Shackleton and 27 men have struggled for months across the melting ice pack in search of land.

n April 7 at daylight the long-desired peak of Clarence Island came into view, bearing nearly north from our camp. At first it had the appearance of a huge berg, but with the growing light we could see plainly the black lines of scree and the high precipitous cliffs of the island, which were miraged up to some extent. The dark rocks in the white snow were a pleasant sight. So long had our eyes looked on icebergs that apparently grew or dwindled according to the angles at which the shadows were cast by the sun; so often had we discovered rocky islands and brought in sight the peaks of Joinville Land, only to find them, after some change of wind or temperature, floating away as nebulous cloud or ordinary berg, that not until Worsley, Wild, and Hurley had unanimously confirmed my observation was I satisfied that I was really looking at Clarence Island. The land was still more than sixty miles away, but it had to our eyes something of the appearance of home, since we expected to find there our first solid footing after all the long months of drifting on the unstable ice. We had adjusted ourselves to the life on the floe, but our hopes had been fixed all the time on some possible landing-place. As one hope failed to materialize, our anticipations fed themselves on another. Our drifting home had no rudder to guide it, no sail to give it speed. We were dependent upon the caprice of wind and current; we went whither those irresponsible forces listed. The longing to feel solid earth under our feet filled our hearts.

In the full daylight Clarence Island ceased to look like land and had the appearance of a berg not more than eight or ten miles away, so deceptive are distances in the clear air of the Antarctic. The sharp white peaks of Elephant Island showed to the west of north a little later in the day. "I have stopped issuing sugar now, and our meals consist of seal-meat and blubber only, with 7 ozs. of dried milk per day for the party," I wrote. "Each man receives a pinch of salt, and the milk is boiled up to make hot drinks for all hands. The diet suits us, since we cannot get much exercise on the floe and the blubber supplies heat. Fried slices of blubber seem to our taste to resemble crisp bacon. It certainly is no hardship to eat it, though persons living under civilized conditions probably would shudder at it. The hardship would come if we were unable to get it." I think that the palate of the human animal can adjust itself to anything. Some creatures will die before accepting a strange diet if deprived of their natural food. The Yaks of the Himalayan uplands must feed from the growing grass, scanty and dry though it may be, and would starve even if allowed the best oats and corns. "We still have the dark water-sky of the last week with us to the southwest and west, round to the north-east. We are leaving all the bergs to the west and there are few within our range of vision now. The swell is more marked to-day, and I feel sure we are at the verge of the floe-ice. One strong gale followed by a calm would scatter the pack, I think, and then we could push through. I have been thinking much of our prospects. The appearance of Clarence Island after our long drift seems, somehow, to convey an ultimatum. The island is the last outpost of the south and our final chance of a landing-place. Beyond it lies the broad Atlantic. Our little boats may be compelled any day now to sail unsheltered over the open sea with a thousand leagues of ocean separating them from the land to the north and east. It seems vital that we shall land on Clarence Island or its neighbour, Elephant Island. The latter island has an attraction for us, although as far as I know nobody has ever landed there. Its name suggests the presence of the plump and succulent sea-elephant. We have an increasing desire in any case to get firm ground under our feet. The floe has been a good friend to us, but it is reaching the end of its journey, and it is liable at any time now to break up and fling us into the unplumbed sea."

A little later, after reviewing the whole situation in the light of our circumstances, I made up my mind that we should try to reach Deception Island. Clarence and Elephant Islands lay comparatively near to us and were separated by some eighty miles of water from Prince George Island, which was about 150 miles away from our camp on the berg. From this island a chain of similar islands extends westward, terminating in Deception Island. The channels separating these desolate patches of rock and ice are from ten to fifteen miles wide. But we knew from the Admiralty sailing directions that there were stores for the use of shipwrecked mariners on Deception Island, and it was possible that the summer whalers had not yet deserted its harbour. Also we had learned from our scanty records that a small church had been erected there for the benefit of the transient whalers. The existence of this building would mean to us a supply of timber, from which, if dire necessity urged us, we could construct a reasonably seaworthy boat. We had discussed this point during our drift on the floe. Two of our boats were fairly strong, but the third, the *James Caird*, was light, although a little longer than the others. All of them were small for the navigation of these notoriously stormy seas, and they would be heavily loaded, so a voyage in open water would be a serious undertaking. I fear that the carpenter's fingers were already itching to convert pews into topsides and decks. In any case, the worst that could befall us when we had reached Deception Island would be a wait until the whalers returned about the middle of November.

Another bit of information gathered from the records of the west side of the Weddell Sea related to Prince George Island. The Admiralty "Sailing Directions," referring to the South Shetlands, mentioned a cave on this island. None of us had seen that cave or could say if it was large or small, wet or dry; but as we drifted on our floe and later, when navigating the treacherous leads and making our uneasy night camps, that cave seemed to my fancy to be a palace which in contrast would dim the splendours of Versailles.

The swell increased that night and the movement of the ice became more pronounced. Occasionally a neighbouring floe would hammer against the ice on which we were camped, and the lesson of these blows was plain to read. We must get solid ground under our feet quickly. When the vibration ceased after a heavy surge, my thoughts flew round to the problem ahead. If the party had not numbered more than six men a solution would not have been so hard to find; but obviously the transportation of the whole party to a place of safety, with the limited means at our disposal, was going to be a matter of extreme difficulty. There were twenty-eight men on our floating cake of ice, which was steadily dwindling under the influence of wind, weather, charging floes, and heavy swell. I confess that I felt the burden of responsibility sit heavily on my shoulders; but, on the other hand, I was stimulated and cheered by the attitude of the men. Loneliness is the penalty of leadership, but the man who has to make the decisions is assisted greatly if he feels that there is no uncertainty in the minds of those who follow him, and that his orders will be carried out confidently and in expectation of success.

The sun was shining in the blue sky on the following morning (April 8). Clarence Island showed clearly on the horizon, and Elephant Island could also be distinguished. The single snow-clad peak of Clarence Island stood up as a beacon of safety, though the most optimistic imagination could not make an easy path of the ice and ocean that separated us from that giant white and austere. "The pack was much looser this morning, and the long rolling swell from the north-east is more pronounced than it was yesterday. The floes rise and fall with the surge of the sea. We evidently are drifting with the surface current, for all the heavier masses of floe, bergs, and hummocks are being left behind. There has been some discussion in the camp as to the advisability of making one of the bergs our home for the time being and drifting with it to the west. The idea is not sound. I cannot be sure that the berg would drift in the right direction. If it did move west and carried us into the open water, what would be our fate when we tried to launch the boats down the steep sides of the berg in the sea-swell after the surrounding floes had left us? One must reckon, too, the chance of the berg splitting or even overturning during our stay. It is not possible to gauge the condition of a big mass of ice by surface appearance. The ice may have a fault, and when the wind, current, and swell set up strains and tensions, the line of weakness may reveal itself suddenly and disastrously. No, I do not like the idea of drifting on a berg. We must stay on our floe till conditions improve and then make another attempt to advance towards the land."

At 6:30 p.m. a particularly heavy shock went through our floe. The watchman and other members of the party made an immediate inspection and found a crack right under the *James Caird* and between the other two boats and the main camp. Within five minutes the boats were over the crack and close to the tents. The trouble was not caused by a blow from another floe. We could see that the piece of ice we occupied had slewed and now presented its long axis towards the oncoming swell. The floe, therefore, was pitching in the manner of a ship, and it had cracked across when the swell lifted the centre, leaving the two ends comparatively unsupported. We were now on a triangular raft of ice, the three sides measuring, roughly, 90, 100, and 120 yds. Night came down dull and overcast, and before midnight the wind had freshened from the west. We could see that the pack was opening under the influence of wind, wave, and current, and I felt that the time for launching the boats was near at hand. Indeed, it was obvious that even if the conditions were unfavourable for a start during the coming day, we could not safely stay on the floe many hours longer. The movement of the ice in the swell was increasing, and the floe might split right under our camp. We had made preparations for quick action if anything of the kind occurred. Our case would be desperate if the ice broke into small pieces not large enough to support our party and not loose enough to permit the use of the boats.

The following day was Sunday (April 9), but it proved no day of rest for us. Many of the important events of our Expedition occurred on Sundays, and this particular day was to see our forced departure from the floe on which we had lived for nearly six months, and the start of our journeyings in the boats. "This has been an eventful day. The morning was fine, though somewhat overcast by stratus and cumulus clouds; moderate south-south-westerly and south-easterly breezes. We hoped that with this wind the ice would drift nearer to Clarence Island. At 7 a.m. lanes of water and leads could be seen on the horizon to the west. The ice separating us from the lanes was loose, but did not appear to be workable for the boats. The long swell from the north-west was coming in more freely than on the previous day and was driving the floes together in the utmost confusion. The loose brash between the masses of ice was being churned to mudlike consistency, and no boat could have lived in the channels that opened and closed around us. Our own floe was suffering in the general disturbance, and after breakfast I ordered the tents to be struck and everything prepared for an immediate start when the boats could be launched." I had decided to take the *James Caird* myself, with Wild and eleven men. This was the largest of our boats, and in addition to her human complement she carried the major portion of the stores. Worsley had charge of the *Dudley Docker* with nine men, and Hudson and Crean were the senior men on the *Stancomb Wills.*

Soon after breakfast the ice closed again. We were standing by, with our preparations as complete as they could be made, when at 11 a.m. our floe suddenly split right across under the boats. We rushed our gear on to the larger of the two pieces and watched with strained attention for the next development. The crack had cut through the site of my tent. I stood on the edge of the new fracture, and, looking across the widening channel of water, could see the spot where for many months my head and shoulders had rested when I was in my sleeping-bag. The depression formed by my body and legs was on our side of the crack. The ice had sunk under my weight during the months of waiting in the tent, and I had many times put snow under the bag to fill the hollow. The lines of stratification showed clearly the different layers of snow. How fragile and precarious had been our resting-place! Yet usage had dulled our sense of danger. The floe had become our home, and during the early months of the drift we had almost ceased to realize that it was but a sheet of ice floating on unfathomed seas. Now our home was being shattered under our feet, and we had a sense of loss and incompleteness hard to describe.

The fragments of our floe came together again a little later, and we had our lunch of seal-meat, all hands eating their fill. I thought that a good meal would be the best possible preparation for the journey that now seemed imminent, and as we would not be able to take all our meat with us when we finally moved, we could regard every pound eaten as a pound rescued. The call to action came at 1 p.m. The pack opened well and the channels became navigable. The conditions were not all one could have desired, but it was best not to wait any longer. The *Dudley Docker* and the *Stancomb Wills* were launched quickly. Stores were thrown in, and the two boats were pulled clear of the immediate floes towards a pool of open water three miles broad, in which floated a lone and mighty berg. The *James Caird* was the last boat to leave, heavily loaded with stores and odds and ends of camp equipment. Many things regarded by us as essentials at that time were to be discarded a little later as the pressure of the primitive became more severe. Man can sustain life with very scanty means. The trappings of civilization are soon cast aside in the face of stern realities, and given the barest opportunity of winning food and shelter, man can live and even find his laughter ringing true.

The three boats were a mile away from our floe home at 2 p.m. We had made our way through the channels and had entered the big pool when we saw a rush of foam-clad water and tossing ice approaching us, like the tidal bore of a river. The pack was being impelled to the east by a tide-rip, and two huge masses of ice were driving down upon us on converging courses. The *James Caird* was leading. Starboarding the helm and bending strongly to the oars, we managed to get clear. The two other boats followed us, though from their position astern at first they had not realized the immediate danger. The *Stancomb Wills* was the last boat and she was very nearly caught, but by great exertion she was kept just ahead of the driving ice. It was an unusual and startling experience. The effect of tidal action on ice is not often as marked as it was that day. The advancing ice, accompanied by a large wave, appeared to be travelling at about three knots, and if we had not succeeded in pulling clear we would certainly have been swamped.

We pulled hard for an hour to windward of the berg that lay in the open water. The swell was crashing on its perpendicular sides and throwing spray to a height of sixty feet. Evidently there was an ice-foot at the east end, for the swell broke before it reached the berg-face and flung its white spray on to the blue ice-wall. We might have paused to admire the spectacle under other conditions; but night was coming on apace, and we needed a camping-place. As we steered north-west, still amid the ice-floes, the *Dudley Docker* got jammed between two masses while attempting to make a short cut. The old adage about a short cut being the longest way round is often as true in the Antarctic as it is in the peaceful countryside. The *James Caird* got a line aboard the *Dudley Docker*, and after some hauling the boat was brought clear of the ice again. We hastened forward in the twilight in search of a flat, old floe, and presently found a fairly large piece rocking in the swell. It was not an ideal camping-place by any means, but darkness had overtaken us. We hauled the boats up, and by 8 p.m. had the tents pitched and the blubber-stove burning cheerily. Soon all hands were well fed and happy in their tents, and snatches of song came to me as I wrote up my log.

Some intangible feeling of uneasiness made me leave my tent about 11 p.m. that night and glance around the quiet camp. The stars between the snow-flurries showed that the floe had swung round and was end on to the swell, a position exposing it to sudden strains. I started to walk across the floe in order to warn the watchman to look carefully for cracks, and as I was passing the men's tent the floe lifted on the crest of a swell and cracked right under my feet. The men were in one of the dome-shaped tents, and it began to stretch apart as the ice opened. A muffled sound, suggestive of suffocation, came from beneath the stretching tent. I rushed forward, helped some emerging men from under the canvas, and called out, "Are you all right?" "There are two in the water," somebody answered. The crack had widened to about four feet, and as I threw myself down at the edge, I saw a whitish object floating in the water. It was a sleeping-bag with a man inside. I was able to grasp it, and with a heave lifted man and bag on to the floe. A few seconds later the ice-edges came together again with tremendous force. Fortunately, there had been but one man in the water, or the incident might have been a tragedy. The rescued bag contained Holness, who was wet down to the waist but otherwise unscathed. The crack was now opening again. The *James Caird* and my tent were on one side of the opening and the remaining two boats and the rest of the camp on the other side. With two or three men to help me I struck my tent; then all hands manned the painter and rushed the *James Caird* across the opening crack. We held to the rope while, one by one, the men left on our side of the floe jumped the channel or scrambled over by means of the boat. Finally I was left alone. The night had swallowed all the others and the rapid movement of the ice forced me to let go the painter. For a moment I felt that my piece of rocking floe was the loneliest place in the world. Peering into the darkness, I could just see the dark figures on the other floe. I hailed Wild, ordering him to launch the *Stancomb Wills*, but I need not have troubled. His quick brain had anticipated the order and already the boat was being manned and hauled to the ice-edge. Two or three minutes later she reached me, and I was ferried across to the camp.

We were now on a piece of flat ice about 200 ft. long and 100 ft. wide. There was no more sleep for any of us that night. The killers were blowing in the lanes around, and we waited for daylight and watched for signs of another crack in the ice. The hours passed with laggard feet as we stood huddled together or walked to and fro in the effort to keep some warmth in our bodies. We lit the blubber-stove at 3 a.m., and with pipes going and a cup of hot milk for each man, we were able to discover some bright spots in our outlook. At any rate, we were on the move at last, and if dangers and difficulties loomed ahead we could meet and overcome them. No longer were we drifting helplessly at the mercy of wind and current.

The first glimmerings of dawn came at 6 a.m., and I waited anxiously for the full daylight. The swell was growing, and at times our ice was surrounded closely by similar pieces. At 6:30 a.m. we had hot hoosh, and then stood by waiting for the pack to open. Our chance came at 8, when we launched the boats, loaded them, and started to make our way through the lanes in a northerly direction. The *James Caird* was in the lead, with the *Stancomb Wills* next and the *Dudley Docker* bringing up the rear. In order to make the boats more seaworthy we had left some of our shovels, picks, and dried vegetables on the floe, and for a long time we could see the abandonded stores forming a dark spot on the ice. The boats were still heavily loaded. We got out of the lanes and entered a stretch of open water at 11 a.m. A strong easterly breeze was blowing, but the fringe of pack lying outside protected us from the full force of the swell, just as the coral-reef of a tropical island checks the rollers of the Pacific. Our way was across the open sea, and soon after noon we swung round the north end of the pack and laid a course to the westward, the *James Caird* still in the lead. Immediately our deeply laden boats began to make heavy weather. They shipped sprays, which, freezing as they fell, covered men and gear with ice, and soon it was clear that we could not safely proceed. I put the *James Caird* round and ran for the shelter of the pack again, the other boats following. Back inside the outer line of ice the sea was not breaking. This was at 3 p.m., and all hands were tired and cold. A big floeberg resting peacefully ahead caught my eye, and half an hour later we had hauled up the boats and pitched camp for the night. It was a fine big blue berg with an attractively solid appearance, and from our camp we could get a good view of the surrounding sea and ice. The highest point was about 15 ft. above sea-level. After a hot meal all hands, except the watchman, turned in. Every one was in need of rest after the troubles of the previous night and the unaccustomed strain of the last thirty-six hours at the oars. The berg appeared well able to withstand the battering of the sea, and too deep and massive to be seriously affected by the swell; but it was not as safe as it looked. About midnight the watchman called me and showed me that the heavy north-westerly swell was undermining the ice. A great piece had broken off within eight feet of my tent. We made what inspection was possible in the darkness, and found that on the westward side of the berg the thick snow-covering was yielding rapidly to the attacks of the sea. An ice-foot had formed just under the surface of the water. I decided that there was no immediate danger and did not call the men. The north-westerly wind strengthened during the night.

The morning of April 11 was overcast and misty. There was a haze on the horizon, and daylight showed that the pack had closed round our berg, making it impossible in the heavy swell to launch the boats. We could see no sign of the water. Numerous whales and killers were blowing between the floes, and Cape pigeons, petrels, and fulmars were circling round our berg. The scene from our camp as the daylight brightened was magnificent beyond description, though I must admit that we viewed it with anxiety. Heaving hills of pack and floe were sweeping towards us in long undulations, later to be broken here and there by the dark lines that indicated open water. As each swell lifted around our rapidly dissolving berg it drove floe-ice on to the ice-foot, shearing off more of the top snow-covering and reducing the size of our camp. When the floes retreated to attack again the water swirled over the ice-foot, which was rapidly increasing in width. The launching of the boats under such conditions would be difficult. Time after time, so often that a track was formed, Worsley, Wild, and I climbed to the highest point of the berg and stared out to the horizon in search of a break in the pack. After long hours had dragged past, far away on the lift of the swell there appeared a dark break in the tossing field of ice. Æons seemed to pass, so slowly it approached. I noticed enviously the calm, peaceful attitudes of two seals which lolled lazily on a rocking floe. They were at home and had no reason for worry or cause for fear. If they thought at all, I suppose they counted it an ideal day for a joyous journey on the tumbling ice. To us it was a day that seemed likely to lead to no more days. I do not think I had ever before felt the anxiety that belongs to leadership quite so keenly. When I looked down at the camp to rest my eyes from the strain of watching the wide white expanse broken by that one black ribbon of open water, I could see that my companions were waiting with more than ordinary interest to learn what I thought about it all. After one particularly heavy collision somebody shouted sharply, "She has cracked in the middle." I jumped off the look-out station and ran to the place the men were examining. There was a crack, but investigation showed it to be a mere surface-break in the snow with no indication of a split in the berg itself. The carpenter mentioned calmly that earlier in the day he had actually gone adrift on a fragment of ice. He was standing near the edge of our camping-ground when the ice under his feet parted from the parent mass. A quick jump over the widening gap saved him.

The hours dragged on. One of the anxieties in my mind was the possibility that we would be driven by the current through the eighty-mile gap between Clarence Island and Prince George Island into the open Atlantic; but slowly the open water came nearer, and at noon it had almost reached us. A long lane, narrow but navigable, stretched out to the south-west horizon. Our chance came a little later. We rushed our boats over the edge of the reeling berg and swung them clear of the ice-foot as it rose beneath them. The *James Caird* was nearly capsized by a blow from below as the berg rolled away, but she got into deep water. We flung stores and gear aboard and within a few minutes were away. The *James Caird* and *Dudley Docker* had good sails and with a favourable breeze could make progress along the lane, with the rolling fields of ice on either side. The swell was heavy and spray was breaking over the ice-floes. An attempt to set a little rag of sail on the *Stancomb Wills* resulted in serious delay. The area of sail was too small to be of much assistance, and while the men were engaged in this work the boat drifted down towards the ice-floe, where her position was likely to be perilous. Seeing her plight, I sent the *Dudley Docker* back for her and tied the James Caird up to a piece of ice. *The Dudley Docker* had to tow the Stancomb Wills, and the delay cost us two hours of valuable daylight. When I had the three boats together again we continued down the lane, and soon saw a wider stretch of water to the west; it appeared to offer us release from the grip of the pack. At the head of an ice-tongue that nearly closed the gap through which we might enter the open space was a wave-worn berg shaped like some curious antediluvian monster, an icy Cerberus guarding the way. It had head and eyes and rolled so heavily that it almost overturned. Its sides dipped deep in the sea, and as it rose again the water seemed to be streaming from its eyes, as though it were weeping at our escape from the clutch of the floes. This may seem fanciful to the reader, but the impression was real to us at the time. People living under civilized conditions, surrounded by Nature's varied forms of life and by all the familiar work of their own hands, may scarcely realize how quickly the mind, influenced by the eyes, responds to the unusual and weaves about it curious imaginings like the firelight fancies of our childhood days. We had lived long amid the ice, and we half-unconsciously strove to see resemblances to human faces and living forms in the fantastic contours and massively uncouth shapes of berg and floe.

At dusk we made fast to a heavy floe, each boat having its painter fastened to a separate hummock in order to avoid collisions in the swell. We landed the blubber-stove, boiled some water in order to provide hot milk, and served cold rations. I also landed the dome tents and stripped the coverings from the hoops. Our experience of the previous day in the open sea had shown us that the tents must be packed tightly. The spray had dashed over the bows and turned to ice on the cloth, which had soon grown dangerously heavy. Other articles of our scanty equipment had to go that night. We were carrying only the things that had seemed essential, but we stripped now to the barest limit of safety. We had hoped for a quiet night, but presently we were forced to cast off, since pieces of loose ice began to work round the floe. Drift-ice is always attracted to the lee side of a heavy floe, where it bumps and presses under the influence of the current. I had determined not to risk a repetition of the last night's experience and so had not pulled the boats up. We spent the hours of darkness keeping an offing from the main line of pack under the lee of the smaller pieces. Constant rain and snow-squalls blotted out the stars and soaked us through, and at times it was only by shouting to each other that we managed to keep the boats together. There was no sleep for anybody owing to the severe cold, and we dare not pull fast enough to keep ourselves warm since we were unable to see more than a few yards ahead. Occasionally the ghostly shadows of silver, snow, and fulmar petrels flashed close to us, and all around we could hear the killers blowing, their short, sharp hisses sounding like sudden escapes of steam. The killers were a source of anxiety, for a boat could easily have been capsized by one of them coming up to blow. They would throw aside in a nonchalant fashion pieces of ice much bigger than our boats when they rose to the surface, and we had an uneasy feeling that the white bottoms of the boats would look like ice from below. Shipwrecked mariners drifting in the Antarctic seas would be things not dreamed of in the killers' philosophy, and might appear on closer examination to be tasty substitutes for seal and penguin. We certainly regarded the killers with misgivings.

Early in the morning of April 12 the weather improved and the wind dropped. Dawn came with a clear sky, cold and fearless. I looked around at the faces of my companions in the *James Caird* and saw pinched and drawn features. The strain was beginning to tell. Wild sat at the rudder with the same calm, confident expression that he would have worn under happier conditions; his steel-blue eyes looked out to the day ahead. All the people, though evidently suffering, were doing their best to be cheerful, and the prospect of a hot breakfast was inspiriting. I told all the boats that immediately we could find a suitable floe the cooker would be started and hot milk and Bovril would soon fix everybody up. Away we rowed to the westward through open pack, floes of all shapes and sizes on every side of us, and every man not engaged in pulling looking eagerly for a suitable camping-place. I could gauge the desire for food of the different members by the eagerness they displayed in pointing out to me the floes they considered exactly suited to our purpose. The temperature was about 10° Fahr., and the Burberry suits of the rowers crackled as the men bent to the oars. I noticed little fragments of ice and frost falling from arms and bodies. At eight o'clock a decent floe appeared ahead and we pulled up to it. The galley was landed, and soon the welcome steam rose from the cooking food as the blubber-stove flared and smoked. Never did a cook work under more anxious scrutiny. Worsley, Crean, and I stayed in our respective boats to keep them steady and prevent collisions with the floe, since the swell was still running strong, but the other men were able to stretch their cramped limbs and run to and fro "in the kitchen," as somebody put it. The sun was now rising gloriously. The Burberry suits were drying and the ice was melting off our beards. The steaming food gave us new vigour, and within three-quarters of an hour we were off again to the west with all sails set. We had given an additional sail to the *Stancomb Wills* and she was able to keep up pretty well. We could see that we were on the true pack-edge, with the blue, rolling sea just outside the fringe of ice to the north. White-capped waves vied with the glittering floes in the setting of blue water, and countless seals basked and rolled on every piece of ice big enough to form a raft.

We had been making westward with oars and sails since April 9, and fair easterly winds had prevailed. Hopes were running high as to the noon observation for position. The optimists thought that we had done sixty miles towards our goal, and the most cautious guess gave us at least thirty miles. The bright sunshine and the brilliant scene around us may have influenced our anticipations. As noon approached I saw Worsley, as navigating officer, balancing himself on the gunwale of the *Dudley Docker* with his arm around the mast, ready to snap the sun. He got his observation and we waited eagerly while he worked out the sight. Then the *Dudley Docker* ranged up alongside the *James Caird* and I jumped into Worsley's boat in order to see the result. It was a grievous disappointment. Instead of making a good run to the westward we had made a big drift to the south-east. We were actually thirty miles to the east of the position we had occupied when we left the floe on the 9th. It has been noted by sealers operating in this area that there are often heavy sets to the east in the Belgica Straits, and no doubt it was one of these sets that we had experienced. The originating cause would be a north-westerly gale off Cape Horn, producing the swell that had already caused us so much trouble. After a whispered consultation with Worsley and Wild I announced that we had not made as much progress as we expected, but I did not inform the hands of our retrograde movement.

The question of our course now demanded further consideration. Deception Island seemed to be beyond our reach. The wind was foul for Elephant Island, and as the sea was clear to the south-west, I discussed with Worsley and Wild the advisability of proceeding to Hope Bay on the mainland of the Antarctic Continent, now only eighty miles distant. Elephant Island was the nearest land, but it lay outside the main body of pack, and even if the wind had been fair we would have hesitated at that particular time to face the high sea that was running in the open. We laid a course roughly for Hope Bay, and the boats moved on again. I gave Worsley a line for a berg ahead and told him, if possible, to make fast before darkness set in. This was about three o'clock in the afternoon. We had set sail, and as the *Stancomb Wills* could not keep up with the other two boats I took her in tow, not being anxious to repeat the experience of the day we left the reeling berg. The *Dudley Docker* went ahead, but came beating down towards us at dusk. Worsley had been close to the berg, and he reported that it was unapproachable. It was rolling in the swell and displaying an ugly ice-foot. The news was bad. In the failing light we turned towards a line of pack, and found it so tossed and churned by the sea that no fragment remained big enough to give us an anchorage and shelter. Two miles away we could see a larger piece of ice, and to it we managed, after some trouble, to secure the boats. I brought my boat bow on to the floe, whilst Howe, with the painter in his hand, stood ready to jump. Standing up to watch our chance, while the oars were held ready to back the moment Howe had made his leap, I could see that there would be no possibility of getting the galley ashore that night. Howe just managed to get a footing on the edge of the floe, and then made the painter fast to a hummock. The other two boats were fastened alongside the *James Caird*. They could not lie astern of us in a line, since cakes of ice came drifting round the floe and gathering under its lee. As it was we spent the next two hours poling off the drifting ice that surged towards us. The blubber-stove could not be used, so we started the Primus lamps. There was a rough, choppy sea, and the *Dudley Docker* could not get her Primus under way, something being adrift. The men in that boat had to wait until the cook on the James Caird had boiled up the first pot of milk.

The boats were bumping so heavily that I had to slack away the painter of the *Stancomb Wills* and put her astern. Much ice was coming round the floe and had to be poled off. Then the *Dudley Docker*, being the heavier boat, began to damage the *James Caird*, and I slacked the *Dudley Docker* away. The *James Caird* remained moored to the ice, with the *Dudley Docker* and the *Stancomb Wills* in line behind her. The darkness had become complete, and we strained our eyes to see the fragments of ice that threatened us. Presently we thought we saw a great berg bearing down upon us, its form outlined against the sky, but this startling spectacle resolved itself into a low-lying cloud in front of the rising moon. The moon appeared in a clear sky. The wind shifted to the south-east as the light improved and drove the boats broadside on towards the jagged edge of the floe. We had to cut the painter of the *James Caird* and pole her off, thus losing much valuable rope. There was no time to cast off. Then we pushed away from the floe, and all night long we lay in the open freezing sea, the *Dudley Docker* now ahead, the *James Caird* astern of her, and the Stancomb Wills third in the line. The boats were attached to one another by their painters. Most of the time the *Dudley Docker* kept the *James Caird* and the *Stancomb Wills* up to the swell, and the men who were rowing were in better pass than those in the other boats, waiting inactive for the dawn. The temperature was down to 4° below zero, and a film of ice formed on the surface of the sea. When we were not on watch we lay in each other's arms for warmth. Our frozen suits thawed where our bodies met, and as the slightest movement exposed these comparatively warm spots to the biting air, we clung motionless, whispering each to his companion our hopes and thoughts. Occasionally from an almost clear sky came snow-showers, falling silently on the sea and laying a thin shroud of white over our bodies and our boats.

The dawn of April 13 came clear and bright, with occasional passing clouds. Most of the men were now looking seriously worn and strained. Their lips were cracked and their eyes and eyelids showed red in their salt-encrusted faces. The beards even of the younger men might have been those of patriarchs, for the frost and the salt spray had made them white. I called the *Dudley Docker* alongside and found that the condition of the people there was no better than in the *James Caird*. Obviously we must make land quickly, and I decided to run for Elephant Island. The wind had shifted fair for that rocky isle, then about one hundred miles away, and the pack that separated us from Hope Bay had closed up during the night from the south. At 6 a.m. we made a distribution of stores among the three boats, in view of the possibility of their being separated. The preparation of a hot breakfast was out of the question. The breeze was strong and the sea was running high in the loose pack around us. We had a cold meal, and I gave orders that all hands might eat as much as they pleased, this concession being due partly to a realization that we would have to jettison some of our stores when we reached open sea in order to lighten the boats. I hoped, moreover, that a full meal of cold rations would compensate to some extent for the lack of warm food and shelter. Unfortunately, some of the men were unable to take advantage of the extra food owing to seasickness. Poor fellows, it was bad enough to be huddled in the deeply laden, spray-swept boats, frost-bitten and half frozen, without having the pangs of seasickness added to the list of their woes. But some smiles were caused even then by the plight of one man, who had a habit of accumulating bits of food against the day of starvation that he seemed always to think was at hand, and who was condemned now to watch impotently while hungry comrades with undisturbed stomachs made biscuits, rations, and sugar disappear with extraordinary rapidity.

We ran before the wind through the loose pack, a man in the bow of each boat trying to pole off with a broken oar the lumps of ice that could not be avoided. I regarded speed as essential. Sometimes collisions were not averted. The *James Caird* was in the lead, where she bore the brunt of the encounters with lurking fragments, and she was holed above the water-line by a sharp spur of ice, but this mishap did not stay us. Later the wind became stronger and we had to reef sails, so as not to strike the ice too heavily. The *Dudley Docker* came next to the *James Caird* and the *Stancomb Wills* followed. I had given orders that the boats should keep 30 or 40 yds. apart, so as to reduce the danger of a collision if one boat was checked by the ice. The pack was thinning, and we came to occasional open areas where thin ice had formed during the night. When we encountered this new ice we had to shake the reef out of the sails in order to force a way through. Outside of the pack the wind must have been of hurricane force. Thousands of small dead fish were to be seen, killed probably by a cold current and the heavy weather. They floated in the water and lay on the ice, where they had been cast by the waves. The petrels and skua-gulls were swooping down and picking them up like sardines off toast.

We made our way through the lanes till at noon we were suddenly spewed out of the pack into the open ocean. Dark blue and sapphire green ran the seas. Our sails were soon up, and with a fair wind we moved over the waves like three Viking ships on the quest of a lost Atlantis. With the sheets well out and the sun shining bright above, we enjoyed for a few hours a sense of the freedom and magic of the sea, compensating us for pain and trouble in the days that had passed. At last we were free from the ice, in water that our boats could navigate. Thoughts of home, stifled by the deadening weight of anxious days and nights, came to birth once more, and the difficulties that had still to be overcome dwindled in fancy almost to nothing.

During the afternoon we had to take a second reef in the sails, for the wind freshened and the deeply laden boats were shipping much water and steering badly in the rising sea. I had laid the course for Elephant Island and we were making good progress. The *Dudley Docker* ran down to me at dusk and Worsley suggested that we should stand on all night; but already the *Stancomb Wills* was barely discernible among the rollers in the gathering dusk, and I decided that it would be safer to heave to and wait for the daylight. It would never have done for the boats to have become separated from one another during the night. The party must be kept together, and, moreover, I thought it possible that we might overrun our goal in the darkness and not be able to return. So we made a sea-anchor of oars and hove to, the *Dudley Docker* in the lead, since she had the longest painter. The *James Caird* swung astern of the *Dudley Docker and* the *Stancomb Wills* again had the third place. We ate a cold meal and did what little we could to make things comfortable for the hours of darkness. Rest was not for us. During the greater part of the night the sprays broke over the boats and froze in masses of ice, especially at the stern and bows. This ice had to be broken away in order to prevent the boats growing too heavy. The temperature was below zero and the wind penetrated our clothes and chilled us almost unbearably. I doubted if all the men would survive that night. One of our troubles was lack of water. We had emerged so suddenly from the pack into the open sea that we had not had time to take aboard ice for melting in the cookers, and without ice we could not have hot food. The *Dudley Docker* had one lump of ice weighing about ten pounds, and this was shared out among all hands. We sucked small pieces and got a little relief from the thirst engendered by the salt spray, but at the same time we reduced our bodily heat. The condition of most of the men was pitiable. All of us had swollen mouths and we could hardly touch the food. I longed intensely for the dawn. I called out to the other boats at intervals during the night, asking how things were with them. The men always managed to reply cheerfully. One of the people on the Stancomb Wills shouted, "We are doing all right, but I would like some dry mitts." The jest brought a smile to cracked lips. He might as well have asked for the moon. The only dry things aboard the boats were swollen mouths and burning tongues. Thirst is one of the troubles that confront the traveller in polar regions. Ice may be plentiful on every hand, but it does not become drinkable until it is melted, and the amount that may be dissolved in the mouth is limited. We had been thirsty during the days of heavy pulling in the pack, and our condition was aggravated quickly by the salt spray. Our sleeping-bags would have given us some warmth, but they were not within our reach. They were packed under the tents in the bows, where a mail-like coating of ice enclosed them, and we were so cramped that we could not pull them out.

At last daylight came, and with the dawn the weather cleared and the wind fell to a gentle south-westerly breeze. A magnificent sunrise heralded in what we hoped would be our last day in the boats. Rose-pink in the growing light, the lofty peak of Clarence Island told of the coming glory of the sun. The sky grew blue above us and the crests of the waves sparkled cheerfully. As soon as it was light enough we chipped and scraped the ice off the bows and sterns. The rudders had been unshipped during the night in order to avoid the painters catching them. We cast off our ice-anchor and pulled the oars aboard. They had grown during the night to the thickness of telegraph-poles while rising and falling in the freezing seas, and had to be chipped clear before they could be brought inboard.

We were dreadfully thirsty now. We found that we could get momentary relief by chewing pieces of raw seal-meat and swallowing the blood, but thirst came back with redoubled force owing to the saltness of the flesh. I gave orders, therefore, that meat was to be served out only at stated intervals during the day or when thirst seemed to threaten the reason of any particular individual. In the full daylight Elephant Island showed cold and severe to the north-north-west. The island was on the bearings that Worsley had laid down, and I congratulated him on the accuracy of his navigation under difficult circumstances, with two days' dead reckoning while following a devious course through the pack-ice and after drifting during two nights at the mercy of wind and waves. The *Stancomb Wills* came up and McIlroy reported that Blackborrow's feet were very badly frost-bitten. This was unfortunate, but nothing could be done. Most of the people were frost-bitten to some extent, and it was interesting to notice that the " old-timers," Wild, Crean, Hurley, and I, were all right. Apparently we were acclimatized to ordinary Antarctic temperature, though we learned later that we were not immune.

All day, with a gentle breeze on our port bow, we sailed and pulled through a clear sea. We would have given all the tea in China for a lump of ice to melt into water, but no ice was within our reach. Three bergs were in sight and we pulled towards them, hoping that a trail of brash would be floating on the sea to leeward; but they were hard and blue, devoid of any sign of cleavage, and the swell that surged around them as they rose and fell made it impossible for us to approach closely. The wind was gradually hauling ahead, and as the day wore on the rays of the sun beat fiercely down from a cloudless sky on pain-racked men. Progress was slow, but gradually Elephant Island came nearer. Always while I attended to the other boats, signalling and ordering, Wild sat at the tiller of the *James Caird*. He seemed unmoved by fatigue and unshaken by privation. About four o'clock in the afternoon a stiff breeze came up ahead and, blowing against the current, soon produced a choppy sea. During the next hour of hard pulling we seemed to make no progress at all. The *James Caird* and the *Dudley Docker* had been towing the Stancomb Wills in turn, but my boat now took the *Stancomb Wills* in tow permanently, as the *James Caird* could carry more sail than the *Dudley Docker* in the freshening wind.

We were making up for the south-east side of Elephant Island, the wind being between north-west and west. The boats, held as close to the wind as possible, moved slowly, and when darkness set in our goal was still some miles away. A heavy sea was running. We soon lost sight of the *Stancomb Wills*, astern of the *James Caird* at the length of the painter, but occasionally the white gleam of broken water revealed her presence. When the darkness was complete I sat in the stern with my hand on the painter, so that I might know if the other boat broke away, and I kept that position during the night. The rope grew heavy with the ice as the unseen seas surged past us and our little craft tossed to the motion of the waters. Just at dusk I had told the men on the *Stancomb Wills* that if their boat broke away during the night and they were unable to pull against the wind, they could run for the east side of Clarence Island and wait our coming there. Even though we could not land on Elephant Island, it would not do to have the third boat adrift.

It was a stern night. The men, except the watch, crouched and huddled in the bottom of the boat, getting what little warmth they could from the soaking sleeping-bags and each other's bodies. Harder and harder blew the wind and fiercer and fiercer grew the sea. The boat plunged heavily through the squalls and came up to the wind, the sail shaking in the stiffest gusts. Every now and then, as the night wore on, the moon would shine down through a rift in the driving clouds, and in the momentary light I could see the ghostly faces of men, sitting up to trim the boat as she heeled over to the wind. When the moon was hidden its presence was revealed still by the light reflected on the streaming glaciers of the island. The temperature had fallen very low, and it seemed that the general discomfort of our situation could scarcely have been increased; but the land looming ahead was a beacon of safety, and I think we were all buoyed up by the hope that the coming day would see the end of our immediate troubles. At least we would get firm land under our feet. While the painter of the *Stancomb Wills* tightened and drooped under my hand, my thoughts were busy with plans for the future.

Towards midnight the wind shifted to the south-west, and this change enabled us to bear up closer to the island. A little later the *Dudley Docker* ran down to the *James Caird*, and Worsley shouted a suggestion that he should go ahead and search for a landing-place. His boat had the heels of the *James Caird*, with the *Stancomb Wills* in tow. I told him he could try, but he must not lose sight of the *James Caird*. Just as he left me a heavy snow-quall came down, and in the darkness the boats parted. I saw the *Dudley Docker* no more. This separation caused me some anxiety during the remaining hours of the night. A cross-sea was running and I could not feel sure that all was well with the missing boat. The waves could not be seen in the darkness, though the direction and force of the wind could be felt, and under such conditions, in an open boat, disaster might overtake the most experienced navigator. I flashed our compass-lamp on the sail in the hope that the signal would be visible on board the *Dudley Docker*, but could see no reply. We strained our eyes to windward in the darkness in the hope of catching a return signal and repeated our flashes at intervals.

My anxiety, as a matter of fact, was groundless. I will quote Worsley's own account of what happened to the *Dudley Docker*: "About midnight we lost sight of the *James Caird* with the Stancomb Wills in tow, but not long after saw the light of the *James Caird*'s compass-lamp, which Sir Ernest was flashing on their sail as a guide to us. We answered by lighting our candle under the tent and letting the light shine through. At the same time we got the direction of the wind and how we were hauling from my little pocket-compass, the boat's compass being smashed. With this candle our poor fellows lit their pipes, their only solace, as our raging thirst prevented us from eating anything. By this time we had got into a bad tide-rip, which, combined with the heavy, lumpy sea, made it almost impossible to keep the *Dudley Docker* from swamping. As it was we shipped several bad seas over the stern as well as abeam and over the bows, although we were 'on a wind.' Lees, who owned himself to be a rotten oarsman, made good here by strenuous baling, in which he was well seconded by Cheetham. Greenstreet, a splendid fellow, relieved me at the tiller and helped generally. He and Macklin were my right and left bowers as stroke-oars throughout. McLeod and Cheetham were two good sailors and oars, the former a typical old deep-sea salt and growler, the latter a pirate to his finger-tips. In the height of the gale that night Cheetham was buying matches from me for bottles of champagne, one bottle per match (too cheap; I should have charged him two bottles). The champagne is to be paid when he opens his 'pub' in Hull and I am able to call that way. . . . We had now had one hundred and eight hours of toil, tumbling, freezing, and soaking, with little or no sleep. I think Sir Ernest, Wild, Greenstreet, and I could say that we had no sleep at all. Although it was sixteen months since we had been in a rough sea, only four men were actually seasick, but several others were off colour.

"The temperature was 20° below freezing-point; fortunately, we were spared the bitterly low temperature of the previous night. Greenstreet's right foot got badly frost-bitten, but Lees restored it by holding it in his sweater against his stomach. Other men had minor frost-bites, due principally to the fact that their clothes were soaked through with salt water. . . . We were close to the land as the morning approached, but could see nothing of it through the snow and spindrift. My eyes began to fail me. Constant peering to windward, watching for seas to strike us, appeared to have given me a cold in the eyes. I could not see or judge distance properly, and found myself falling asleep momentarily at the tiller. At 3 a.m. Greenstreet relieved me there. I was so cramped from long hours, cold, and wet, in the constrained position one was forced to assume on top of the gear and stores at the tiller, that the other men had to pull me amidships and straighten me out like a jack-knife, first rubbing my thighs, groin, and stomach.

"At daylight we found ourselves close alongside the land, but the weather was so thick that we could not see where to make for a landing.

Having taken the tiller again after an hour's rest under the shelter (save the mark!) of the dripping tent, I ran the *Dudley Docker* off before the gale, following the coast around to the north. This course for the first hour was fairly risky, the heavy sea before which we were running threatening to swamp the boat, but by 8 a.m. we had obtained a slight lee from the land. Then I was able to keep her very close in, along a glacier front, with the object of picking up lumps of fresh-water ice as we sailed through them. Our thirst was intense. We soon had some ice aboard, and for the next hour and a half we sucked and chewed fragments of ice with greedy relish.

"All this time we were coasting along beneath towering rocky cliffs and sheer glacier-faces, which offered not the slightest possibility of landing anywhere. At 9.30 a.m. we spied a narrow, rocky beach at the base of some very high crags and cliffs, and made for it. To our joy, we sighted the *James Caird* and the *Stancomb Wills* sailing into the same haven just ahead of us. We were so delighted that we gave three cheers, which were not heard aboard the other boats owing to the roar of the surf. However, we soon joined them and were able to exchange experiences on the beach."

Our experiences on the *James Caird* had been similar, although we had not been able to keep up to windward as well as the *Dudley Docker* had done. This was fortunate, as events proved, for the *James Caird* and *Stancomb Wills* went to leeward of the big bight the *Dudley Docker* entered and from which she had to turn out with the sea astern. We thus avoided the risk of having the Stancomb Wills swamped in the following sea. The weather was very thick in the morning. Indeed at 7 a.m. we were right under the cliffs, which plunged sheer into the sea, before we saw them. We followed the coast towards the north, and ever the precipitous cliffs and glacier-faces presented themselves to our searching eyes. The sea broke heavily against these walls and a landing would have been impossible under any conditions. We picked up pieces of ice and sucked them eagerly. At 9 a.m. at the north-west end of the island we saw a narrow beach at the foot of the cliffs. Outside lay a fringe of rocks heavily beaten by the surf but with a narrow channel showing as a break in the foaming water. I decided that we must face the hazards of this unattractive landing-place. Two days and nights without drink or hot food had played havoc with most of the men, and we could not assume that any safer haven lay within our reach. The *Stancomb Wills* was the lighter and handier boat—and I called her alongside with the intention of taking her through the gap first and ascertaining the possibilities of a landing before the *James Caird* made the venture. I was just climbing into the *Stancomb Wills* when I saw the *Dudley Docker* coming up astern under sail. The sight took a great load off my mind.

Rowing carefully and avoiding the blind rollers which showed where sunken rocks lay, we brought the *Stancomb Wills* towards the opening in the reef. Then, with a few strong strokes we shot through on the top of a swell and ran the boat on to a stony beach. The next swell lifted her a little further. This was the first landing ever made on Elephant Island, and a thought came to me that the honour should belong to the youngest member of the expedition, so I told Blackborrow to jump over. He seemed to be in a state almost of coma and in order to avoid delay I helped him, perhaps a little roughly, over the side of the boat. He promptly sat down in the surf and did not move. Then I suddenly realized what I had forgotten, that both his feet were frost-bitten badly. Some of us jumped over and pulled him into a dry place. It was a rather rough experience for Blackborrow, but, anyhow, he is now able to say that he was the first man to sit on Elephant Island. Possibly at the time he would have been willing to forego any distinction of the kind. We landed the cook, with his blubber-stove, a supply of fuel, and some packets of dried milk, and also several of the men. Then the rest of us pulled out again to pilot the other boats through the channel. The *James Caird* was too heavy to be beached directly, so after landing most of the men from the *Dudley Docker* and the *Stancomb Wills* I superintended the transhipment of the *James Caird*'s gear outside the reef. Then we all made the passage, and within a few minutes the three boats were aground. A curious spectacle met my eyes when I landed the second time. Some of the men were reeling about the beach as if they had found an unlimited supply of alcoholic liquor on the desolate shore. They were laughing uproariously, picking up stones and letting handfuls of pebbles trickle between their fingers like misers gloating over hoarded gold. The smiles and laughter, which caused cracked lips to bleed afresh, and the gleeful exclamations at the sight of two live seals on the beach made me think for a moment of that glittering hour of childhood when the door is open at last and the Christmas-tree in all its wonder bursts upon the vision. I remember that Wild, who always rose superior to fortune, bad and good, came ashore as I was looking at the men and stood beside me as easy and unconcerned as if he had stepped out of his car for a stroll in the park.

from I May Be Some Time
by Francis Spufford

We didn't know Scott or his men, though we make free with them and their memory. Francis Spufford (born 1964) wants us to know the expedition members by their beliefs, their motives, their behavior: the fundamentals and the details that matter in men's lives. In pursuing this, Spufford provides one answer to this question: Why tell a story that's been told many times before? We begin on the Terra Nova, *heading south from New Zealand.*

Then dawn came and with it everything began to go wrong again at once.' Wilson wakes in one of the few bunks still dry on the ship, and finds that the *Terra Nova* is no longer floating because it rides on top of the sea, but because its wooden hull and deck planks enclose a roller-coasting bubble of air, outside which water hammers on all sides for entry. Yesterday's 'fairly manageable' westerly gale has grown into the familiar monster of the South Fifties, a hurricane mangling sea and sky together, which the *Terra Nova*, overloaded, heavy in the water, is in no state to resist. They guess that the waves coming at them from the west are thirty-five feet high, but they can only guess as the ship pitches up a crest, wallows down into the dangerous troughs between, the engine labouring to keep the prow pointed safely. If the angles of floor and bulkheads shift less violently than they did, that is a sign of dwindling buoyancy. Solid green heaves of water cover the waist of the *Terra Nova* almost continuously, tearing at the mounds of coal and pyramided petrol cans there, which have begun to flex and slide about in an unpredictable rushing mass, like a random battering ram. Birdie Bowers has spent much of the night diving for petrol, trusting to his grip on a rope when the ship rolls and he slides sideways underwater towards the rails; the dogs tethered on deck wash about around him, snatching breaths. Even on the bridge Scott is often waist-deep in the sea. All this weight of water on deck wrenches the planking. It pulls open the seams between, in rhythm with the arriving waves. All through the night, Wilson has heard 'the thud of a sea on the decks overhead and a water cart full of water pour down upon the wardroom floor'. With the water, trickling downward into the hold to reduce their besieged bubble of air, come little greasy balls of coaldust from the ruined sacks. Around dawn these clog the pumps down below; and in rapid consequence, the water in the stokehold where the steam-boilers are fuelled, already sloshing knee-deep from wall to wall, rises suddenly to threaten the furnaces. The fires have to be put out. The engine stops. They are now in a logical impasse. They cannot get at the clogged mechanism of the main pump to clear it without opening a deck hatch: the pump is only reachable from above. They cannot open any hatch on deck without inviting the whole Southern Ocean in. 'It would have meant less than ten minutes to float,' Bowers will explain in a letter to his mother. They try a small hand-pump, but the pressure is too low, and it will not raise the water from the hold up to the deck. Lieutenant Evans takes the Chief Engineer and the carpenter below and starts cutting through the steel wall isolating the blocked intakes, a twelve-hour job at least. Meanwhile at 7 a.m. all the ship's officers who are not working the ship at that moment, and all the scientific staff and gentlemen volunteers not absolutely incapacitated by seasickness, are called to the narrow well that rises the whole height of the ship, from engine-room to the lee doorway up top. Puking (some of them) every few minutes, they cluster on the iron ladders clumped in the well, the bottom-most men naked in the steaming bilgewater hissing off the engines, those higher up progressively more and more dressed. 'A couple of engineroom oil-lamps whose light just made the darkness visible' (Wilson) swing as the well—an inky tube—itself sways back and forth across the vertical, like the arm of a metronome. They are passing buckets of water up the well; and as they bale, as they vomit, they sing. 'I went to bale with a strenuous prayer in my heart', Bowers writes, 'and "Yip-I-Addy" on my lips . . .'

'Yip-I-Addy' is a patter song in waltz time. It began as a Broadway hit of 1908, but London music halls took it up quickly. Really you need a female voice and a cello for the full comic effect. The twenty-odd inaccurate tenors, basses, and baritones on the ladder do the deep tones and the girlish tones as best they can:

> Young Herman Von Bellow, a musical fellow,
> Played on a big cello each night;
> Sweet melodies rare, in a dance garden where
> Dancers danced round and round with delight.
> One night he saw dancing a maid so entrancing,
> His heart caught on fire inside,
> And music so mellow he sawed on his cello,
> She waltzed up to him and she cried:
> Yip-I-Addy-I-Ay, I-Ay!
> Yip-I-Addy-I-Ay!

Even in these straits, a measure persists of the larkiness with which the gentry aboard the *Terra Nova* go about routine shipboard tasks. 'How the custom of the ship arose I do not know,' says Cherry-Garrard, 'but in effect most things were done by volunteer labour.' It's a small world where 'unselfishness' determines your social standing. When the call goes out, eager young men compete to act as dogsbodies, to be the donkeys for donkey-work. Geologists reef sails; naval autocrats in the making help in the galley; Cherry-Garrard himself has had a try at stoking the furnaces. (It was 'a real test of staying power', he decided.) Some, older or more sceptical, chafe at the atmosphere that results; the greater part of them like it. Many have already tasted authority in their professions. Before he signed up as Scott's stores monitor, Bowers had commanded a 255-ton Royal Indian Marine gunboat, alone for days on the gray-green River Irrawaddy with a crew of Lascars. Oates was the lackadaisically efficient adjutant of his regiment in India (as well as Master of the Mhow Foxhounds). By joining the expedition they have voluntarily demoted themselves, but the tasks they do on board are so far beneath their class's roster of possible destinies that doing them does not feel like any conceivable backward step, it feels like a holiday.

They have become gloriously junior again, responsible to each other yet free of the persona of responsibility. And they are allowed to pitch in and get dirty. Jobs that are ordinary for the sailors are fun for them. Work about the ship has become a sort of social comedy, with a comedy's lightning mobility of roles. You exit as a specialist in geomagne-tism, you re-enter immediately as a bilge-scrubber. Perhaps too the tasks they stumble through under the expert gaze of the crew revive the earliest thwarted ambitions of middle-class boyhood. Oh, to make things go! Oh, to have a set of tools of your own! What Papa does is mysterious, but the lordly men who drive trains and mend clocks know something worth knowing. Oates has enjoyed himself so much like this that a practical joke practically had to be played on him. At Lyttleton, while he was perched on the foremast helping the ship's carpenter, his head shaved, his shirt filthy, his mouth full of nails, 'a parson came up belonging to the Missions to Seamen. He heard I was a soldier and came up to me. He said he had been a private soldier and had raised himself to a parson and it was sad that I who had been a Captain of a Cavalry Regiment should have come down to be a carpenter's mate. I think somebody had been pulling his leg.'

But Oates is not among the band forming the bucket-chain, and trying not to think about what will happen if baling does not hold the water level down. (They have been baling for hours now, in two-hour shifts.) Since the storm began his station has been in the fo'c'sle, where he and another notably silent man, the second surgeon Atkinson, have been struggling to keep fifteen frightened ponies on their feet, and therefore alive. Each wave rushes through the makeshift stalls: 'on occasions', Lieutenant Evans notices when he and Scott visit from time to time, 'he seemed to be actually lifting the poor little ponies to their feet as the ship lurched heavily to leeward and a great sea would wash the legs of his charges from under them'. Oates lifts and coaxes and soothes and shoves and lifts and coaxes and soothes and shoves. One horse has already drowned. Probably a mounting anger helps propel him through his invariable cycle of actions. The ponies were a set of wind-sucking old crocks in the first place, a botched buy. They ought not (no horse ought) to be exposed to this battering. Yet Oates is responsible for them. Scott's travel plans in the Antarctic may depend on them, or on whatever demoralised quota of horseflesh Oates can contrive to bring through this; and Scott may blame him for the deficiency. It is striking him more and more that all this altruism makes for a rather vulnerable social contract. You give your best, and then you rely on the other man being equally just and self-sacrificing. What if he isn't? 'Scott has always been very civil to me . . . but the fact of the matter is', he will fume later, 'he is not straight, it is himself first the rest nowhere and when he has got all he can out of you it is shift for yourself.' Oates is probably the only man to say 'fuck' on Scott's Last Expedition. Soon another pony dies.

Yip-I-Addy-I-Ay, I-Ay!
Yip-I-Addy-I-Ay!
I don't care what becomes of me,
When you play that sweet melody.

Nobody else quite feels Wilson's relish for the situation ('I must say I enjoyed it all from beginning to end'). Oates says, 'I can't remember having a worse time.' But everyone, without exception, is responding with understatement. They grow universally clipped, imperturbable. 'I thought things were becoming interesting,' writes Wilson. 'Captain Scott was simply splendid, he might have been at Cowes,' Bowers notes admiringly. By maintaining this yachting demeanour, Bowers adds, Scott 'behaved up to our best traditions at a time when his outlook must have been the blackness of darkness'. Bowers himself likes to pop on his dressing-gown—'a lovely warm thing'—whenever a pause in the action allows. The words *death* and *drowning*, present in everybody's minds, are banished from speech. Instead they use the code-words *interesting* and *exciting*, which will be convenient many times over later. It is a group style, and (though they find it inside themselves, ready for an emergency) it also has an immediate group imperative behind it. While every single account of the storm they write afterwards reveals a perfect comprehension of their peril, most of them imagine at the time that there are innocents close by who must be protected from the dreadful knowledge: 'None of our landsmen who were working so hard knew how serious things were,' says Bowers, and in turn each scientist in the well labours under the same illusion where his neighbours are concerned. So they converge, unknowing, on the same manner, reinforcing it in each other, offering each other a constant mutual display of sang-froid. Ignorance of the true state of affairs is not, after all, completely impossible in theory. Suppose you are a 'landsman', a non-sailor accustomed to earth beneath your feet. You go to sea, and to begin with every lurch of the ship seems potentially dangerous. You don't say so of course. Only the bearing of your companions aboard reassures you that all is well, that ships do naturally move like that. You accustom yourself to pitching, tossing, rolling, yawing, dripping water in your bed, sudden painful creaking sounds from the timbers in the middle of the night. You know your own starts of fright furnish no guide to this wet world: the point at which real trouble begins seems, if anything, still more obscure, till experience teaches you. Just conceivably then you might ride out a hurricane unaware, if the sailors stay calm, that this time matters have genuinely slid past the incalculable danger line. But 'calm' does not exactly describe the behaviour of those in command now. It is an intensification of calm until calm becomes something else; something else perfectly intelligible. If any scientist balancing on the ladder had not made the obvious deduction from the rising water, he would have been able to read it like a book in the short answers and uniform good cheer of those around him. In fact the last person aboard to have grasped the situation is probably Oates, not because his reasoning powers are defective, but because, isolated in the fo'c'sle, he has had to wait for the evidence of his senses rather than taking the quicker cues in faces and voices. 'About 4 in the morning the fo'castle got half-full of water and on looking out I found the whole forrard part of the ship deserted and one solitary dog washing about. I began then to think that things were getting a bit serious . . .' Oates needed no group around him to turn stoical. 'He . . . appeared quite unconscious of any personal suffering,' Lieutenant Evans notices when he looks in on the struggle in the fo'c'sle, 'although his hands and feet must have been absolutely numbed by the cold and wet.' With Oates, it is only a deepening of his habitual reserve.

As will become famously clear in the British trenches of the Great War, the understated style, the phlegmatic manner, when apt to a dreadful situation can be extremely expressive. Then it will register a sense of horror that would leak away in ordinary description, and vanish completely if you try to match horror with hyperbole. 'Move to trenches Hebuterne', Private R. W. Mitchell will write in his diary in June 1916. 'Strafing and a certain dampness.' Now, it is true, the voices to be heard on the *Terra Nova* register less bleakly, they aim at lighter tones; but still they achieve irony, not euphemism, to those who share the mortal knowledge producing the light tone. (Which is everybody.) They can catch the absurdity in sinking to the bottom of the Southern Ocean only a couple of days after setting out to astonish the world with polar feats. 'It looked as though [the storm] had come', writes Wilson, 'to save us a great deal of trouble and two years' work . . .' Bowers is tickled by the contrast between today's waterlogged chaos and Tuesday's big send-off. 'God had shown us the weakness of man's hand,' he writes cheerfully, 'and it was enough for the best of us—the people who had been made such a lot of lately—the whole scene was one of pathos really.' The baling party joke glancingly about their own impotence.

Nor does their manner exclude fleeting moments at which they register the unwanted grandeur of the forces beating on them. Burke would not recognise the conditions for the sublime being met here: there's no real place of safety here from which to find satisfaction in this swirling flood: yet still the absorption of the work in the well interposes a kind of frail shelter in the mind between them and the hurricane. They are thinking constantly of what they can do, the hurricane still lies just beyond the confines of the present instant. When Wilson calls the waves 'really terrific', he does not only mean they are terrifying. When the moment the logic-trap closes is described as 'thrilling', fear is not the only component of the word, bravado and denial of danger not the sole motives for employing a term from the vocabulary of appreciation. 'Thrilling' half-expresses, half-mocks a sensation that pierces with wonder even as they bale for their lives.

Frank Debenham, a young Australian geologist, staggers back below decks, his mind full of the vista above, 'an abomination of watery desolation, giant waves . . . racing towards me whipped by a shrieking wind'. Birdie Bowers, overtaking, slaps him on the back. 'Isn't that a wonderful sight—didn't I tell you that a sailor's life is the only one worth living?'

Yip I-Addy-I-Ay, I-Ay!
My heart wants to holler 'hurray!'

Bowers is terrified. Bowers is also profoundly happy, as high as a kite on the continuous exertion the emergency demands. He has not slept except in snatches for something like sixty hours, which gives all his perceptions an exhilarated clarity. He craves work and he has got it in abundance; he craves a hero to worship and he has found one in Scott; he loves good company, and all around him a constellation of nicknamed friends, Uncle Bill and Titus and Deb and Cherry and Sunny Jim, are labouring away. They call him Birdie, latest in a long line of nose names. And if the ship doesn't sink he is on his way to the place he has most desired to see since he was seven, when he mixed Antarctica up with the picture-book igloos of his geography lesson, and wrote: 'Dear Eskimo, Please write and tell me about your land. I want to go there some day. Your friend Henry.' Jesus came to Henry one night when he was nineteen, on the deck of a merchant ship homeward bound from Australia. He had just learned that girls were put off by his turkey-cock appearance.

> Jesus showed me why we are here, and what the purpose of life really is. It is to make a great decision—to choose between the material and the spiritual, and if we choose the spiritual we must work out our choice, and then it will run like a silver thread through the material. It is very difficult to express in words . . . but I can never forget that I did realize, in a flash, that nothing that happens to our bodies really matters.

Bowers has a very kind heart. 'There was nothing subtle about him,' Cherry-Garrard will remember; but he brings a kind of jocular delicacy to bear on the mysterious areas of life in which he does not expect to be included. If he senses your heart is troubled, he slams you heartily between the shoulder-blades, he ducks you in ice-cold water, he wishes you all the best. In all the world, he is only frightened of one thing, spiders. And only the thought of his mother gives him pain now. His father dead at sea before his first birthday, she raised him alone. (Perhaps in some ways he is a religious woman's idea of what a manly man ought to be.) She never wanted him to become a sailor; she certainly does not welcome him disappearing now to the ends of the earth. Again and again in letters he has tried to reconcile her wishes and his. It does not work. He cannot find a way to fit together the pleasures of decorating the house for Christmas, or playing athletic tennis while his mother looks on, with these present sensations. Instead it seems to him that he must simply be a person who pulls in two directions. 'Why did you give me this nature that loves and longs more than anything else to be at home, and yet when away at sea glories in the fact.' Glorying, he heads down for his next turn at the buckets. See him: a compact sphere of adrenalin bouncing along the companion-way.

> Sing of joy, sing of bliss,
>   Home was never like this,
>   Yip-I-Addy-I-Ay!

• • •

They have baled long enough. The borehole to the pump succeeds. The holds empty. The storm abates. The ship sails on.

31 December 1910–4 January 1911

Out of the rolling storm, into the rigid pack-ice; at a snail's pace through the tricksy lanes between the floes where the Adélie penguins squark 'a guttural Aha or Wahah' at the sight of humans, and grow 'most excited' when Bowers sings to them; released from the metamorphic ice, thick with resemblances and reflections, into the open Ross Sea beyond, as if they had passed ringed defences on their way to the core of the Antarctic. The New Year approaches like (says Teddy Evans) 'the opening of a new volume of an exciting book', and the *Terra Nova* moves sweetly in the bright night of Antarctic summer over shadowed and silvery waves. It is still a few hours short of midnight; surgeon Atkinson shakes Cherry-Garrard's shoulder. 'Have you seen the land? Wrap your blankets round you, and go and see.' Men of all watches are gazing off the starboard bow at 'the only white in a dark horizon': mountains 'like satin', high and so far away that they seem to float untethered above a band of dark. The clearing air transmits the peaks pin-sharp across 110 miles of sea, and over the next days, the last of the voyage, as they cruise to the Ross Sea's terminus at the Great Ice Barrier, then round the shore of Ross Island in search of winter quarters, the weather steadily takes on a fragile summer perfection. The sea calms, the wind goes gentle, clouds abolish themselves, the air dries completely. This is the air that cured Wilson's TB; it is a pleasure to breathe. It has a slight edge to it that you feel when you inhale, tingling when it meets the warm blood in your lungs, as if the vestige of a shiver were dissolved in each chestful, but the result is a heightened wakefulness, and a sense of your body working superlatively well. Scott calls it 'inexpressibly health-giving', Bowers says it is 'permeated with vitality'. Rather than sleeping, they sit on the deck in the nighttime sun. During the final approach to landfall, Cherry-Garrard writes, 'Many watched all night, as this new world unfolded itself, cape by cape and mountain by mountain.' The air conducts light extraordinarily. First they see a stark white Hollywood glow on the horizon dead ahead—the 'ice-blink' announcing the Barrier. Out of it rises the cone of Mt Erebus, then, as Wilson describes it, 'a brilliant white line' running away to the left as far as the eye can see, which thickens until it has 'developed' into the unmistakable wall of ice. Wilson ransacks his paint-box to name the colours that the light infuses into sea and ice, the colours that will withdraw too when the light does. Cobalt blue, 'inky' blue, sage green, emerald green, holly green. The sage green is the result of 'innumerable yellow and orange tinted diatoms floating in blue water', like the overloaded field of psychedelic flecks used for testing colour blindness. Suddenly a swarm of penguins ('brown from above with white edges') are in wild submarine motion in the clear depths siding the ship, 'leaping in and out like little dolphins', 'and the water was as though hundreds of rifle bullets were dropping in around us everywhere'. At the Barrier wall, pitted and luminous wherever wave action has scooped a cavern, they turn for Cape Crozier, where the long ice sheet runs aground on basalt rocks, but to land is impossible—too much surf, too much rotten ice in the surf—and they steer on towards the next likely landing sites in McMurdo Sound. Ponting wishes Scott would slow the ship as planned for cinematography, but this little frustration drowns in his tide of excitement. Like the expedition artist, the photographer is recording the sun-shot scenery for all he's worth. He has only a few frames of an experimental colour film, but he is scurrying to do all the justice he can to the light on monochrome plates, and at least in words. 'Ponting is enraptured', writes Scott, 'and uses expressions which in any one else and alluding to any other subject might be deemed extravagant.' Ponting actually has two styles of enraptured expression. Number One: 'The midnight sun was shining with such brilliance that I was able to make focal-plane photographic exposures with an aperture of F11, using a Zeiss Protar lens of 16 inches focus, with a K3 colour screen in conjunction with an orthochromatic plate.' Number Two: 'In these wondrous grottoes played hundreds of Peter Pan fairies—rainbow-hued flashes of light, mirrored by the dancing, lapping wavelets.' Both are professional. Scott allows that this is Ponting's rightful area of expertise, but he finds the photographer ever so slightly vulgar: he thinks constantly in terms of *effects*, both visual and verbal, both the 'remarkable pictures of priceless educational value' these scenes might become, and the picturesque patter that will go with them when he darkens a room and a magic-lantern-show of the Antarctic appears on a wall. Effects do come constantly. The ship is in motion, glittering icebergs are in motion, near shores and far peaks seem to move against each other with the parallax of the ship's passing. As McMurdo Sound— calm today—opens around them, cape slides out from cape, new reaches of still water open and close, forming and re-forming a kaleidoscope of views, a little light pack-ice here and there 'composing well into foregrounds'. It is not long after the *Terra Nova* finally moors that Ponting takes his famous photograph of the ship framed by an ice-cave's mouth shaped like the cross-section of an aeroplane wing.

These are rare days, and in fact these are rare perspectives. The Southern Continent will scarcely ever again show them this serene face, or offer such perfect visibility. Sometimes from their base at Cape Evans the mountains thirty miles westward across McMurdo Sound will return into focus, to remind them of their first pristine vision of the place. In the ordinary run of things the air will not be glass-clear, or permit this level, sustained, revealing light; it will be bright but not clear, clear but only moon-lit; at worst the endless permutations of cloud and darkness will lock down their vision to objects a mile away, a hundred yards away, five feet ahead of a groping arm. And only with the advantage of a far perspective is it possible to see Antarctica spread wide and whole, as it was before they closed with it. Bowers writes, 'The inhospitable mountains look from the distance inviting and grand beyond conception.' *The inhospitable mountains*: they sound like the Delectable Mountains in *Pilgrim's Progress*, always unreachably far, only requiring a human eye to read their invitation. They fill Bowers with the restless, acquisitive desire to do more with a landscape than look at it, to go among the peaks and put his foot on them. Closer to (like the tempting islands seen by St Brendan that turned brackish and foul when approached) the line of sight shortens, the angles go against you. Already the creased, intricate heights around Erebus and Terror have scrunched together, until, as they sail close under the bulk of Ross Island, only a single swart volcanic cliff can be seen, and one sufficiently forbidding first foothill above it. And the white shoulders of the mountains prove to be snow fissured in all directions, the edges of the island to be crevassed ice-falls. It is all dangerous. There is none of the land, none of the sea, that you can cross without laborious planning. You would not want to set your foot on anything you were not sure of.

Of the sixty-five men on the *Terra Nova*, eight have been here before, on the *Discovery* expedition or with Shackleton only two years ago, in the *Nimrod*. They had these vistas as memories and dreams while they worked at ice-less jobs in England; now memory rises up into overlap with all they see, and continues in phase with it. The polar landscape does its trick of freezing time. Wilson writes: 'All these things are strangely familiar and it seems but yesterday that I was clambering over them roped up with Cross and Whitfield . . .' They pass a message post hammered into a beach 'which we put up ten years ago and on it the two cylinders, the lower one of which I attached myself ': all preserved, all immunised against change, as the remains of this present expedition will also be, down to the last half-eaten biscuit. Scott's heart lifts at the 'sight of the old well-remembered landmarks'. (During the weeks in the pack-ice he hardly spoke, Wilfred Bruce remarked.) 'It was good to see them again . . . It gives one a homely feeling to see such a familiar scene.'

The newcomers find it all familiar in a different sense. It is prepared for, hoped for, expected; Antarctica comes to them as a confirmation as much as a revelation. They bring ready images, if not memories. 'As for the Barrier,' Cherry-Garrard explains, 'we seemed to have known it all our lives, it was so exactly like what we had imagined it to be, and seen in the pictures and photographs.' But they cannot feel the veterans' sense that they have a place in it. It's exciting, it's even—on these particular fair days—seductive. But its calm and its hugeness make for a beauty utterly detached from human uses and human needs. Teddy Evans is placed midway between veterans and tyros, for he has called here before, on the *Discovery*'s relief ship *Morning*, yet never lived with these views, never felt his way into this landscape. Usually so rapid-fire chatty, he has been feeling 'odd thrills'. 'To me those peaks always did and always will represent silent defiance,' he remembers afterwards; 'there were times when they made me shudder,' as if the shiver in the air amplified at the sight. Least of all can the newcomers find the panorama homely. Their prefabricated house of matchboard and rubberoid is packed in the hold, and in all the thousands upon thousands of square miles of the continent only the two indistinguishable dots of the previous expedition huts keep out the weather. It's homely's opposite, for which the German language has the perfect word. *Unheimlich*: uncanny. They stare and stare.

18 February–3 March 1911

White-out. Compared to the Great Ice Barrier, Ross Island is only a volcanic bobble. Across the sea-ice twenty miles south from Cape Evans, where the carpenters are still fitting out winter quarters, the Barrier seals the end of McMurdo Sound. Beyond, a huge plated wedge of ice larger than France fills the whole indentation in this side of the continent; a cracked white tabletop stretching poleward all the way to the foot of the Beardmore Glacier. Blown snow freezes into rippled ridges, or sets to a crust that hisses sharply when your foot goes through, or gathers into powdered, floundery drifts. Moving fast to seize the remainder of the summer sledging season Scott and ten others leading ponies or driving dog-teams have laid a curved line of supply dumps out here for next spring. 'Let's leg it,' he likes to say. Now, about 150 miles south of Cape

Evans, Scott has decided that the ponies can go no further. They have built the bulk of their food and fuel into a neat heap called One Ton Depot, and turned for base, split into separate parties. They travel by night so that the ponies may rest during the warmer daytime hours. Northward in a thick whiteness, then, step Bowers, Oates, and Tryggve Gran—a young skier who is finding it quite hard being Norwegian in this company just now, but promised Oates a few days ago he would fight for England in a war, and won a handshake. Each guides an exhausted horse by the head. The horses are roped together in series; their breath whiffles beside the walking men.

'That march was extraordinary,' writes Bowers,

> the snowy mist hid all distant objects and made all close ones look gigantic. Although we were walking on a flat, undulating plain, one could not get away from the impression that the ground was hilly—quite steep in places with deep hollows by the wayside. Suddenly a herd of apparent cattle would appear in the distance, then you would think: 'No, it's a team of dogs broken loose and rushing towards you.' In another moment one would be walking over the black dots of some old horse droppings which had been the cause of the hallucinations.

The foot-high snow ridges, *sastrugi*, float off the ground and become white downland lying across the route ahead. Stepping up onto what seemed the beginning of a long incline, their feet lift right over the whole hill. 'After going about ten miles we spotted a tiny black triangle in the dead white void ahead, it was over a mile away and was the lunch camp of the dogs.' The following night it is much clearer, and the optical effects reverse. The same unending plain lies before them, but now the horizon is further away than the senses suggest. The white sheet they look forward over comprises miles of snow, instead of yesterday's few yards, and mirages lift even remoter expanses into view, the shimmer producing a persistent illusion of open water. One of the cairns marking the route appears in the distance and then stays there: 'the only trouble about seeing things so far off is that they take such an awful time to reach'. Resolved not to make yesterday's mistake twice they overcompensate and identify another 'dark object' ahead as the dog-teams' encampment again. More steps, and 'it turned out to be an empty biscuit tin, such is the deceptive nature of the light'. February 22 brings a single night of ideal conditions, 'clear as a bell'; otherwise they march in growing obscurity night after night, in an atmosphere of imminent blizzard. Autumn is coming, 'the midnight sun was already cartwheeling the southern horizon . . . also the season had undoubtedly broken up'. They pass unexpected snow-cairns that prove to contain the corpses of two beasts belonging to the other pony party. Their own, emaciated from twenty-four-hour exposure to the Barrier, need constant nursing. Gran has dropped a small but crucial component of the primus stove, somewhere in the 'fuzzy nothingness' that engulfs them, on and off, all the way to the rendezvous at Safety Camp on the Barrier's edge. 'Cold food stared us in the face!' Still, 'we legged it into the void . . .'

The juggling confusions of the Barrier are new to Bowers; they disconcert him, but do not overbear his imagination; he even finds them amusing, till the 'novelty' wears off. He records them with a navigator's accuracy and an ingenuous curiosity that such things can be. Bowers has the quality Melville praised in whales and recommended for humans, 'the rare virtue of thick walls'. Seeing the Barrier phenomena through his eyes is like gazing through a thick, square block of glass. It is different for Scott, up ahead with a dog-team. Scott has been hammered thin by anxious calculations of weight and distance, by, too, the evident suffering of the horses as blizzard winds on the way out wasted their flesh under its thin hair coat. His eye is wide and scarcely defended against the loom and waver of objects in the mist. He notices acutely the forms of the snow, the hugeness of the Barrier, the sounds you hear from the tent when you are on the verge of sleep. In his diary he has been writing a series of 'Impressions' which show that, at however many removes, he has picked up hints from the new poetry of concise images beginning to shape the literary scene in London. If his notes do not quite match the prototypical Imagist comparison of faces in the Underground to 'petals on a wet black bough', they are none-theless hyper-attentive. 'The wind blown furrows', he writes. 'The small green tent and the great white road.' 'The gentle flutter of our canvas shelter.' 'The drift snow like finest flour penetrating every hole and corner—flickering up beneath one's head covering, pricking sharply as a sand blast.' Then, more ominously, the impressions gathering speed and turning into something like the hyphenated précis of contents at the head of a chapter of disasters in a Victorian travel book, 'The blizzard, Nature's protest—the crevasse, Nature's pitfall—that grim trap for the unwary—no hunter could conceal his snare so perfectly—the light rippled snow bridge gives no hint or sign of the hidden danger, its position unguessable till man or beast is floundering, clawing and struggling for foothold on the brink.'

This *is* a chapter of disasters, logistically speaking. The experience of the outward journey has proved that ponies cannot work in the blizzards which prevail at the beginning and end of the 'sledging season': therefore next year's departure for the pole must wait for a month after the date Scott had in mind. And perhaps, Scott thinks wretchedly, there may not be a departure. Since he overruled Oates' advice that they should write off the weakest ponies, and push One Ton further south, stashing pony-meat for dogfood as each horse failed, the ponies have been keeling over anyway on the road back. 'I have had more than enough of this cruelty to animals,' he had said. Now 'Blossom' and 'Blucher' are dead in the snow where they cannot do any good, and when Bowers' party catches up at Safety Camp 'Weary Willy' promptly expires too. Next year's essential transport is steadily disappearing. As if he had foreseen it, Scott has also had a sudden, scrabbling close shave with a crevasse. And, to ice his cake, a message has just arrived from the *Terra Nova*: Amundsen is ashore at the Bay of Whales with 110 dogs. Beside this item 'every incident of the day pales'. But this is not the end of the skein of catastrophes. There follows an astonishingly intricate final piece of ill-fortune. As they set off once more from Safety Camp in their different groupings for the last leg of the journey, across the frozen sea to Cape Evans, Bowers loses sight of Wilson, whose dog-team is supposed to be acting guide for the following ponies; in 'a black mist' he leads four ponies, Cherry-Garrard, and Seaman Crean onto ice that creaks underfoot and leaks black water along fracture lines, and though he thinks he has found safe ice for their camp that night, Bowers wakes in the small hours on a broken ice-floe drifting out to sea. Elaborate rescue operations and much bravery save the humans, but 'poor Guts' vanished when the sea opened, 'Punch' and 'Uncle Bill' have to have the *coup de grâce* administered. Oates, who had advised a humane revolver shot at One Ton, ends up driving a pickaxe through Punch's brain as the animal struggles in the water. 'I shall be sick if I have to kill another horse like I did the last,' he says. Bowers sees to Uncle Bill. Around them a dozen or more killer whales ram their heads up methodically through the masking ice: all teeth, all appetite. Six ponies gone of eight. 'Everything out of joint,' writes Scott.

Scott puts the expedition's incessant stumbling down to bad luck. He does not cease to find nervous fault with his companions, or to make minor distributions of blame; but he takes the stricken Bowers aside and comforts him with words about the impossibility of some situations. In the face of the biggest blow of all, Amundsen's arrival, he takes a stance part dignified, part denying. 'The proper, as well as the wiser, course for us is to proceed exactly as though this had not happened.' The others are proud to see him so 'philosophical', when they have felt a momentary gust of rage at the news. Of course, it conveniently relieves Scott of personal responsibility if the last day's events have been fated accidents. This is what Oates sees, and what will still madden him six months afterwards: 'the loss of the ponies,' he will write, 'was Scott's fault entirely'. But Scott's state of mind is altogether less comfortably evasive than Oates allows. Wrought-up, wound-up, Scott may be salving his nerves when he talks about luck, but he has always believed that he was ill-starred, bound to stumble. He takes events personally in another way: they seem targeted at him. Out here, to a man who jumpily monitors every shift of cloud or change in snow texture beneath the sled runners, who feels events as a pressure mounting from the subtly invasive flick of flakes inside a balaclava to the eruptive attack of the killer whales, it can begin to seem that an obscure message is being delivered. Scott's ordinary feeling that an impersonal fate obstructs him germinates into something else, his sense of the mammoth indifference of the physical universe to his efforts shades further over with each successive mishap into a nudging conviction that there is a purpose at work. It's a perception common on the expedition. You can't not try to read the great document of Antarctica for meaning. In these surroundings the pattern-seeking habit of the human mind wakes a vague instinct of faith even in the most secular and scientific of Scott's men. As Debenham will put it years later: 'one cannot live for a while amidst the vast, lonely and yet magnificent scenery of the Antarctic . . . without feeling dwarfed by the scale of everything one sees and in the hands of a Providence or a Power. An intelligent man cannot really be satisfied with saying it is a matter of Chance, or if he does he really means that there is Something behind the Chance.'

Wilson and Bowers, now, are sure they know what lies behind. Bowers: 'My own opinion is that it just had to be, the circumstances leading to it were too devious for mere coincidence . . . everything fitted in to place us on the sea-ice during the only two hours of the whole year that we could possibly have been in such a position.' Wilson: 'The whole thing was just a beautiful piece of education on a very impressive scale.'

There is another candidate than providence. Scott is not a believer, but he is a romantic, conscious of Nature's ambiguous force; conscious as well of its blind selecting violence. 'I'm obsessed with the view of life as a struggle for existence,' he explained to Kathleen in 1909. In a world without God, the purpose you detect in your setbacks may be the fearsome otherness of the natural order, orchestrated for a moment to extinguish you. A Something never defined stirs behind Scott's conventional images of a hostile Nature; Something wakes in those deliberate pitfalls, traps, and snares. 'All visible objects, man, are but as pasteboard masks,' said Ahab to Ishmael. 'But in each event—in the living act, the undoubted deed—there some unknown but still reasoning thing puts forth the mouldings of its features from behind the unreasoning mask.'

But you cannot harpoon Antarctica; and Scott—who is not crazy, only driven to distraction, heaped and tasked by schemes that fall apart, until he sees malignity out of the corner of his eye—knows you cannot even fight it. Sledging is like swimming. If you lose your temper with the sluggish medium you move in, you only thrash about and sink. You can only defy the snow by a held-in persistence, which keeps you going, impatient perhaps, but steadily butting forward at whatever speed the snow permits. Scott lacks the technical, the tactical, and the cultural qualities which ease progress. If he were Amundsen, schooled by the Inuit, ingenious and perfectionist, he could take the continent at a dog-powered glide. He has, though, the moral component: determination. It's his strength as an explorer, 'sheer good grain,' says Cherry-Garrard, 'which ran over and under and through his weaker self and clamped it together'. Whatever opposes him, whatever mistakes of his own return to thwart him under the name of 'bad luck', he will interpret as tests of behaviour. This means that in the end, in a curious way, he is less vulnerable to setbacks than Wilson, certainly than Bowers, both of whom subscribe to the Edwardian spiritual commonplace that you are never tested beyond your power to endure. Scott will never recognise his own contribution to the malignancy of his fate, but by the same token expects no favours from providence. He sees no limit to how wrong things can go. He's on his own. He just grips tighter.

When the party at last returns to Cape Evans, via a chafing wait at the old *Discovery* quarters while the sea freezes again, to contemplate the ten ponies remaining for the attempt on the pole, the rhythm of winter life soothes Scott. The white features that had seemed infiltrated with intent—imperceptibly fatted with presence, on the verge of writhing into hostile movement—still themselves. The mask is only a mask. Scott writes a diagnostic letter to Kathleen. He says, 'I am quite on my feet now, I feel both mentally and physically fit for the work.' He says that he has shaken off a malaise which had spread through his relations with the men he leads. 'The root of the trouble was that I had lost confidence in myself.' Next summer, as they slug their way up the Beardmore Glacier towards the pole, he will cry lightly 'How's the enemy, Titus?', when a stint of man-hauling looks about to end. Oates will look at his watch, report the hour. 'Oh, well, I think we'll go on a little bit more then . . .' Knackered, underfed, the others will curse under their breaths and follow.

4 June 1911

Rising bread dough. Sour-sweet yeast working in the lobed white mass, swelling it slowly in the night hours, carrying upward the steel disc placed neatly on top in the dead centre of the bowl. The disc touches the metal lid. Contact: a small red bulb goes on in the dark hut, the only light except for the oil-lamp beside the man on night watch. He picks his way among the sleepers at the other-ranks' end of the wooden building, finds Thomas Clissold, the cook. The bread machine Clissold invented used to ring an electric bell, but there were complaints. 'Clissold!' (A whisper.) 'Your bread!' Clissold, early twenties, Navy crewcut, little blond beard—who looks as if he'd be renting Kung Fu films from a video shop, if there were Kung Fu films, if there were video shops—rouses, and silently begins to knead his breakfast loaves at the galley table. The watchman settles back to his station by the acetylene plant in the porch. He must patrol for fire every couple of hours, and check the ponies in their icicle-encrusted stable alongside. Otherwise this time is his, to write or think or be private. Teddy Evans has contributed a canister of China tea for the watchman's comfort. On stormy nights, when the blizzard blows down off Erebus, whichever officer or scientist has the watch may have to wrap up, go out through three successively colder doors, and feel along the side of the hut in the whirling drift for the ladder secured there. The intake pipe of 'Dines' Anemometer' on the roof tends to clog if too much loose snow flies in. If it's blizzing, too, the Anemometer becomes the most spectacularly noisy of Simpson's meteorological devices. The bottom end of the pipe broadcasts a continuous moaning howl, rising and falling like a banshee's wail, waking Ponting (who sleeps lightly) in his cubicle near by, or giving the photographer peculiar dreams of waterfalls and cataracts. The hut vibrates. The warm dark space, fifty feet by twenty-five, seems truly besieged then. But tonight is quiet, yesterday's wind a memory by midnight. Outside an enormous frosted hush; inside the ticking of all the chronometers from the far corner where Teddy Evans sleeps. At 5 a.m. or thereabouts a candle lights at the table next to Evans: Wilson is up, has prayed, and is painting. His brush jiggles against glass in his water-jar, moves to the box of colours in obedience to the pencil notes he made when he was sketching, hands out of mittens just long enough to snatch down a line of coast, a smudge of smoke, a mountain contour in the autumn afterglow. 'Put Hut Point in darkness—deep brown & purple snow against any western summit of deep orange.' 'Cambridge blue of the ice foot.' 'Greenish ice.' Clocks counting the minutes, preserving the exact deviation from Greenwich time necessary for navigation; Wilson working fast on wetted paper; Clissold baking; the watchman's last night rounds. Nothing else disturbs the dreamers' mutters from the remaining twenty-two sleepers, or the profound snores from Bowers, until, with no lightening of the sky, 7.30, designated as morning, arrives. The acetylene gas is switched on, flows to the shaded gas mantles around the long room; is ignited, with a soft fierce *woomf* of white light.

'*Good morning*, Farmer Hayseed,' cries Bowers to Oates, one bunk along from him in the genteel-squalid district of the hut known as The Tenements. 'How's the hay?' Oates grunts, stirs, swears with a delightful predictability, while around him the other Tenement dwellers collect themselves under the imperious eye of Oates' single ornament, a small print of Napoleon. Cherry-Garrard hooks his thick glasses round his ears. Across the way the rival encampment of Australian scientists dress behind their curtain, the only curtain in the Antarctic, they boast, which Oates declares makes their quarters look like an 'opium den' or 'a lady's boudoir'. Then Oates gathers up Anton—a Siberian groom who has been leaving cigarettes outside as nervous offerings to the aurora, and finds Oates' solidity very reassuring—and goes indeed to feed the horses with him in companionable silence, on wheat and hay chaff, the morning diet. Those of the seamen who have not darted navy-quick outdoors to fetch ice for drinking water look on with completely concealed amusement as the watchman quits his post yawning. They do not have to sit night watches. Scott has decreed this for the sake of morale: it is one of the winter's little gestures of deference towards the 'lower deck', little turnings of the world upside-down, that co-exist with the social wall of packing-cases dividing the hut in two. Every morning brings the men a spectacle of upper-class blear. And now Bowers and Wilson meet naked at the porch-end for their daily bath with a basin of snow. They grin, they grimace; and 'proceed to rub glistening limbs with this chilling substance' writes Scott, who like everybody except these two Spartans prefers washing in a rationed pint of warm water from a jug. Sounds of the weekly shave mix with the clatter as Hooper the steward sets the tables for breakfast. The ice detail, returned, report an iron-hard stillness outdoors and the moon on the rise. One by one the places fill; Clissold serves fresh bread, marmalade, porridge. Sometimes they have scrambled 'Truegg', a dehydrated yellow powder out of catering-size tins. When Nelson, the biologist, has caught some specimens of *Notothenia* in his fish trap under the sea-ice, and Atkinson has put aside the nematodes and trematodes from their guts for his parasite research, they eat those too.

The breakfasters chat amiably, reinforcing their points with the occasional wave of a fork. Griffith Taylor, the Australian geologist, is trying to get Oates' goat by advocating female suffrage: Oates' ripostes to these outrages tend to come in a slow, slow drawl. A few nights ago his voice was heard from his bunk saying, 'Poor old Griff. [Pause] Poor old Griff. [Long pause] He's not a bad fellow. . . [Very long pause] . . . but he's a bit *mouldy*.' Elsewhere around the table, someone is seeking artistic advice from Wilson. Someone else is proposing the kind of hypothetical question much valued during the winter because it keeps them all arguing for hours. They've thought of this one overnight: What would the wine-waiter at the Ritz say (and do) if you demanded a pint of bitter? Further along again, Cherry-Garrard is refusing to be drawn on the contents of the *South Polar Times*, which will be published on Midwinter Day, and is strictly secret till then, no matter how sly the approach. No, it's no *use* you asking. You'll just have to wait. No! not even a hint. Scott casts a sharp eye up the table, and is glad. Badinage; shop-talk polar and shop-talk scientific. It's a happy company. They all think so. Something pleasing has gelled from the 'diverse assortment of our company', as Scott put it in his diary a fortnight ago: 'I am very much impressed with the extraordinary and general cordiality of the relations which exist amongst our people . . . With me there is no need to draw a veil' over frictions or clashes that would be unfit for print later. The heavy-handed teasing, like the lump of lead in the keel of a toy boat, keeps conversation bobbing along upright; the gents and scientists can go to Wilson, the seamen to Bowers or Evans or Oates when the 'many rubs' of life cramped together need arbitrating or defusing. Those who are finding the constant darkness hard to bear can lean surreptitiously on the good humour for support. Scott himself finds it particularly helpful that the scientists are so willing to share their work, creating an atmosphere of amateur study among the rest that they're calling 'the University of the Antarctic'. To Scott this is the chief distinction of the 'modern style' of overwintering. It's worth working up, he thinks, when he turns his diary into a book: 'compare the interests of a winter spent by the old Arctic voyagers with our own, and look into the causes. The aspect of everything changes as our knowledge expands.' He finds it exciting to learn. He lacks scientific training (because of his naval career he missed the ordinary sort of university) but he has a sharp syllogistic mind that reasons forward unstoppably from the premises he picks up in conversation. At the thrice-weekly lectures he takes copious notes on ice physics, the aurora, physiographic techniques; and he also likes to quiz the scientific staff, mostly twenty years his junior, about their progress. Some actually find these talks rather intimidating. Scott may not know the material, but when the delight of logic grips him he is alarmingly quick at spotting a flawed deduction. Any chagrin this causes, they hide, for the key to the harmony reigning in the hut is a deliberate withdrawal from sight, on everybody's part, of disruptive emotions. Scott wants to believe the opposite. 'I do not believe there can be any life quite so demonstrative of character,' he wrote a month ago. 'Here the outward show is nothing, it is the inward purpose that counts . . . Pretence is useless.' Pretence is essential. The companionship of the winter life, the easing of the loneliness of command for Scott as he quietly communes now with Wilson at the table's head, rest on a constant demonstration by everyone to each other of truthful but partial versions of their characters. For his part Scott maintains a safety-valve by penning critical estimates of those around him. These are certainly not for publication.

On an ordinary day they would scatter now to their winter tasks; the men to sew sleeping bags and refurbish kit in a workspace lined with butter boxes, the others to lab and darkroom and typewriter and stables and meteorological post and planning session. Today is Sunday, though. The pace is easier. After breakfast comes an interval of tidying and straightening: then Scott does what ship's captains do *ex officio* on clement Sundays, whatever their beliefs, and holds a service pieced together from the Book of Common Prayer. His congregation of twenty-three stand bunched beside the piano no-one can really play. Scott's expressive voice sounds the Jacobean English of the Whitsun prayers and readings; he feels an obligation to do reverent justice, at least, to the drama of the words, and as he reads them in the wooden house on the black volcanic shore under Erebus, some passages seem to speak directly of this very gathering.

When the day of Pentecost was fully come, they were all with one accord in one place. And suddenly there came a sound from heaven, as of a rushing mighty wind, and it filled all the house . . . From all blindness of heart; from pride, vainglory, and hypocrisy; from envy, hatred, and malice, and all uncharitableness, Good Lord, deliver us . . . Thou shalt break the ships of the sea: through the east wind . . . O God, according to thy Name, so is thy praise unto the world's end.

The hymns are another matter. Wilson plinks the piano for the first note 'and I try to hit it after with doubtful success!' Next week Scott will get Cherry-Garrard 'to vamp the accompaniment', but nothing can make them any more tuneful than they were with 'Yip-I-Addy'.

Bowers sings loud. As a matter of fact, he is writing a hymn himself to celebrate the return of the sun, due in late August. When nobody is looking he will drop it into the contributions box for the *South Polar Times*. He is turning the already appropriate

> Thou, whose almighty word
> Chaos and darkness heard,
> And took their flight;
> Hear us, we humbly pray,
> And where the Gospel-day
> Sheds not its glorious ray,
> Let there be light!

—which is excellent for singing your head off to, especially the splendid crash you make at the end of the verse—into

> Thou whose far-reaching ray
> Heralds the dawn of day,
> At last begun,
> Scatt'ring with glorious light
> Darkness of winter night,
> Dazzling in brilliance bright,
> Hail mighty Sun!

Around noon a faint greyness comes into the sky, then goes, the solitary trace at present of the mighty sun; until Midwinter Day on 22 June they will still be on the year's downward slope into darkness. Some excitement: while the men are exercising the ponies outside, small black figures moving to and fro on the sea-ice at the heads of snorting duffel-clad beasts, Cherry and Bowers spot a crabeater seal flumping up from an open ice-hole near the beached bergs in the bay. Crabeaters, slim and elegant, are much less common in this area than the tubby Weddell species. They corner the seal in the moonlight and succeed in killing it. Clissold joins the scientists admiring the catch. When they've done drawing, measuring, skinning, and dissecting it, it will be his. Sometimes he feels frustrated at the unvarying raw material he has to work with. He eyes the seal: if you remove every speck of blubber, seal meat does not taste fishy. Rissoles? Steaks? Perhaps another galantine. . . . Scott applauded the seal soup, followed by seal steak-and-kidney pie, that Clissold conjured up last week. 'I cannot think we shall get scurvy,' he wrote.

After lunch a party of five sally out to make an experiment. Wilson, Bowers, and Cherry-Garrard will be leaving soon after Midwinter Day for their effort to reach the Cape Crozier rookery of the Emperor Penguin during the pitch-dark, sub-zero nesting season. They hope that if they can place themselves at Cape Crozier at the right time, they will be able to place in the hands of science an Emperor embryo in such an early stage of development that the link will be visible between present bird-life and its remote evolutionary ancestor, the flying saurian archaeopteryx. The embryo locked in the egg is supposed to recapitulate the primitive history of the species. The travellers will have their tent, but it would be handy if they could put more than canvas between themselves and the winter temperatures while they ornithologise. Another kind of recapitulation is in order. Along with the three directly concerned, Scott and Petty Officer Lashly choose a level patch of moonlit snow behind the hut 'to start the building of our first "igloo"'. Stamping of feet, energetic activity with a variety of competing tools. Bowers has a trowel, Wilson has a saw, Cherry has a big flat-bladed toothed knife. 'There is a good deal of difference of opinion as to the best implement with which to cut snow blocks . . .

I'm inclined to think the knife will prove most effective,' writes Scott, who designed it, 'but the others don't acknowledge it *yet*.' It's hard to cut the blocks, hard to lift them, and hard to translate the mental picture of a round Eskimo home-sweet-home into architectural reality. By tea-time they have to stop. The sinking moon is casting long shadows, turning their handiwork to a confusion of light and dark planes. The igloo only stands thigh-high: they've only managed three layers of blocks. 'We must go on with this hut building till we get good at it,' writes Scott. 'I'm sure it's going to be a useful art.' Wilson is cheerfully unsanguine. He writes: 'Played at building an igloo—with no success.' At Cape Crozier the egg collectors will end up building a compromise, a hut of rock chunks with a canvas lid held down by snow slabs. Unfortunately its flapping edges will offer a little too much purchase to a blizzard, which will blow the roof off vertically; 'and ended for ever "The Age of Stone"', as a light-verse account in the *South Polar Times* will put it. The three will return from the Winter Journey pinched and dull-eyed, reminding Ponting of starved POWs. Even so, Eskimo skills do not seem specially attractive to the explorers. If they must play at being primitive, they would much rather imagine themselves as ancient Egyptians. They have a running gag about future tourists on Ross Island admiring pyramids and obelisks left behind by the expedition. Wilson paints joke pictures of stone tablets, 'Antarctic Archives', showing red cartoon people sashaying hieratically across the snow in loincloths.

Solitary excursions in safe weather, like night-watch duty, offer the opportunity for privacy. As Hooper clears away the tea things, Scott kneels in the lean-to porch to fix his ski lashings, and heads into the Antarctic night alone. Out he goes past Teddy Evans' old survey-points on the sea-ice, dubbed Sardine and Shark and other fishy S-names, towards Inaccessible Island. The ice rings sound and solid, the surface is 'the best possible', compact and smooth. Cold sorts the moisture in his breath and crystallises it in rime on his balaclava and twinkling showers when he exhales. He hears the noises of his body working but no other human sound, though sound carries in still air here over amazing distances: you can overhear conversations at miles'-range. Instead there come only the sharp cracks now and again of ice expanding on the distant Barrier, like pistols fired at random. The moon is almost down, but the sky is afire with green light, drifting and changing, blushing rose. Scott lifts his face, solemn, and drinks the aurora in. He has an endless appetite for its substanceless beauty. The twisting arches and wavering curtains of light above seem almost animated by a kind of stately life, 'and in that lies its charm', he noted a fortnight ago:

> the suggestion of life, form, colour, and movement never less than evanescent, mysterious—no reality. It is the language of mystic signs and portents—the inspiration of the gods— wholly spiritual—divine signalling. Remindful of superstition, provocative of imagination. Might not the inhabitants of some other world (Mars) controlling mighty forces not thus surround our globe with fiery symbols, a golden writing which we have not the key to decipher?

Tonight there is something new: three sudden white flashes at sea level, over away by the grounded Castle Berg. Lightning? thinks Scott. Actually it is Ponting getting pictures with his flash-gun, a contrivance you load with magnesium powder and hold above your head. Ponting likes the brilliant, instantaneous smash of candlepower onto ice walls. Shadows flee into crevices, inking shapes far back for the lens. The fissured detail of the ice leaps out in deep relief. Once, though, this winter Ponting has found himself overwhelmed. He was taking the famous photograph of the sublime wall of ice. As the neon afterimage of the flash fades on his retina, and the moon reasserts itself, he gazes at the two-hundred-foot sheer edge of the Barne Glacier, enormously shattered, hugely unper- turbed by tiny men with cameras, and feels 'an intense and wholly indescribable loneliness'. It's too big, too silent, too cold. It's all too much. 'Coo-ee!' shouts Ponting. Pause. Moonstruck immensity. 'Coo- ee!' replies the Barne Glacier. A perfect echo!

Among the bags and bundles festooning The Tenements are some whose contents must not be revealed till the grand Midwinter party. Bowers seizes spare evening moments to work—back turned, shoulders hunched—on a secret Christmas tree. The branches are split and jointed lengths of ski pole, the leaves are to be gull feathers. When everyone is carousing under the massed sledging banners, and the snapdragon has just been lit, he plans to have it brought forth with a flourish, hung with little satirical gifts for each man there. Oriana Wilson's sister bought them for him. He has a popgun reserved for Oates. (Who'll be delighted. 'If you want to please me very much you will fall down when I shoot you,' Oates will say, firing to left and right.) They rejoice in festivities, which distinguish the days from one another and absorb your attention entirely in the moment, while they last. Lectures are popular for the same reason. Apart from Simpson on ice physics and Taylor on physiography, they have had Wilson on sketching, Ponting on Japan, and Meares on the bloodthirsty Lolo people of Tibet. 'Going to the pictures tonight, dearie?' says Oates. But, supper done, today closes quietly. Everybody is indoors. A comfortable fug of pipe-smoke floats over the arguments—the wine-waiter at the Ritz still has plenty of mileage left in him—and the feeble efforts at the piano. Oates re-opens his one book, Napier's *History of the Peninsula War*. Scott brings his diary up to date for another day, seated at the plan-table by his bed, surrounded by pictures of Peter and Kathleen, behind the L-shaped partition that keeps him separate from the rest. Perhaps he searches out a quotation from Browning, or the library of polar voyages presented by Sir Albert Markham and Sir Lewis Beaumont. He heads new notebooks with quotations, loads literary crannies with them, and sometimes sketches out a thought not quite expressed—about history, or the difference between courage as it is seen and as it feels—in a short assembly of borrowed words. At ten the acetylene lights go off. They settle to sleep. Wilson pads out in stockinged feet across the floor to the gramophone; selects a record, winds the handle, adjusts the horn. Though the wind is rising again, and Dines' Anemometer will wail soon, they can all hear, through the premonitory whoops of the accelerating air, and the thick crackle of the record itself, Clara Butts singing 'Abide with Me'. It is Uncle Bill 'saying goodnight to us all'.

4 October 1911

Scott's plan for reaching the pole is a baroque mechanism, like one of those whimsical clockwork devices presented to a Renaissance prince: a gilded rhinoceros model as big as a carthorse, whose horn, twisted, sets a line of silver cockerels crowing in succession along its back, until a fist-sized strawberry in red enamel drops into a tray at its back end. Scott's plan co-ordinates men, dogs, horses, and motor-sledges into a pyramid of effort, from whose apex will pop a little team of men aimed at 90° S. By now any plan he makes has to be a composite job. After the losses of the autumn he needs to extract the maximum use from all his remaining resources. The logistics of such assorted transport have been fiendish to work out, with different loads to be pulled by different methods for different distances, each having to be factored into the equation governing the relationship between mouths to be fed and miles to be covered. And still he has no margin for error. Amundsen, starting for the pole using only one scheme of transport that he has stripped and refined and rebuilt for the task, is taking more dogs than he thinks he'll need, and far more food, just in case. The difference is not lost on Scott, who writes to Kathleen: 'I don't know what to think of Amundsen's chances. If he gets to the Pole it must be before we do, as he is bound to travel fast with dogs, and pretty certain to start early.' He does not think he is in a position to do things any other way, though. 'Any attempt to race must have wrecked my plan, besides which it doesn't appear the kind of thing one is out for.' The plan has all the defects of complexity. When Scott's faith in one of his resources wavers (as it does, up and down through this Antarctic spring, upon the news from the stables that Jehu is sickly; then that Jehu is doing better; or on the news from Day, the motor engineer, that the steel rollers have cracked; then that they can be replaced with wooden ones) his hopes slide tacitly towards another. His confidence wanes in the ponies, waxes in the motors; and vice versa, a cycle of anxiety and refuge of which he is growing heartily sick. As for the expedition's own dogs, he has decided for certain that they are an 'unpredictable element'. Before the experience with the crevasse last autumn he considered taking them to the pole. 'What a pity he didn't!', Teddy Evans will write in his memoirs—never Mr Tactful.

The plan *will* be rich in photogenic moments, dog paws whisking through the snow, caterpillar tracks crunching in a (very brief) triumph of machine over matter, faithful horses stepping on. Ponting is coming along for the first twenty-five miles to film them. But Scott cannot take him further, and there will be scenes lacking in the world's first Antarctic movie if they abide too closely by the strict rules of truth, so Ponting is seizing the opportunity of these last spring weeks before departure to mock up the missing pieces. The verb 'to pont' has taken root in the expedition. If Ponting is getting still pictures, to pont means to stand motionless in the cold, always with the interesting chance that you may fall off something if he's asked you, say, to hold a posture balanced on an iceberg. When the cinematograph comes out, pont-ing, writes Wilson, is more like 'amateur theatricals'. Today Ponting wants to capture the routine of making camp on the polar march. His camera is a slim, upright box on a tripod, with the main lens projecting out of the front and a second attached to the side as viewfinder. It attaches to the tripod like a theodolite—rigidly, with screws. Ponting cannot swivel it while he is filming. The camera must be lugged to face the subject, or else an event constructed right in front of it, on the stage of snow before the camera's eye. It looks absurdly small for its function; it's hard to believe that the world can be finessed into this repository. Ponting has no lighting, cannot in fact film indoors or anywhere the world's light does not reach. Therefore his actors today, Wilson and Scott and Petty Officer Evans and Bowers, by chance the whole party who will reach the pole bar Oates, carefully rig half a tent as backdrop. Ponting films from where the other canvas wall would be. Lens cap off, gloved hand ready for the cinematographer's even cranking of the celluloid through the gate. Action, gentlemen, please.

'We did it in sections,' reports Wilson,

> first we changed our footgear and lit the primus and hung up our socks and cooked the hoosh. Second, we opened up the steaming cooker and whacked it out in the pannikins, and had our meal. Third, we packed up the cooker, tied up the provision bag, put both out of the tent and then unrolled our sleeping bags. Fourth, we had our sleeping bags out and were sitting in them writing diary, winding watch, sewing, etc., and then all got inside the bags and went to sleep!

They are giving Ponting an idealised, or maybe burlesque, record of the

exact actions they will perform at each stop on the high plateau above
the Beardmore Glacier, when they are propelling themselves by pure
reliance on their own muscles; when there are no more dogs or ponies
in view to worry about, and the punishing effects of the plan become a
private matter, between themselves and their bodies. ('After all,' writes
Bowers to Kathleen Scott, 'it will be a fine thing to do that plateau with
man-haulage in these days of the supposed decadence of the British
race.' 'I hope your little boy is as lively and strong as he appears in the
many photographs of him I see round the Captain's table,' he adds.)
Even Oates, who does not want to go on to the pole, who thinks Scott
'should buy a shilling book about transport', will feel a certain
relaxation when his horses no longer need coaxing or slavedriving. 'I
thank you, Titus,' Scott will say, the Barrier crossing accomplished and
all the horseflesh depoted at Shambles Camp; and suddenly, one
memorable evening, Oates will turn chatty and expansive, telling stories
in the tent for hours. 'You funny old thing, you have quite come out of
your shell, Soldier,' Scott will say, and throw an arm around his
shoulder. Just so, then, the men in the tent will poise themselves so as
not to upset the cooker, while the night's designated cook boils
pemmican into hot 'hoosh'. They'll wriggle into their sleeping bags like
a nest of very polite caterpillars. No matter how crowded the tent (more
crowded still when Scott impulsively adds a fifth man at the last
moment) they'll contrive to nestle, and to reach over each other,
without forfeiting the manners which preserve privacy. Or social
separation, in the case of Petty Officer Evans. They'll sleep like this
through a night as white as this illusion of one, and wake every day to
do the same again. Ponting's film cannot show, though, the
predominant silence of the polar marches. By the time they pitch camp
Scott will have paced them through a day of sticky snow surface, or
sastrugi, himself withdrawn deep in calculation, the sole decision-
maker, and they prey to the bitter little resentments that fill your mind
automatically as you jerk and heave in harness, only waiting for the
signal to stop. You forget, Cherry-Garrard writes, 'how the loss of a
biscuit crumb left a sense of injury which lasted for a week; how the
greatest friends were so much on one another's nerves that they did not
speak for days for fear of quarrelling; how angry we felt when the cook

ran short on the weekly bag . . .' These things vanish after sledging; seem negligible before, too. The film cannot show the way the hot food will hit their bloodstreams like a drug, replacing the sullen mood with an equally physiological flush of gaiety, during which they must get into their bags to radiate the heat that makes sleep bearable.

And they move *fast* for Ponting's camera: quick movements by well-fed men who've left the warm hut minutes ago, to be accelerated yet further, till they skitter through polar bedtime when Ponting's film gets shown in later decades at slightly too many frames-per-second. If the new medium Ponting uses yet had a technique appropriate to the antique sport of man-hauling, it would be slow-mo. Night after night the polar journey will pause on sluggish replays of these same few actions: the cooker assembled with painful concentration piece by piece, feet melting a passage inch by inch between the frost-stiffened sides of a sleeping bag.

The trick of film acting, writes Wilson, is 'to try and be absolutely natural . . . you have to completely ignore and forget the cinematograph'. Petty Officer Evans keeps his head down, never looks towards the lens. Scott finds the whole thing fascinating. Bowers and Wilson cannot help grinning.

18 January 1912

'All the day-dreams must go,' writes Scott: all the dreams predicated on the vacancy of this imaginary place. The void has let them down. The mad geometricians were right. Jules Verne was right. Poe was right. There is something at the South Pole. It is a Norwegian flag.

30 March 1912

Sometimes you wake from a dream of guilt or horror that has filled your whole sleeping mind, a dream that feels final, as if it held a truth about you that you cannot hope to evade, and the kind day dislodges it bit by bit, showing you exits where you had thought there were none, reminding you of a world where you still move among choices. Day has always done this for you. It seems unfair that it should not, today. Scott's eyes open. Green canvas wall of tent, rush of snow outside seen only as a tireless random spatter of porous dark. The canvas rustles. He has not been sleeping. He has been trying to drift, but the habit of self-command cuts him off, calls him back over and over to the realisation that it is all true. This irrevocable position *is* the whole, waking truth, and the tent is his life's last scene, beyond any possibility of alteration. He can make no effort that would change anything. If he had taken Oates' advice last autumn and pushed One Ton Depot further south, he might not be lying eleven miles short of it now. If he had left different instructions about the dog-teams, even now help might be on its way, rather than receding through the Barrier blizzard as Cherry-Garrard, unknowing, drives for Cape Evans. But these are ironies that have lost their power to torment, through many repetitions. Edgar Evans is dead under a shallow mound of snow on the Beardmore: brain haemorrhage, Wilson thought. Oates 'left us the other day', as it says in Birdie's letter to his mother, neatly folded on the groundsheet. Oates is a white hummock now somewhere a little to the side of the line of march. And Wilson and Bowers lie one each side of Scott in the tent, their sleeping bags pulled over their faces. How many hours ago he does not know, the breathing first of one and then of the other turned briefly ragged and then stopped. The breath sighed out and never drew in again. Except for the silence they might be sleeping. Scott has a terrible desire that he must keep quelling, to reach and shake them, to try and summon again their company. He can imagine all too well the way the illusion of sleep would break if he did; and the moment when he asked for an answer and got none would be beyond bearing. So he must not break down and ask. He must not touch them at all. He is entirely alone, beyond all hope. For who knows what scoured and whirling distance all about, he is the only living thing. There is nothing left to do but die. But he is still here. He composes himself as best he can (it is difficult to want to stop, your mind is not adjusted to it) but nothing happens. The greater nothing which he supposes will replace this tiny green space when he goes—still unimaginable—does not arrive. His heart beats in his chest with stupid strength.

It was better when he was writing. Twelve days ago Scott's feet froze at last and crippled him. Eleven days ago, the immobilising blizzard began. Ten days ago they ran out of fuel. Eight days ago they ate the last of the food, and soon the thing became absolutely certain. Everyone

wrote, though the pencil was hard to hold, and the paper glazed over
with ice if you exhaled on it. Wilson wrote a letter to Oriana, a letter to
his parents in Cheltenham (carefully adding the address anew on the
second page in case it should be separated) and a note to his friends the
Smiths. Bowers apologised to his mother that his letter should be 'such
a short scribble', and for other things. 'It will be splendid however to
pass with such companions as I have . . . Oh how I do feel for you when
you hear all, you will know that for me the end was peaceful as it is only
sleep in the cold. Your ever loving son to the end of this life and the next
when God shall wipe away all tears from our eyes—H. R. Bowers.' But
Scott wrote and wrote and wrote. He paid his professional debts. He
told Mrs Bowers that her son had been magnificent to the end, and Mrs
Wilson that her husband had the 'comfortable blue look of hope' in his
eyes. He told his mother that 'the Great God has called me'. There are
twelve letters by him in the tent, besides his diary and a Message to the
Public. His teeth are loose in his gums from scurvy, his feet would be
gangrenous if the cold were not slowing up the bacteria, his face is
cracked with snow-burn and marked with unhealed red and purple
sores where the frost bit at the points of the bones; but while he wrote
he commanded the kingdom of words. He was *making*. He could see the
story of the expedition as a parabola that descended to earth at its
completion, and might be made to do so with a power and a grace that
justified the whole; that gave the whole an inevitable fall, like any good
story whose end is latent in its middle and beginning. He knew exactly
what to do. A century and more of expectations were to hand,
anonymous and virtually instinctive to him: he shaped them. Scarcely
a word needed crossing out. One, inside the cover of his diary: 'Send
this diary to my wife.' Correction: 'widow'. With the authority of death
he insisted 'The causes of the disaster are not due to faulty organisation
but to misfortune in all risks which had to be undertaken.' Into the
syntax of his best sentences, he wove appeals to the practical charity of
the nation, so that—like a politician on television taking care his
soundbite cannot be edited into smaller units—the emotion and the
appeal should be indivisible. 'These rough notes and our dead bodies
must tell the tale, but surely, surely, a great rich country like ours will
see that those who are dependent on us are properly provided for.'

Grand sombre cadences, funeral music in words, came to him; long sentences running parallel in sound to each other, inviting a voice to work its way through the scored heights and depths of the phrasing.

> We are weak, writing is difficult, but for my own sake I do not regret this journey, which has shown that Englishmen can endure hardships, help one another, and meet death with as great a fortitude as ever in the past. We took risks, we knew we took them; things have come out against us, and therefore we have no cause for complaint, but bow to the will of Providence, determined still to do our best to the last.

But he had to stop. 'It seems a pity but I do not think I can write more.' When the writing stopped, so did all that words can do to give this situation meaning. His words are exhausted. The tale is told; but he is still here, in the silence afterwards, waiting. Some people wear their roles so closely they become their skin. There is nothing left of them besides, no residue that does not fit the proper emotions of a judge, or a salesman, or an explorer. Scott is wonderfully good at his role, but he is not one of these; he has always been self-conscious. Tucked beneath him, 'I have taken my place throughout, haven't I?' says the letter to Kathleen—whether with pride, or anxiety, or final bitterness at the explorer's place and its mortal demands, he hardly knows. 'What tales you would have had for the boy, but oh, what a price to pay.' After the storied death it seems there remains all of you to die that you had only glimpsed sidelong as you subdued yourself to the part. You cannot die in a story; you have to die in your body. He wonders if the other two travelled, invisibly to him, sometime in the night hours, past the end of their belief, their belief not quite stretching all the way to the fact of death, and faced this horrible vacancy. He thinks not, and is glad. They were certain enough, so far as he could judge, that the eyes they closed here would open again elsewhere. They still looked forward, 'slept' only to wake. Sleep, sleep: all at once he hates this lulling metaphor for the disappearance of every slightest speck of forty-three years of thinking and feeling. Such a lie. It is not sleep, this formless prospect from which his mind recoils helplessly though it is imminent.

But whatever he thinks, whatever he wants, here he is still, both holding death at bay, he cannot *help* it, and wishing it would hurry. He wants to see Kathleen again. He wants the world to expand again from this narrow trap to the proportions you learn to trust, living. He thinks that he would very much like to go indoors. The tent is a feeble cone perched beneath a huge sky on a bed of ice sustained by black, black water. He left Cape Evans five months ago: for almost a hundred and fifty nights he's been in the open, or within this portable fiction of shelter. You never realise until you come out here that the world divides so absolutely into outdoors and indoors. It is almost metaphysical. It seems marvellous to him now that people take open space, and floor it and wall it and roof it, and transform it utterly. He thinks of doors opening, and himself passing through. The door at Cape Evans, of course; but also he stands on the steps by the railings in Buckingham Palace Road knocking at the coloured front door of his own house. He waits at the bigger door of the Geographical Society, and through the glass panes he can see the porter in the vestibule coming to let him in, quite unflustered by the balaclava and the drip of melting frost off his windproof smock. Thresholds: the thick metal door in the corridor of a destroyer, whose rivets are cool bulges in a skin of paint, whose foot-high sill is shiny steel in the centre where feet touch it. A screen-door in the verandah of an American house on a hot day, which has an aquarium cool you are glad of on the inside of it, and a remote buzz of insects and traffic. Doors squeaking, grating, gliding ajar with huge solidity. He thumps for entry at the doors of St Paul's, not on the lime gateway inset in the greater but on the vast sculpted panels of the great door itself, which swing wide on a chessboard floor where his footsteps fall echoey yet distinct. The gates of ivory and of horn in the *Odyssey*, from whose parted leaves stream out true visions and false dreams . . . *Have the gates of death been opened unto thee? or hast thou seen the doors of the shadow of death? Hast thou perceived the breadth of the earth? declare if thou knowest it all. Where is the way where light dwelleth? and as for darkness, where is the place thereof, that thou shouldest take it to the bound thereof, and that thou shouldest know the paths to the house thereof? . . . Hast thou entered into the treasures of the snow? or hast thou seen the treasures of the hail . . . Out of whose womb came the ice? and the hoary frost of heaven who hath gendered it? The waters are hid as with a stone, and the face of the deep is frozen. Canst thou bind the sweet influences of Pleiades, or loose the bands of Orion?* Drift . . . Drift . . . Stop! Get a grip, man. Or, no, he supposes perhaps he ought not to take hold again. But it is already done. He has tightened whatever it is in him that lashes a crumbly fear together into a block strong enough to face things. And the tent returns. The tent, the place, the two corpses, the bottle of opium tablets that would dissolve him away irresistibly if he once chose to swallow them. He is still here.

Scott kicks out suddenly, like an insomniac angry with the bedclothes. Yes, alright, but *quickly* then, without thinking. He pulls open the sleeping bag as far down as he can reach, wrenches his coat right open too, lays his arm deliberately around the cold lump of the body of his friend Edward Wilson (who is not sleeping, no, but dead) and holds tight. It is forty below in the tent. The cold comes into him. Oh how it hurts. His skin, which was the frontier of him this whole long time past, is breached: he is no longer whole: the ice is inside his chest, a spearing and dreadful presence turning the cavities of him to blue glass. His lips pull back from his teeth in an enormous snarl; but Scott has left the surface of his face, and does not know. At its tip the cold moves inside him like a key searching for a lock. An impersonal tenderness seems to be watching as it finds the latch of a box, a box of memories, and spills them out, the most private images, one by one, some that would never have been expected because they were scarcely remembered and it was never known that they had been diligently stored here all the time; one by one, each seen complete and without passion, until the last of them is reached, and flutters away, and is gone.

12 November 1912

After eight months a hand opens the tent-flaps. But it is too dark inside to see what lies on the floor: the blizzards and the great winds of the long winter, through which the three bodies lay in mineral stillness, have piled up snow upon snow until nothing shows now in the spring sunshine on the Barrier except a bamboo pole. The search party from Cape Evans burrow the tent free. Now everything is clear. Those who enter can read the macabre physical evidence of the heads, the hands, the feet. Atkinson is a doctor; Petty Officer Lashly had prophesied that scurvy would prove to have been the cause of the deaths. Cherry-Garrard writes in this diary that Wilson 'had died very quietly', and Bowers 'also quietly'. He does not care to guess how Scott died; only he will add at today's end, 'It is all too horrible—I am almost afraid to go to sleep now.' But they also see that the tent was pitched as tidily as ever; that there are rolls of photographs waiting to be developed; that the sledge buried alongside the tent carries an orderly load, part of which is made up of decayed coal specimens from the rock strata beside the Beardmore Glacier. Turn these and you can see the delicate fossils of plants in them, vestiges of the Cambrian era when Antarctica was green: just as the presence of the coal in the baggage of the dead, and the proud neatness of the final camp, are vestiges of will and intention. These speak to the discoverers as loudly as the tent's dead cargo does. While they collect up the letters and the documents they can be, they *are*, reverent as well as horrified.

And then there is Scott's diary. Atkinson takes charge of it, as Scott had instructed: 'Hour after hour, so it seemed to me,' says Cherry-Garrard, 'Atkinson sat in our tent and read.' When he has the gist of it, he summons the rest and reads aloud to them. The Message to the Public, the account of Oates' very last laconicism. The story is not alive any more than the huddled corpses are. It will be told because it makes good propaganda for the war that is coming, or because it prompts reticent passion in the passionately reticent, or because—in endless ways—it serves. The life of stories is just another metaphor. But this story has already spread to ten minds, very much as if it had been one cell eager to reproduce that Atkinson had brought out of the tent; and now they carry it northward to multiply unimaginably in the warmer world.

They collapse the tent gently. They build a cairn over it that stands black against 'sheets and sheets of iridiscent clouds'. And they turn away; so shall we.

from Beyond Cape Horn
by Charles Neider

Four men followed Scott to the South Pole and then to their deaths. Charles Wright was among the group that turned back early at Scott's behest after helping to haul supplies partway to the Pole. More than 60 years later, at age 86, Wright drank rye and whiskey and answered the questions of writer and polar aficionado Charles Neider (born 1915). Here is Neider's account of their talk.

I n May 1973 I had flown to Vancouver after a stopover in Boulder, Colorado, to visit my Antarctic friend Dale Vance, who had wintered over with the Russians at Vostok Station and to whom I had devoted part of a chapter in *Edge of the World*. I spent a night in Vancouver and early the next morning took a crowded bus to Tsawwassen (pronounced without the first "s"), where I boarded the ferry for Saltspring Island, on which, in Ganges, Sir Charles Wright lived.

As a working scientist Wright had made three trips to Antarctica. At the time of my visit he had recently turned eighty-six (he was born on April 7, 1887) but, as I would soon discover, he was still energetic, witty and full of enthusiasm regarding Antarctica. Living with him and his mementos of those early days, I found it eerie to think he had known Scott and those other now legendary figures of the *Terra Nova* Expedition. He had had a long and distinguished career as a scientist and a scientific administrator and had been knighted for his work as an administrator in the Admiralty during the Second World War. Far from being formidable, which I feared he might be, he proved to be a delight to live and work with, as well as an adequate drinker who plied us both with various liquids in order to keep our voices well oiled, as he explained.

In his first letter to me, dated early February 1973, he said he found my article on Taylor Valley "extremely interesting" and hoped I would let him know when my book came out, for he wanted to get a copy. He explained that he was the only survivor now of Taylor's geological party and of several other parties, including the Pole Party of 1912 that returned from the top of the Beardmore Glacier. He said he still tried to keep in touch with what went on in the Dry Valleys and especially in his namesake valley and added he was almost sure it was Brandau, in a 1965 visit to Wright Valley, "who put the wind up me" (meaning scared him) when he seemed about to land on one of the sharpest of ridges, which fell away on each side at about 70 degrees.

I replied on February 25.

"What a marvelous surprise to have a letter from you. Of course, I know about your work with Scott's last expedition and about Wright Valley. Although I was scheduled to visit Wright Valley during my last trip to Antarctica, I was prevented from doing so because I was involved in a helicopter crash close to the summit of Mount Erebus, as a result of which my hands were not very good for field work for a time.

"My book is being dedicated to Brandau, whom I admire extremely. It will be my pleasure and honor to send you a copy as soon as one is available. For your interest I enclose a copy of the Table of Contents. I also enclose a booklet about Ross Island that I wrote at the request of the National Science Foundation."

I sent another letter to Wright on the 27th.

"You have been much on my mind since I wrote to you the other day. I hope you won't mind hearing from me again so soon. I'd like to ask you several questions. Did you publish an account of your experiences as a member of the party that found Scott, Bowers and Wilson in November 1912? Do you have any theories or hunches regarding the Scott tragedy that differ from those of Cherry-Garrard, Atkinson, Debenham and Amundsen? Had you returned to Antarctica between the time of the Terra Nova Expedition and 1965? If not, you must have had some striking impressions in 1965, given the contrast between the sledging days and the days of aircraft, and given all the changes that had taken place at what had become McMurdo Station. Did you stay long in Antarctica in '65? Have you published your impressions of the '65 visit?

"I have other questions that come to mind and would very much like to interview you for my book. Will you kindly tell me if the idea of an interview appeals to you?"

Wright responded on March 2, saying he had published nothing about his early Antarctic experiences but that he was now, with the help of his daughter Pat, trying to interpret the pencil diaries he had kept in the old days and which had become difficult to decipher as well as to interpret. The Scott Polar Research Institute in Cambridge, England, had offered to copy them, but Wright preferred to keep things in his own hands. At any rate, the diaries were not intended for publication. As for a taped interview by telephone, he was definitely interested. He expressed the wish to be helpful so far as he could. I wrote to him again on March 30.

"I'm increasingly inclined to believe that the best and perhaps the only way to conduct a really productive interview is in person. If you wish, it could be held in successive days if we found we had a great deal to talk about."

I phoned him the evening of April 18 and had a pleasant and productive conversation. And so I went to Saltspring Island.

Exiting from the ferry's car deck, I ascended a slope and saw Wright standing beside his daughter, recognizing him from the two photos Dale Vance had given me. He was thinner than in the photos, possibly more bent, had spectacles, and in general I had no trouble spotting him because of his great age. I walked up to them, introduced myself, and to my amusement had to decline their determined offers to take my heavy blue airline bag. Even Wright really tried to take it from me. He directed me to sit on the front seat of the car and he got in the back seat and we drove not through a hamlet or settlement as I had expected—where and what was Long Harbour?—but on a narrow asphalt road through heavy woods, seeing cyclists starting up hills from the ferry slip, some families at a picnic ground, then only road and trees.

When we arrived at Wright's property at around 1 p.m., he got out to open and shut a long wire gate to keep out a neighbor's geese. His place was indeed quite rustic—and attractive—simple, informal, with views of saltwater inlets. Pat Wright showed me to a room, which, as it turned out, was her own, and said I could use the top drawer of the chest of drawers (which had been left partly open for guidance), but I said I preferred to live out of my bag, which I was used to doing.

One of my first and most vivid impressions was of a large sepia print, framed, of the famous photo by Ponting of Scott seated at his collapsible desk in his cubicle in the Terra Nova Hut on Cape Evans. Herbert G. Ponting was a great photographer of the Antarctic. I guess the negative was 8310. The print in Wright's house was a good deal larger than that and very effective. Above and to the left of it was a large print of young Wright on his knees, peering upwards through a theodolite. This too appears, as I seem to recall, in *Scott's Last Expedition*. I became vividly aware of other memorabilia: rare first editions, even rarer photographic scrapbooks, a bookcase made of a Nansen polar sledge cut in half, a large, wood-cased thermometer, a wooden 435 camera, a theodolite, a penguin-shaped menu from the last midwinter's feast of the Terra Nova Expedition signed by many of the expedition members.

Without delay, after lunch I set up my equipment in Sir Charles's room. He wore a tie and a sports jacket with a white handkerchief in the breast pocket. He was lean and had almost all his hair, now white and cut very short. The fingers of his darkened hands were gnarled. I wondered if he had arthritis pain. He had a habit of stroking his hands lengthwise, one above the other. Brown, age-darkened hands, with much extra, paperlike skin that he sometimes absently pursed into mountain ranges, then, catching himself, smoothed out. His habit of saying, during pauses, "Hm-hm," the first on a higher note than the second. Once he said to me he remembered only poorly events of last week but recalled very well what had happened fifty years ago.

So we taped a good deal. We took a lunch break when his voice began to fade. His fading voice was a problem Pat had warned me about. He corrected it by drinking plenty of rye while insisting that I drink also. I chose scotch and soda with ice. The rye did seem to improve his voice considerably.

Neider: Let me just read to you what Cherry-Garrard says. "That scene can never leave my memory. We with the dogs had seen Wright turn away from the course by himself and the mule party swerve right-handed ahead of us. He had seen what he thought was a cairn and then something looking black by its side. A vague kind of wonder gradually gave way to a real alarm. We came up to them. All halted. Wright came across to us. 'It is the tent.' I do not know how he knew." You don't take exception to that?

Wright: No, not at all. It's very precise and very correct.

Neider: The reason I'm interested, as somebody who's trying to get the facts straight about the history of Ross Island, is that by an irony of history that I think is well justified Scott in his great tragedy made a more lasting mark on Western civilization than Amundsen in his great triumph.

Wright: It's very interesting.

Neider: And I think it's for two reasons. One, Scott's style as a man, and two, his style as a writer. Therefore I think that any revelation that we have of this primal, terrible scene is important to our society, increasingly important because of the difference in moral values that we are experiencing today. To think back on Scott, for all his possible errors of judgment, is to think back on a time and a man when a certain nobility of conduct was to be taken for granted.

Wright: Yes, I agree with you entirely.

Neider: Cherry-Garrard seems to be certain that Scott died last. Do you share his opinion?

Wright: I'm not prepared to be certain about that. He bases it on the fact that Scott was sort of half out of his bag, leaning over with his diary toward Dr. Bill [Edward A. Wilson].

Neider: To your knowledge did Wilson or Bowers also write final messages?

Wright: I don't think so. Otherwise it would appear in Dr. Bills's diary.

Neider: I was fascinated by a little anecdote you mentioned at breakfast, and that is that going up the Beardmore you had a sleepless—

Wright: I felt sleepless, shall I say. I lay awake the whole night.

Neider: This was only at around 3000 feet.

Wright: Yes, it was about that, I should think.

Neider: The idea of being sleepless on a sledging traverse, is that something to be concerned about?

Wright: I wasn't concerned about it in the least. It was an interesting thing and I thought back and I remembered—I was quite a youngster—people talking about sleeplessness at elevation.

Neider: But Atkinson [Edward L.] then reported it to Scott, did he?

Wright: Oh, it got through to Scott.

Neider: But in what sense? Do you think Atkinson was actually worried about you because you hadn't slept well that night?

Wright: I don't know. I never spoke about it to Atch.

Neider: What interests me here is that Atkinson reported to Scott that perhaps one of the people in his group was not feeling too well on the basis of this, and that may have affected Scott's decision in sending you back.

Wright: Might be, I don't know.

Neider: If that indeed was the case, then how extraordinary an event that was for your life, as it turned out.

Wright: Yes, I would have liked to have gone further, but I never had any expectation of being one of the party going right to the Pole. I knew who I thought it should be.

Neider: You went to the top of the Beardmore. How far is that from the Pole?

Wright: We must have been 250 or 300 miles from the Pole.

Neider: One of the men, when told off to go back, burst into tears, according to Scott. I forget who it was, it's in Scott's diary. Apparently everyone wanted to go.

Wright: Scott would certainly go, one knew this. Scott always had Wilson in his train, and Birdie Bowers and Wilson and Cherry-Garrard had done a wonderful job with the winter journey, you see. You could almost put your finger on the people who were almost certain to go. And they had all proven themselves very fit for this sort of thing.

Neider: One of the things that is never mentioned by the early explorers, and it seems to me to be rather vitally important for a complete understanding of life in the Antarctic, is toilet habits in the field. For example, Cherry-Garrard never talks about the fact that it's sometimes necessary to leave the tent at minus seventy [Fahrenheit].

Wright: Yes, well that's insane, of course. But we did it. We all did it.

Scott wanted it that way and we all went out of the tent if we had to. Well! It's quite a business, because the first thing that happens if you go outside in that sort of temperature, everything freezes solid. You see, you've come from your sleeping bag, you've taken into the sleeping bag all the frozen sweat of the previous day, and the previous day and the previous day and the previous day. There's a lot of it at the end. And during the night you first melt that frozen sweat. And very often it freezes at the bottom of the bag, where your feet are. And if you're going to have a decent night you've got to melt all that before you have a chance. And even then it's not comfortable because whatever is next door is wet and cold, and every breath you take brings some of the cold stuff into the small of your back. So a winter's night when you're sledging is not a comfortable thing at all. But you've got to, before you get anywhere, you've got to melt the ice. And sometimes there's fifteen pounds of ice or something like that that's got to be turned into water before you begin to sleep. But that's not what you were thinking of when you asked that.

Neider: No. But when you leave the tent you're wet, actually.

Wright: Oh yes. You freeze straightaway. You manage to get in again and you tie it up again and hope that you get to sleep again before you have to get out. It's not comfortable. But in summer it's quite different. Your sleeping bag loses its condensed water vapor and you have a relatively dry bag. And there's all the difference in heat conductivity between a wet bag and a dry bag, as you can imagine. Worst of all is the frozen bag.

Neider: You were very pleased that Scott wanted you, as he calls it, to saturate your mind with ice problems?

Wright: Yes, yes indeed. It was not very respectable but I dearly wanted the opportunity of seeing some of the country, you see, and if I hadn't taken on glaciology I'd have spent my time, I'm afraid, in headquarters. And I couldn't bear to think of that.

Neider: I gather that you have fallen into many a crevasse. There are not many people in modern times who fall into crevasses. What was it like?

Wright: The unpleasant part is the jerk that comes at the end of your fall. You've got a harness, you see, with a rope. In crevasse country there's usually at least one man well ahead, an extended line ahead. And there *is* an art in walking, something like walking on slippery ice. You walk from your knees and not from your toes. You walk flatfooted, and it helps enormously, if you're not to fall into a crevasse, if that's the way you do it.

Neider: I gather that there were times when one just accepted the notion of falling into crevasses and was very cool about it.

Wright: I can remember Scott, about opposite the Cloudmaker [a mountain], up the Beardmore. He stopped just before we got to some rough level stuff and said, "Well, here are the crevasses. Somebody's got to fall into them." He was the first one in. [Both laugh.] That pleased us all immensely.

Neider: Did you fall very far?

Wright: Not as a rule. You haven't got a very long stretch between yourself and the sledge. You lengthen the distance at least for one man so that the whole outfit doesn't go down at once. But the thing that surprised me was to find out how much more difficult it is to see what's ahead of you coming down than going up. Extraordinary. I went badly astray coming down to the Mid-Glacier Depot. Got to a tangle of crevasses. Not crevasses so much as separate seracs, spikes filled up on the surface with snow. And I was very ashamed of myself that time, almost as ashamed as the time when, later on, I led our party in a complete circle to meet our own sledge tracks again.

Neider: When was this?

Wright: On the way back from the Beardmore. And the funny thing— it's really quite interesting. Normally I had no real difficulty in navigating. Something went wrong this day. I don't know what it could have been. But it was a bad day. Couldn't see the horizon, couldn't see the sky, couldn't see anything. Nothing to look at. No wind. Just a sheer white wall. But the interesting thing was that once I'd done this I lost my confidence in the ability to keep a straight line and I had to tell Atch, "I can't go on, I can't trust myself any more." It was very curious.

Neider: And what did he say?

Wright: He said, "Yes, right-o." It's the most interesting phenomenon. Having made a muck of it, I didn't trust my ability any more—till we camped next day. [Laughs.]

Neider: And then it was over.

Wright: Oh yes. Yes, yes. No trouble after that.

Neider: When Shackleton was coming back down the Beardmore after his farthest south the party developed dysentery.

Wright: One of our own people picked that up—Keohane [Patrick]. We'd had our Christmas dinner at the Mid-Glacier Depot, and we put it down to the cubic inch of Christmas pudding that was too much for his tender stomach. That was spartan fare. *He* got it then. What sort of confirmed our idea was that we all ate enormously when we came into One Ton Depot—rations of everything, you know, and I remember eating three days' meal at one whack. It was not very much. That didn't affect me but it started Atkinson off and he had quite an unpleasant time of it for three or four days. By that time Keohane had recovered.

Neider: That's a disaster in itself, to have something like dysentery when you're manhauling sledges.

Wright: Oh, it is. You're not there all the time and you have to catch up.

Neider: Did you ever have any signs of scurvy?

Wright: No. When I saw my legs on getting back, saw them for the first time—you don't take your clothes off—I was surprised. They were really swollen up. Which I put down to having stopped marching. I don't know whether it was incipient scurvy or not. I never went into it. I never mentioned it to anybody except to Priestley [Raymond], who said, "Oh yes, I had the same when *we* came in." And then he said [whispers], "I put on ten pounds in three weeks after I got back."

Neider: It occurs to me that being out in the field for so long in those conditions you have a very unusual relationship with your own body. You don't see parts of your body for a long time.

Wright: You wear windproof trousers, and puttees over them.

Neider: At night did you undress to get into the sleeping bag?

Wright: Oh no. I put another pair of socks on, maybe. You see, our allowance of personal stuff was eleven pounds apiece, and I should say that three pounds of that went for tobacco, and another two pounds for reading matter, and a sledging diary (just a few ounces)—but it didn't leave much room for spare clothing. We all had a pair of spare socks but they were really wet. A woolly thing gets really wet and there's quite a weight in them. In that abortive attempt to relieve the northern party— that would be the autumn of 1912, I guess—I weighed the sweater I had on, when I came back, and it was thirteen pounds overweight.

Neider: Scott and Cherry-Garrard often said there was never any bad feeling among the men. As a matter of fact, Cherry-Garrard says that during the entire winter journey he almost cannot remember one swear word despite the desperation that they felt. Do you think this is romanticizing?

Wright: Yes. It's impossible when we're with seamen to go along with the kind of things happening, you see, and not to have a few words, seamen's language. I just don't believe it. It wasn't meant in any special sense.

Neider: Did Scott react to seamen's language?

Wright: He was used to it. Of course, so was Dr. Bill, he'd been from before.

Neider: But you do feel that the reports that have come out, of really good behavior under very trying circumstances, are true?

Wright: Absolutely. Yes, there was nothing in it. If a few unpleasant words were used it just meant nothing at all. It was normal seamen's language or normal Londoner's language.

Neider: But under desperate circumstances men did behave very well?

Wright: Extraordinarily well.

Neider: So this was not an exaggerated report?

Wright: Not a bit.

Neider: Now you mentioned at lunch today that you felt—it came out quite naturally—that in some ways Cherry-Garrard is not appreciated. I'd like to hear you talk about that.

Wright: I feel it quite strongly because, first of all, Cherry was one of the nicest people. He was a real gentleman of the nicest kind you find in England. Although he was educated in Oxford he didn't have any Oxford accent, it didn't stick out at all. And he was one of the nicest of the party. Now, he also had a stake in every really sticky journey. The depot journey, where they lost some of the ponies to killer whales. The winter journey, which was a terrible thing, terrible. The Pole journey, although he was with us all the time when I was there—that was the only easy time. And then this awful journey with Dmitri [a dog and pony handler] and the dogs to help Scott and the party get back quickly to catch the ship at Hut Point, you see, a quick journey to catch the ship, and then keep remembering, when you're inclined to think that things needn't to have gone wrong. I dare say Scott's orders to be at a certain place by a certain time were arranged by him in order to catch the ship on the way back, he didn't want to stay another winter if it wasn't necessary. Well, there we are. What I started to say was Cherry had a stake in all these difficult things. The only not difficult part was on the polar journey and the return journey. On the return journey we came through without any trouble at all except for dysentery for a short time on the part of Keohane and a little bit on the part of Atkinson. When we met all the food in the world and all the oil that anyone could use we took our proper share of that and a bit more, I think. So Cherry had a hard time. He stuck it extraordinarily well. Mind you, he rowed when he was at Oxford, he was a tougher guy than he looked, much tougher, but he wasn't as tough on that winter journey as Wilson and Birdie Bowers. He was not in quite such good shape when he got back, at any rate. I'd say asleep on his feet.

Neider: Why do you feel he's not appreciated? In what sense?

Wright: Well, he's written a book, and like most Englishmen in similar cases he understates everything in which he's involved, and I think that people reading his book don't realize, because he understates something he really knows, don't appreciate that he had really, really difficult times. And I know that many other people who were down there feel the same as I do.

Neider: Did you feel a distinction being made between the civilians and the noncivilians of the expedition, let's say at winter quarters? Did you feel that you and Cherry-Garrard had a great deal more in common because you were civilians?

Wright: No, they didn't come the naval officer over us. We were really part of the gang, and as a matter of fact what welded us into the right position very firmly was when we had to take over bailing the ship out, two hours on and two hours off. About a day and a half. [Chuckles.] On deck, trying to keep the dogs and the ponies alive.

Neider: This was during the storm.

Wright: This was during the storm about four days after we left New

Zealand. And we did a pretty good job, if you ask me. Man the buckets. [Laughs.]

Neider: Somebody I read recently—I don't know if it was Atkinson or Taylor—remarked on your awareness of beauty in Antarctica and as an example they said that during a field trip studying ice crystals in crevasses you were the only one who was fascinated by and remarked on the beauty of the crystals. This convinces me that you were very much aware of the beauty in Antarctica.

Wright: It wasn't so much the beauty of it as the geometrical designs and the reasons for it. It's the reasons for it that are really interesting. You see some funny shape and you wonder, "Now how did that come about? Did this part of it get made at night, and this part in the daytime?" All that business, you see. It's fascinating, really, if you don't know.

Neider: And you became very adept at photographing ice crystals. Some of your photographs are reproduced in *Scott's Last Expedition*, volume two. They're beautiful against a black background. Ponting says that he gave you some tips on that. The grotto by Ponting, by the way, is very beautiful.

Wright: I'll never forget that. That was an iceberg that tilted over, and there were killer whales in the open water. When we were told officially, Griff [Griffith Taylor] and I, to go with Pont—naval people were scared of him, he had the reputation of a Jonah—things didn't happen to him, they happened to people *with* him. [I laugh. Wright joins me.] At any rate he said, "I'll take several pictures of you going up," and I said, "Look here, that's rather too steep, we'll have to cut steps to get up." He said, "Oh that's all right, you go and cut the steps first and then you go up and pretend to cut the steps." And we did that. Griff and I had sense enough to rope ourselves together. Up I went [chuckles] and at the top, at an unguarded blow, a great bit of ice fell down amongst the killer whales. And Ponting said [shouting]: "That's wonderful! Do it again!" [Both laugh.] You'd see these darn killer whales, waiting for you, hoping.

Neider: When you returned to Antarctica was it always in connection with scientific work or did you ever embark on what they used to call a sentimental journey?

Wright: Well, it's very difficult, you know, to answer a question like that because you go, ostensibly anyway, you make an excuse, possibly, to go, but when you get there then you find, or at least I found, that one is regarded as one of the old gang. They used to talk of the heroic age. I've heard that word several times. Heroic age. The Americans *make* it so. They *make* it so. By their attitude and by what they say and so on. But the sentimental part, as far as I was concerned, was an inescapable thing over which I had no control.

Neider: You wouldn't disagree with the fact that it's referred to as the heroic age of Antarctic exploration?

Wright: I don't know, it's very difficult to say. It depends on how one's brought up. I spent most of my life in England, and the British attitude is quite different from the American, you know.

Neider: Can we go into that briefly, that difference?

Wright: I don't know what it's based on, this is the trouble. The U.S. of A. no doubt is a frightful mixture of people, races. And so is England. But the mixture had been formed umpteen years ago in England—the Angles and the Saxons and all the other people. And we've come to expect this difference, but why it comes about, unless it's a mixture of races that does it, I don't know.

Neider: Is it also partly a difference in what was happening in the Anglo-Saxon world in the years just before the first war? Wasn't Britain undergoing a kind of inspirational surge of patriotism in preparation for the contest with Germany?

Wright: Yes, that's true enough.

Neider: Let me read you this from Scott, who says, "One of the greatest successes is Wright. He is very thorough and absolutely for anything. Like Bowers, he has taken to sledging like a duck to water, and although he hasn't had such severe testing I believe he would stand it pretty nearly as well. Nothing ever seems to worry him, and I can't imagine that he ever complained of anything in his life."

Wright: [Chuckles.] Well, on the last thing he's certainly gone astray. What does he mean by complain? I think you can complain to yourself, very often, without complaining to anybody else. With these glasses, which I had to wear, and another pair of glasses, snowglasses, goggles, as well—it was quite a burden. When the weather was cold you couldn't see where you were going and I used to complain to myself, "What a silly ass. Why didn't I get some special lenses made of snow goggle glass?" Because with two of these things, you see, you have four surfaces on which you can either have condensation of ice or water vapor or actual stuff sticking to the outside lens. So that it was a dreadfully stupid thing not to have got some special glasses made. That's what I call complaining. I was complaining to myself.

Neider: Scott of course had something else in mind, and what he had in mind was your willingness and eagerness—

Wright: It was all very interesting, you see.

Neider: And your optimism and your enthusiasm. Have you enjoyed your life, on the whole?

Wright: Until a little while ago I was thinking very seriously of writing a memoir, and the title I had was *Diary of a Fortunate Man.*

Neider: How do you account for your extraordinary longevity and vigor?

Wright: Well, I can't account for it now, it's gone. [Laughs.] I don't know. I said I was odd, a long time ago. I think I was odd even when I was a youngster at school, because I remember that for some incredible reason I thought it was a good thing—I was living in Toronto at the time—to toughen oneself a bit, so I wore the same clothes in summer and winter. Not a sensible thing at all to do. [Chuckles.] I don't know what would account for it. My mother didn't last very long. My father only lasted until about 80. Nothing in heredity, anyway.

Neider: Scott said how fit you were. You were very fit, weren't you?

Wright: I was, of course.

Neider: Can you tell me something about your early years? Were they happy ones?

Wright: Oh, very. Although they weren't very happy after my father married again. I had a stepmother and I didn't entirely approve of her, shall we say.

Neider: How old were you then?

Wright: About ten. Not that one was unhappy but, like every youngster, I was very ready to fly elsewhere, to get away from home. Every youngster with any guts wants to clear out.

When in February 1974 I sent Wright a copy of the dust jacket of my forthcoming *Edge of the World*, he remarked that he was sorry to see I was a flat-earth believer. The book was published in April. Early in May he wrote to me, "I am not qualified as a critic in your field of effort, but I think you have written a very fine book." At the end of May he wrote me saying he had been very busy as the result of an "event" at Victoria University, where he was the recipient of an honorary degree of Doctor of Laws. In a footnote he added that this reminded him of the Royal Navy admiral who already was a Knight of the Order of the British Empire (K.B.E.) and who was then made a Knight Commander of the Bath (K.C.B.), and that a message received by the admiral read, "Congratulations. Twice a knight at your age."

He died November 1, 1976, at the age of eighty-nine.

from The Birthday Boys
by Beryl Bainbridge

Beryl Bainbridge (born 1933) divides her superb novel of Scott's Terra Nova *expedition into five sections, each narrated by a member of the doomed polar party. The book draws upon original diaries and letters, but Bainbridge imagines something more about these men and the drama they lived. The results are haunting; they lend new depth to the tragedy and its leading players. Titus Oates narrates this passage.*

I didn't take my sock off because the size of my foot unnerved me. When I last took a peek it was pretty colourful, blotched with red and purple, the skin right up to the ankle shining with that same sort of sweet glaze one sees on rotten meat. Two of my toes were black. I was afraid to remove my sock for fear my toes came with it and we'd all sniff their stink above the smell of that stew in the saucepan. I wish to God I'd listened to Ponting when he said we ought to bring a pistol on with us.

A quarter of an hour ago I begged Bill for a drop of brandy. He refused, giving the tommy-rot excuse it would do my shrunken stomach no good. 'Please believe me, my dear Oates,' he said. 'I'm only thinking of what's best for you.'

He and Bowers still waste an inordinate amount of energy worrying about the welfare of others, whereas my world is no longer large enough to contain anyone but myself. I was trying to get my other boot off and Bill was squatting on his haunches at the cooker, stirring away at the hoosh.

'Do you reckon a man without feet could still ride to hounds?' I asked, and he had the grace to look discomfited. If I hadn't felt so damnably feeble I'd have snatched the bottle from his medical box and to blazes with his permission.

I caught Scott looking at me. I don't know what he saw in my eyes, but a moment later he said, 'For pity's sake, Bill, do as he asks.'

It was a miserly enough measure, yet the effect was immediate. Such a huge smile tugged at my mouth my lips cracked afresh and I could taste the trickling blood.

'Get some food into him,' Bill urged, and selfless old Birdie tried to feed me with a spoon.

'I will lay down my life for Bill,' I said, or something to that effect. I felt absolutely liberated, like a stone hurled into the depths, leaping not falling into that shining abyss where the piebald pony waited . . .

We shot the remaining ponies when we reached the foot of the Glacier early in December. We were all pretty down in the mouth about it, though poor Bowers showed it the most, his horse being the strongest of the lot. For my part, I was thankful Scott had changed his mind yet again and abandoned his damfool notion to take them up the Glacier. They'd suffered enough; the surfaces had been uniformly terrible, and towards the end we'd had to lash them onwards. I think we all felt the inflicting of such cruelty harmed us almost as much as the wretched beasts who bore it.

Bill congratulated me on having got them thus far. 'After all,' he observed, 'they were hardly the best animals money could buy.' He never spoke a truer word. The motors, for which not enough spares had been brought and which now lie under drift on the ice somewhere between Hut Point and Corner Camp had cost £1000 a piece, the dogs thirty shillings and the ponies a fiver—and I reckon that was a good few bob more than they were worth. Scott thanked me too, if a little stiffly.

We named the depot where we buried them Shambles Camp, which was an apt enough name for it, and not just on account of the ponies. What with our late start, the almost immediate failure of the motors, our inexpertise on skis, 'unexpected' weather conditions and Scott's mistrust of dogs, our journey so far had been a catalogue of disasters and miscalculations. Scott puts it down to 'poor luck'.

I've never known such a man for making mistakes and shifting the blame onto others. If it hadn't always been so damned cold I think one or two of us might have got heated enough to forget he was Leader and resorted to fisticuffs. It was pretty shameful the way he laid into Bowers when the hypsometer got broken. Birdie was frightfully cast down at being given a drubbing in front of the seamen.

'It would seem to me,' I said to Scott, 'that it's something of an oversight we're not carrying a spare one.'

He didn't go for me; nor had he, not since Birdie, Cherry and Crean nearly perished on the sea-ice. He turned on his heel and went muttering off to get words of sympathy from old Bill. In the end I don't know what the fuss was about. We didn't need an instrument to tell us what altitude we'd reached on the Glacier; any fool could tell for himself when he was a quarter way up, then half, and so on.

Another time he got himself into a frightful fizz over the fact that Shackleton had apparently travelled on blue ice, whereas we floundered in drift. There was also that business of his not wanting me to shoot Jehu, not until we'd travelled another twenty miles or so. The animal was dying on its feet, but I was forbidden to despatch it until we'd passed the point at which Shackleton shot his first pony. One would have thought we were racing Shackleton rather than Amundsen.

On New Year's Eve, by which time we had slogged, heaved and crawled some 9000 feet up the Beardmore Glacier, we took a half day's halt for the sledges to be adjusted. Once we reached the summit Birdie assured me it was little more than a hundred and fifty miles to the Pole. I took his word for it. In my opinion, without him we could have been moving sideways, or even backwards, he being the only one who appears to have any sense of direction.

Scott still hadn't told us which three he intended to take with him on the final run. Even Bill didn't know, though he said Scott had asked him which of the three seamen he considered the fittest, Taff Evans, Lashly or Crean. Bill had told him he'd put his money on Lashly.

Birdie was convinced he wouldn't be chosen; he's very naive and simply didn't see that Scott would be in Queer Street without him. Quite apart from his doing the work of three men, he's the only competent astronomical navigator among us, and if he'd been left behind it wouldn't have been so much a question of reaching the Pole as finding it. For my part, I neither expected nor wished to be included. My feet were in a sorry state and I was none too happy about my leg.

It had been Scott's intention to make another march before nightfall, but the work on the sledges took longer than expected. Petty Officer Evans was practically rebuilding them, so we had time on our hands. We sat in the tent drinking tea, and for some reason I was seized with a dreadful bout of homesickness. It was Bill's fault really, rambling on about those bluebell woods he's so fond of. I was only half paying attention to the conversation, because my leg was giving me gyp. I had the oddest sensation my old thigh wound was coming apart, so much so I was pretty frightened of touching the skin in case it was gaping open. When I did get up the courage there was nothing under my fingers save that puckered scar. It was rougher than usual and there were one or two pustules, but we all had those. We hadn't washed for weeks, or changed our clothes, and the hell-hole we were in before we reached the Glacier—Scott dubbed it the Slough of Despond—when for four days we were tent-bound in a blizzard and the temperature rose so high we lay waterlogged in our bags, had wrinkled us like washerwomen. The pain in my leg was a blessing in one way—it stopped me thinking of my wretched feet. I suppose it was the remembrance of my time in hospital, my return to England, the delayed twenty-first birthday party in the grounds of Gestingthorpe that pitched me into thoughts of home.

I must have listened for an hour or more to Bill rhapsodising over his nature study excursions, and a further hour while he and Birdie drivelled on about the Greeks and their notion of tragedy. I can't pretend to know what Bill's getting at when he says the 'joy of being' incorporates a delight in annihilation; not unless he means it's all right for a fellow to break his neck coming off his hunter when clearing an eleven-foot hedgerow.

Scott didn't open his mouth. Nor did Teddy Evans. In Scott's case I don't believe he was out of his depth, rather that he had as little sympathy with the argument as I had. I reckon Bill's whole philosophy is damnably unhealthy. Any man who spends years trying to find out why grouse fall sick of a parasitic disease, and is tickled pink at discovering it's to do with some blob clinging to dew on the bracken, must have a very limited love of life. Dear me! Bill is the sweetest old chap in the world—one just gets a mite tired of his being so depressingly good.

He and Birdie got onto another subject which left me equally in the cold—something to do with the birds of Stymphalos being frightened into the air by the shaking of a bronze rattle.

'No,' said Bill. 'That won't do. They were all shot. And besides, surely they were no bigger than kingfishers?'

'Well,' said Bowers, 'what about Phosphoros, son of the Morning Star, and his wife Alkyone? Weren't they turned into birds which nested on the sea in mid-winter?'

'Halcyon days,' Bill enthused. 'Jolly good try, Birdie.'

In the middle of their smiling at each other in mutual if mysterious, gratification Teddy jumped in with a reminiscence of the time he'd sailed as a junior officer on *The Morning*, the relief ship sent out to rescue the *Discovery* expedition. At this Scott looked fit to boil over, though he held his tongue. Teddy made a good joke—he said the ship was known as 'Joy Cometh in the Morning'. He spoilt it by boasting that he and a chap called Dorley had been given the nickname of the Evanly twins, on account of their winning the two most coveted prizes awarded by the *Worcester*, Dorley snatching the Gold Medal and Teddy the cadetship into the Royal Navy.

'Gosh,' said Bowers, 'how ripping. I tried for the Gold but I hadn't a hope.' At which Scott took out his blessed diary and began to scribble furiously.

Teddy would have gone on if one of the seamen hadn't shouted out for Bill. Apparently Petty Officer Evans had cut his hand working on the sledges. Before he could go outside to see how serious it was Evans bawled, 'It's nothing, Dr Wilson, sir. Nothing at all. Hardly a scratch. Don't you disturb yourself.'

Scott said Evans was a marvel, a blooming marvel. 'You realise,' he told us, 'that building a sledge in these conditions is phenomenal. Nobody's ever done it before.' And no doubt recording the fact, he continued to dash his pencil across the page.

Teddy pulled a face. Whether it signified contempt for the Petty Officer or our Leader is a moot point. Most likely both. The animosity between Scott and Teddy hadn't exactly been hidden. Times without number Bill had stepped in to keep the peace, and Teddy wore himself ragged trying to outdo Scott on the marches—not that it did him much good; the one thing Scott thrives on is competition and he's a formidable opponent. In spite of his nervous temperament—I've never known such a chap for tears—he's tremendously strong. I'd go so far as to say he has more stamina than the lot of us rolled up together, and that includes Bowers. Meares said Scott reminded him of one of those natives who could dance about on hot coals; he reckoned they withstood the pain simply because they couldn't stand the thought of the mind being controlled by the body.

Until we reached the Glacier Teddy was in charge of a dog team, and time and again he romped into camp after us, fresh as a daisy. This really got Scott's goat; he couldn't wait to send the teams back. I can't excuse him for having allowed his dislike of Teddy to fuel his already irrational prejudice against the use of dog transport.

Some argue that Teddy hadn't forgiven Scott for reinstating the drunken Petty Officer, others that it went deeper and stemmed from the time he had high hopes of leading the Expedition himself. Then there was that bust-up in South Africa between their respective wives, Mrs Evans blubbing because she'd received an invitation to Government House a day later than Mrs Scott, and Mrs Scott rounding on her and shouting she was a silly gubbins for minding.

The following morning at our hotel in Simonstown, Cherry and I were knocked awake at some ungodly hour and summoned downstairs to join Scott and his wife for breakfast. Cherry couldn't eat anything; he had a fearful crush on Mrs S and shredded the bread rolls into crumbs, which he arranged in rows across the cloth and shoved about as though they were dominoes. Scott was effusively genial, which I took for a bad sign. He would keep saying how well I looked.

'I'm amazed to see you're again wearing bootlaces,' Mrs Scott said—she'd taken an interest in my footwear once before.

'It's possibly Sunday,' I rejoined. 'The two often go together.'

'I've come to the conclusion,' she said, digging viciously into her grapefruit, 'that things ought to be considered in pairs.'

'Darling,' said Scott, 'you're spraying me.'

'If it had been up to me,' she burst out, 'I'd have interviewed the wives first.' Apparently she'd had to read a library book to Mrs E for two hours in order to calm her down, and it was a perfectly ghastly book, all about women simpering over their sewing and reaching for the smelling salts every time a man came within ten yards of them.

'I think that was jolly decent of you,' Cherry said, making sheep's eyes across the table.

'On the contrary,' snapped Scott, 'it was the least she could do, seeing it was her fault Mrs Evans got into such a state in the first place.'

Mrs Scott wasn't at all put out. 'Don't you just hate women?' she asked me, as though she was something quite other.

Things came to a head at a civic reception in New Zealand. Mrs E took it as a personal slight that Scott didn't give her the first dance, and Evans backed her up. Later I learnt from Atkinson there'd been a hullabaloo in the ladies' powder-room. He'd taken a cousin to the ball, who was present when Mrs S and Mrs E began a magnificent battle which lasted fifteen rounds. Mrs Wilson flung herself into the fight after the tenth and there was rumoured to be more blood and hair flying around than you'd find in a Chicago slaughterhouse.

Bill, being Bill, protests that Scott had nothing against Teddy beyond he regarded him as lightweight and something of a slacker. As I tried to warn young Gran, it simply doesn't do to be seen loafing about when Scott has his beady eye on one. A man could march for nine hours, unload the tents, build the snow walls, feed the animals, see to his personal gear, and Scott would still find him something extra to be getting on with. Meares and I got away with it by decamping to the stables; at least there we could lounge in peace.

If it came to it, I'd have to agree that Teddy is lightweight, but I don't suppose any of us will ever forget what a good sport he was during his command of the *Terra Nova*, or the blazing good fun we had those sea nights we sat round the wardroom table, hollering like banshees and laughing until we cried.

'Weren't they good times?' I asked out loud, and they all looked at me. 'I was thinking about home . . . Gestingthorpe,' I lied, not wanting to antagonise Scott by reminding him of how little he'd been missed on the voyage out.

'Tell me about it,' he said, closing his notebook and tucking it into the pouch strapped to his chest. 'I saw the photographs you had pinned up in the hut . . . it's a fine building.'

'I'm going to make a few improvements when I get back,' I said. 'In fact, they're already in hand . . . nothing very ambitious . . . a new dressing-room next to my sister's bedroom, some more shelves in the library, extra kennels beyond the stables . . . that sort of thing. One day I'd really like to build a swimming-pool . . . Trouble is, the best place to put it as regards sunlight would be on the south terrace, and I can't see my mother agreeing to that. I expect I'll have to wait until . . . And here I broke off, because I don't believe I'd ever seriously thought of the possibility of my mother dying. Well, I had, but I'd never linked it to swimming-pools.

'Titus, old chap,' said Bill, ever sensitive, 'when we get home I'd dearly like to meet your mother. You must promise to invite me to tea. I might even do a sketch of the house.'

'There'll be currant cake,' Teddy murmured, and we all laughed.

'You'll get more than tea,' I said. 'My mother's likely to kill the fatted calf. You should have been there on my twenty-first birthday.' And suddenly I wanted to tell them about my mother and my home and all the memories I'd kept bottled up inside me while we dragged those damn sledges mile after mile and my feet froze in my boots.

'I was in hospital in South Africa on my birthday,' I began, 'after I'd copped it in that skirmish with the Boers. I'd lost three stones and was as weak as a kitten. That chap Campbell-Bannerman later accused the army of barbarism in its conduct of the war, but I just did as I was told. In point of fact I was far more alarmed about the proposed reforms—the changing of uniforms, Wolseley's campaign for the abolition of bought commissions, his insistence that promotion should rest on ability rather than seniority. I was young, don't forget, and hidebound, though I did approve of his wanting to break down the barriers between men and "officers and gentlemen", and dub the whole lot soldiers.

'I sailed home on the *Bavarian*, and my mother cried when she saw me so wasted and on crutches. You've never known such a fuss to be made of a fellow. My sister Lilian used to come into my room in the middle of the night and force chicken broth down my gullet. My brother Bryan spent hours poring over jigsaws laid on a tray across my lap, making out he didn't know which piece fitted into the sky. I think he imagined I'd lost my mind along with that three stone in weight. When the weather improved they put me out in the garden on a deckchair and Violet read poetry to me. It was frightful stuff and mostly sent me to sleep. In mid-June,.when I was better, they gave me a birthday party to make up for the one I'd missed the previous March.

'It was a magnificent bash. There was a tea for the village children in the schoolhouse, banners and flags all over the place, coconut-shies and a steam-roundabout juddering away in the Long Meadow, and at four o'clock most of the tenants sat down to a dinner in the main barn, my mother, the vicar and the estate manager taking their respective places at the head of the three trestle tables. My mother's a wonderful woman for catching the mood of the moment, for knowing what's suitable. We had quantities of roast beef washed down with nut beer . . .' And here I stopped my babbling and swallowed, the very utterance of the word beef filling my mouth with saliva. Dear God, at that moment I would have traded my immortal soul for a mouthful of rump steak smeared with horseradish.

'After we'd eaten the plum pudding,' I continued, 'Jordan, the head keeper, stammered through an address of welcome, followed by the vicar waffling on in praise of gallant young men, myself in particular, and ending up with a baffling comparison between my "bravery" and that Frenchman Becquerel's assertion that atoms, thought for almost a century to be the ultimate units of matter, might contain yet smaller particles. None of us had the faintest idea what he was getting at, though most gave him the benefit of the doubt and assumed he was being complimentary. At any rate, my mother looked as proud as punch, so I sat there smirking and pretending it was just the ticket, when all I actually wanted to do was go and admire my new steeplechaser, an absolute ripper of a brute, black as coal and glossy with it.

'There was a dance later. A limp is a marvellous excuse for getting out of all that waltzing rot, and after doing my duty and taking my mother, my sisters and the vicar's wife once each round the floor I was able to slope off to bed. I would have gone to the stables, but, to tell the truth, I was more done in than I cared to admit.

'I didn't notice the picture right away. I read for a bit, and then Chalmers came in to put on more coals and I asked her why she wasn't at the dance and she said she was going as soon as she'd seen to the fires. I told her she could extinguish the light. I wasn't lying flat, because

I was finishing a cigarette, and I blew one of those smoke-rings, an absolute belter, which rose sideways and sailed towards the hearth, drawn by the draught from the chimney. It was then, my gaze following its wobbling lassoo, that I noticed the picture, still in its tarnished green frame, hung on the wall above the mantelshelf. I found out later that my mother had given instructions for it to be removed from the old night nursery only that morning—I told you she was a woman with a remarkable sense of occasion.

'The picture—it was a print—was of Queen Victoria seated side-saddle on a piebald pony, John Brown holding its bridle, taken in the courtyard of Balmoral Castle. It was a very small pony and its rider somewhat stout. One could tell from the expression on the Queen's face that she found the pony restive.

'From the time I could name things the picture had dangled on its cord above the tin soldiers marching along the third shelf in the nursery alcove. I called the pony Boy Charger. Owing to some bulge in the stonework of the wall the picture mostly hung askew. Before going down for her supper my nurse leant on tiptoe against the fireguard and poked it straight with her finger. When I was old enough I shoved it back into place with the handle of my tennis racket.

'Looking at it by firelight, the reflection of the flames licking the glass, it was easy to conjure up the sound of hooves skittering on cobblestones. "Mr Brown," the stout lady said in my dreams, "be so good as to keep Boy Charger under control." "Get away, woman," John Brown replied, "ye canna expect me to hold back the dawn." '

After this somewhat embarrassing outburst I fell silent, and might have remained so if Birdie hadn't asked me if I'd done any pig-sticking while in India. I said I had, but much preferred polo, which struck me as the same thing, though without the screaming, at which Scott and Bill looked fit to poop.

'It's all right, Uncle Bill,' said Birdie. 'If you'd seen what pigs get up to in India you'd feel sticking was too good for them. They root about among corpses, you know. I've never eaten a sausage since.'

It was Birdie's mention of India that set me off again; besides it had been a long time since we'd sat around doing nothing. Usually when we halted we either ate and moved on again, or ate and slept, and now we sat idle in that cramped, wind-torn tent, listening to the hiss of the primus and the occasional burst of hammering as the seamen outside reconstructed the sledges.

I told them of the jackal hunts we'd gone on in Mhow, how we blew the horn at six in the morning. '. . . When the scent was still on the dew and the sun not yet fiery. A sister of one of the adjutants came out with us on several occasions; she was the first woman I'd ever seen riding astride . . . I can't say it was an edifying sight. She was present when one of the jugglers came into camp, the time Maltravers made an ass of himself. This juggler was quite famous. With one stroke of his sword he could cut in half a lime fruit balanced on the palm of his assistant's hand. Pinkie Maltravers was convinced it wasn't possible. Thinking to expose the chap as a fake, he held out his own hand and told the juggler to perform the trick again. After studying his palm for some moments the Indian wallah refused. "I thought so," shouted Pinkie triumphantly, only to have the juggler examine his other hand. "I will do it on this one," he said. "What the deuce difference does it make?" demanded Pinkie. At which the juggler explained that his other palm was too hollow in the centre and the sword would most probably take off his thumb. One could tell that Pinkie was in a bit of a funk, but he couldn't very well show the white flag, not with us all watching, and so he closed his eyes and stretched out his arm. The sword flashed down and the lime collapsed neatly in two. Pinkie said he'd had to bite on his tongue not to snatch back his hand at the last moment, and reckoned the beatings he'd got at school had stood him in good stead. The adjutant's sister fainted before the sword fell.'

On and on I babbled, during and long after we'd finished our evening meal, remembering places visited and things past, my days at Eton, my time in Egypt, the colour of the flowers in the borders of my mother's garden, as though my life was one of Bryan's jigsaws and I was determined to fit in all the pieces, until, the hot food making me drowsy and the picture all but complete, I trailed into silence. Whereupon Scott leaned across and, taking hold of my shoulders and shaking me affectionately, exclaimed, 'You funny old thing, Titus, you've quite come out of your shell.' I admit I blushed.

Birdie said later it was the first time he'd ever seen me so at ease in

Scott's company, and I believe he was right. I put it down to the fact that with the ponies slaughtered and off my hands, and Meares and Cherry no longer with us, I was forced to make the best of things.

The following morning Teddy's team—Lashly, Crean and Bowers— were told to leave their skis behind and march on foot. On the face of it this seemed a pretty strong indication of their not going on to the Pole, but one never knew with Scott. Teddy looked the picture of misery all day and even Bowers had hardly a word to say for himself. I asked Bill what he thought it meant and he snapped that he was as baffled as the rest of us.

'Surely I won't be included?' I said, and he said, 'Is there any reason why you shouldn't be?' I hadn't told him about my leg.

There was a lot of whispering between Scott and Bill when we camped that night. Bowers's name cropped up several times. I woke in the small hours to see the candle still burning and Scott propped up in his sleeping-bag, scribbling in his notebook.

At dawn, while the rest of us were drinking our tea, he went into the other tent and told its occupants what he'd decided. Imagine our astonishment when he returned and said Bowers would be coming on with us for the last slog. Every detail of that final journey—tent, food, fuel, etc.—had been worked out with four men in mind, and now it would be five!

As for me, my inclusion was so unexpected that I didn't know what to feel. It did cross my mind to tell Scott I wasn't fit, but when I thought of how Teddy Evans and his lot had been manhauling three-hundred miles longer than any of us owing to the breakdown of the motors, and still appeared as keen as mustard, I felt ashamed. It seemed foolish, never mind cowardly, to back out when only ten or eleven days of marching separated us from our goal. I came to the decision that even if I didn't much want to go on for myself, I very much wanted to do so for my regiment. It would be a tremendous feather in the Inniskillings' cap if I made it to the Pole.

I had to write a letter to my mother for Teddy to take with him, telling her I wouldn't be home for another year as we'd almost certainly miss the ship. I said I was feeling very well, perhaps better than anyone else with the exception of Bowers. I didn't want her worrying about me.

I asked her to ignore all the unkind comments I'd made about Scott in previous letters, as it was only the cold and the terrible plight of the ponies that had made me sound so scathing and that really he was a good fellow and utterly decent when it came to things that mattered.

I enclosed a list of books I wanted her to send out to the *Terra Nova* at Lyttelton, so that I could study for my major's exam on the voyage home. I knew that would please her. I'm afraid I've always been a fearful dunce, but I did truly feel that the experiences of the last two years had made me altogether steadier and that I was at last ready to apply myself to books and that sort of stuff.

Teddy was awfully cut up at turning back, and Crean wept. I was sorry Lashly wasn't coming with us in place of Taff Evans. None of us, with the exception of Scott, had much time for the Welshman, though he was a splendid worker in the traces and quite the strongest puller among us.

Scott made a gracious speech before we made our farewells, in which he thanked the support party for agreeing to return short-handed and urged them to remember it had been a team effort.

'It may be us four . . . five,' he said, hastily correcting himself, 'who will stand at the Pole in a few days' time, but we will never forget that it was you who sent us there.'

Then Teddy called for three cheers and Scott gave the order to start. With what excitement we set off, what optimism! Every time we looked back those three figures were still standing there, waving, turning black and dwindling as the distance widened.

Our hight spirits lasted all of two days, mostly on account of the smooth surfaces and calm weather. Four in the tent had been cramped enough, five was a squeeze and cooking for five took longer than for four, but it didn't matter when the sun was so warm we could stand about outside the tent in perfect comfort.

Then the weather turned bad and we got amongst sastrugi and had to take off our skis and pull on foot—Bowers, of course, was without his the whole time. Scott got into a frightful dither over whether or not we should dump our skis altogether, and no sooner had he made up his mind and we'd done as he ordered and had struggled on another fearful two miles or so, than the surface improved and he had us plodding back to retrieve them. I think we were all weaker than we let on—I know I was—and we simply couldn't afford to be indecisive and fritter away our meagre resources of energy on such manoeuvres. Cold was one thing, and hunger another, and we'd grown callous to both these forms of torture, but it was simply more than flesh could stand when exhaustion was added to the catalogue of pain. Then it mattered terribly that it took an extra half hour to get the food into our stomachs.

Scott, poor devil, seemed genuinely perplexed at this setback. 'I must admit,' he confessed, 'it hadn't occurred to me that cooking for one more would add thirty minutes to preparation time.' For a moment he seemed cast down. Then he said, 'However, I'm sure we'll get used to it.'

In his ruthlessness of purpose he resembled Napoleon, who, when the Alps stood in the way of his armies, cried out, 'There shall be no Alps.' For Scott there was no such word as impossible, or if there was it was listed in a dictionary for fools. In the dreadful circumstances in which we found ourselves, half-starved and almost always frozen, our muscles trembling from the strain of dragging those infernal sledges, I expect his was the only way. To have faltered at this late stage would have been like pulling in one's horse while it was leaping. He spared no one, not even himself, and he drove us on by the sheer force of his will. And then Birdie spotted that black flag.

I suppose for a mile or two we kidded ourselves it might be a sastrugus, but soon we came to sledge tracks and the clear trace of dog paws—dozens of dogs. Amundsen had beaten us to the Pole. We put up the tent right away. It was curious how we each reacted to the realisation that our fearful labours had been for nothing. Birdie was angry; the Norwegians were poor sports, sneaks, not worth bothering about. When the story came to be told our feat of manhauling would be seen as the greater triumph. Bill busied himself making a sketch of the cairn and the flag and hardly opened his mouth. Scott himself was surprisingly philosophical. I think the shock of disappointment was so severe he could scarcely take it on board. He talked about his state of mind before the sailing of the *Terra Nova* from Cardiff, how he'd told his wife he was not quite himself, that there was some cloud hanging over him.

'Kathleen said it would be all right once we were actually on the move . . . she was right . . . but I can't help thinking it was perhaps too late. If I hadn't been in the grip of such damnable lassitude perhaps the outcome would have been different.'

There was nothing much one could reply to that, and none of us tried, beyond Bill murmuring that we'd achieved what we'd set out to do and at least we could plant the Union Jack at the Pole.

For myself, it was all one, whether we were first or last at that god-forsaken spot. It was obvious that the best team had won.

It was then that Taff Evans began to rock so violently back and forth in his sleeping-bag that we had to hold tight to the cooker for fear he tipped it over. 'For God's sake, man,' cried Scott, thoroughly alarmed, and he tried to restrain him. Taff flung him off so fiercely that Scott fell against the tent pole and jarred his back.

The Welshman was ranting that we'd all be laughing-stocks when we got home, that none of our families would get a penny, that it was all right for the likes of us, but he was done for, finished. 'I won't never get my public house,' he shouted. 'Not now . . . no apples in the orchard, no little skiff at the water's edge . . . all them bloody dreams turned as rotten as this bloody stump.' And he pulled off his mitt and held out his hand for us to see.

Scott turned as white as a sheet. I think if I'd had enough food in my belly I'd have vomited. Taff's hand was vast and purple and most of his nails had gone. There was a great gash across his knuckles which gaped so wide that the bone showed through. It wasn't so much a hand as some grotesquely swollen fruit about to burst asunder.

Bill took it badly. He blamed himself for not having attended to Taff's wound when he first cut himself rebuilding the sledges. He gave the Petty Officer morphia to ease the pain. It took a long while to take effect and Taff kept up his rocking and his moaning until the tears stood in our eyes and we stuffed our fingers into our ears to drown that dreadful keening.

We marched on the following day and came to the Norwegian flag and tent. They'd left us a note—'Dear Captain Scott, As you are probably the first to reach this area after us, I will ask you kindly to forward this letter to King Haakon VII. If you can use any of the articles left in the tent please do not hesitate to do so. With kind regards. I wish you a safe return. Yours truly, Roald Amundsen.'

Scott thought it a bit of an insult, but I reckon it was no more than a wise precaution on Amundsen's part. The Norwegians had no more certainty than we had of getting safely home.

We marched another two miles to the spot Birdie calculated to be the exact geographical location of the Pole. Taff Evans was more or less himself again, though he moved clumsily and once or twice I swear I heard him chuckling.

We halted when Birdie gave the word, built a cairn and stuck the Union Jack on top. We took a photograph of ourselves; I don't think any of us had the heart to smile. Then we started for home.

I don't know when Taff died . . . a week ago, a month. It was somewhere on the Glacier. I know that the day before, we'd got into a frightful pickle. Scott said it was our own fault. We'd started in a wretched wind, pulling on skis in a horrible light that threw fantastic shadows across the snow. Birdie said he was reminded of a pantomime set for *Ali Baba and the Forty Thieves*, all glittering back-cloths and eerie pockets of stagy darkness. As far as I could tell the world was a coffin and the lid of the sky was about to nail me down. It showed up the difference between us, but then I don't imagine Birdie's feet were in the first stages of gangrene.

Around lunchtime—not that we had any food—Scott took the fatal course of steering east. I appear to put the blame on Scott, but none of us disputed his command and all of us followed him like lemmings. Truth to tell, I think he was the only one among us capable of making any decisions. Wilson had snow-blindness, Birdie still suffered under the delusion that it would be worldly to thrust himself forward, and Evans had gone soft in the brain. Scott had insisted Bill give him morphia at regular intervals, for pity's sake, and half the time the Welshman was floundering on in a merciful haze of oblivion. He fell a lot, once raising a bump on his head the size of Bill's blessed Emperor penguin eggs.

When we got up the next morning and had crushed half a biscuit each into our mug of hot water, we had one meal remaining in the bags. If we didn't reach the next depot by nightfall we'd go hungry. I'd got past wanting food, unlike Bill and Evans who were always complaining that they were starving. I could understand Evans's dilemma. He had been a great brute of a man, and doubtless he needed more rations than the rest of us, but it was curious to think that slim old Bill, by nature frugal, should suffer the same pangs as that giant of a seaman. I don't know what torments Birdie was undergoing—he was too busy being helpful, taking readings, being a kindly light in a naughty world to let on what he truly felt.

Half an hour from setting off one of Evans's ski shoes came adrift and he had to leave the sledge. 'On, on,' he shouted, waving his good hand in the air. We stopped after two hours and he slowly caught up with us. We'd hardly started again before he dropped out under the same pretence. He asked Birdie for a piece of string. Scott cautioned him not to lag too far behind, and he replied, 'Goodness, that I won't. It's lonely out here. I'll be with you in a jiffy.'

We had our meagre lunch, and still he didn't appear. Alarmed, we went back to look for him. He was on all fours in the snow, his gloves off and his clothes dishevelled. When we approached he barked like a dog. 'Taff,' said Scott, 'what's wrong, man?' but the Welshman didn't reply. We got him to his feet, supporting him on either side, with the intention of walking him back to the tent, but after no more than a few steps he sagged between us and sank to his knees. He said something then about being sorry.

Scott sent Bowers and Wilson back for the sledge. He seemed terribly affected by Evans's condition and, kneeling, cradled him in his arms.

'You have to understand, Titus,' he told me, 'that a man is often a reflection of another.'

I couldn't make head nor tail of that, and kept silent.

'I know you all puzzle over my regard for Evans,' he said, 'but there's nothing very strange in it.'

'The crevasse,' I said. 'You faced death together.'

'No, Titus, nothing so simple.' And here his face crumpled to such an extent I feared he would howl. I turned away, pretending to look for the sledge.

'Titus,' he said, 'did you love your father?'

'Of course,' I replied.

'And I loved mine,' he said. Then he let go of Taff and got to his feet. 'Stay with him,' he ordered. 'I'm going to help the others.'

I tried to make Taff more comfortable, not that it was possible. I buttoned up his coat and thought of trying to put his gloves back on, but the sight of that awful hand unnerved me. Suddenly he stirred and opened his eyes. 'Lois?' he said.

'Help's coming,' I said. 'The Captain's gone for the sledge.'

He murmured something then about cigars and being sorry, and after that he closed his eyes and didn't speak again, not ever.

We got him into the tent and waited for him to die, which he did around noon. Bowers and Scott buried him. Bill was practically blind, and my fingers were useless with frostbite. They had intended to build a cairn over the body, but when it came to it they were too weak so they just scuffed the snow over him.

Bill thinks it was probably that last blow to his head that really did for him, that and the state of his hand. Scott said he'd noticed a deterioration in his character even before he fell.

'He was usually such a strong man,' he said, 'and utterly reliant, never slack, never slipshod in his work. And he understood what one was on about. Yet the day before we got to the Pole he didn't strap the sleeping bags securely enough onto the sledge. If you remember, one went missing and Birdie had to go and look for it.'

It was the first time the Pole had been mentioned since we'd turned back. God knows, we'd all thought about it and what it meant in regard to our home-coming, but none of us had dared to put our thoughts into words for fear of upsetting Scott. I'd had a dream three nights running in which we approached the Pole and, instead of those paw prints in the snow and that black flag, I stumbled across a small cairn with a blue enamel plate on top with a slab of steak lying across it.

'It's a dreadful thing to say,' Scott said, 'and I know you chaps will take it in the spirit in which it's meant, but Taff's death has considerably enhanced our own chances of survival.'

And that was the first time, too, that survival had been mentioned, or rather the notion that we might not get through. There again, we'd all thought about it—I can't imagine I was the only one who realised the food depots were spaced too far apart, and that blizzards and bad surfaces hadn't been sufficiently taken into account.

'He was holding us back,' said Scott. 'He was simply . . .' and here he broke off and we all saw the tears welling up in his eyes.

None of us knew how to comfort him, not even stalwart old Bill. During the last few weeks I'd revised my opinion of Scott, though I still couldn't fathom why he had been so stupid as to disregard the overwhelming opinion that dogs were the only form of Antarctic transport. I still thought he was a poor leader of men in the military sense, meaning he hadn't given enough attention to strengths, capacity, terrain, superiority of the enemy, but I had none the less come to recognise his other, more important qualities, not least his ability to put himself in another's shoes. One could see in his eyes, even when he wasn't blubbing, that his heart was too big for his boots. God knows how, but he's managed to surmount his naval training and retain his essential humanity.

I haven't. Well, it's all there, buried within myself, and I kid myself that faced with some terrible dilemma I'll be able to drag it to the surface, that I'll act out of an inborn sense of what is right, but I fear it's not true. I'm too rigid, too encased in rules and codes of behaviour.

I'm not explaining myself very well, but I had suddenly come to comprehend why Bill loved him. Scott is the man Bill would have liked to have been. Scott can't draw to save his life, but he sees things.

'You must have wondered,' Scott said, 'why I cared for Evans.'

'That crevasse,' Bill said.

'Exactly what Titus put it down to,' said Scott. He remained silent for some minutes, now and then dashing the moisture from his eyes. Then he launched into a rambling account of his childhood, his love for his mother, his fear of his father. 'My father was a drunk,' he said. 'It was what one would call an occupational disease, seeing he was the manager of a brewery. I daresay he had other problems to contend with . . . the fact that his brothers and sisters were brighter than him, that my mother was a strenuous character. She loved him, yet despised his weaknesses. All through my childhood he alternated between the good father and the bad one. Sometimes he hit us.'

'Con,' said Bill, 'please, there's no need.'

'Once,' Scott said, 'on my mother's birthday he rose up from the dinner-table and hurled the gravy-boat into her lap. Archie and I were on the landing, peering through the banisters. We couldn't see what went on, but we heard that thud and the murmur of disgust that followed.

Then my mother came out into the hall, her dress stained with meat juice, her face blank. She looked up and saw me and Archie on the stairs, and waved. I think she wanted to say something, but words failed her.'

'Con,' said Bill, 'please stop.'

'What I could never forgive,' continued Scott, 'was the way he cried afterwards . . . the way he grovelled in self-pity . . . the way he pleaded for understanding. Taff was an altogether different kettle of fish. He drank because he enjoyed it, not because he wanted to obliterate the moment . . . he never once tried to excuse his alcoholic outbursts. He was a strenuous drunk, and for that I admired him.'

It was later that night that I asked Bill if a man without feet could ride to hounds, and Scott ordered him to give me the brandy.

Birdie says we've walked, there and back, over 1500 miles, or will have done once we reach Cape Evans. We're now two marches from One Ton Camp, wherever that is, where Cherry and the dogs will be waiting for us.

I no longer care about distances or arrivals. I've passed the point when I can visualise anyone waiting in the drive, not unless they're carrying a bedstead. All I long for is sleep. Yesterday Birdie got it in the neck for saying we'd gone too far east. As navigator he's supposed to know where we're going. It must be a dreadful bind to be responsible for direction. If it was left to me I'd stagger into the moon. The only woman I've ever loved is my mother. This is in response to Bill blethering on last night about his Oriana, who is apparently in accord with his soul. We have only his word for it.

I think it's my birthday tomorrow. Last night I showed Bill my left foot. He blenched. Scott saw it too.

'It's all up for me, isn't it? I asked. 'How will it finish? I shouldn't want to end screaming.'

'Nonsense,' said Bill, 'you'll pull through.'

'Stop it,' Scott shouted, 'tell him the truth.'

Poor old Bill pulled a face. One could tell he wanted death to come like a thief in the night.

'I want the morphia,' I said. I knew we had thirty tablets apiece.

'No,' he said. 'It's against my principles.'

'I order you to hand them over, Bill,' Scott said. 'I order you to give every man the means to choose his own time to die.'

There was such a struggle over it that I lost heart. I lay in my bag, hands, feet, nose, hip, rotting to hell. Dozing, I plodded towards the Pole again, towards that blue dish atop the cairn. This time I saw dog prints in the snow.

Bill gave me the morphia, five tablets washed down with tea.

'Pray God I won't wake in the morning,' I said, and sleepily shook hands with Birdie.

What dreams I had! I think the approach of death is possibly heralded by a firework display of days gone by. My mother came to me, bossy, competent, convinced she could nurse my dead feet into life. 'No, Mother,' I said, 'they've gone beyond recall.'

And then she embraced me, and I thought it was her tears that rolled down my cheeks until the pain in my legs jerked me into consciousness, and I realised it was my own eyes that spilled with grief.

I could hear Birdie snoring. There was a little chink of daylight poking through the canvas above Bill's head. In that moment before I struggled upright it came to me that my greatest sin had been that of idleness. I had wasted my days.

Birdie woke when I struggled out of my bag. I put my finger to my lips, enjoining silence. I wanted to kiss him good-bye, but I was too shy.

'I'm just going outside,' I said, 'and may be some time.'

There was a blizzard blowing. I was in my stocking-feet, yet I didn't feel the cold. I had only struggled a few yards, the snow driving against me, when I heard voices. I waved my hand in front of me, as though I was wiping a mirror, and then I saw Boy Charger, skittering backwards and forwards in the drift.

'Be so good as to restrain him, Mr Brown,' a voice said.

'I'm holding back the dawn,' said Mr Brown. 'Captain Oates approaches.'

I only had to crawl a few yards; the pelting snow rained down like music.

'Happy Birthday,' sang the man holding the bridle. And oh, how warm it was.

acknowledgments

Many people made this anthology.

At Thunder's Mouth Press and Avalon Publishing Group:
Neil Ortenberg and Susan Reich offered vital support and counsel.
Dan O'Connor and Ghadah Alrawi also were indispensable.

At Balliett & Fitzgerald Inc:
Designer Sue Canavan is an artist. Production editor Maria Fernandez
skillfully oversaw production with patience, foresight and a wonderful
courtesy. Proofreader Kathryn Daniels did meticulous and skillful work
on this book as well as on three previous Adrenaline titles: High, Rough
Water and The War. Kristen Couse found some wonderful photographs.
Thanks also to Mike Walters and Simon Sullivan.

At the Thomas Memorial Library in Cape Elizabeth, Maine:
The librarians cheerfully worked to locate and borrow books from
across the country. Their help was more important than they know.

At the Writing Company:
Shawneric Hachey did superb work gathering books, permissions and
facts. Meghan Murphy helped copyedit and check text. Mark Klimek,
Nate Hardcastle, Mike Milliard and Taylor Smith cheerfully took up
slack on other projects while I read books for this one.

Among friends and family:
My wife Jennifer Schwamm Willis helped gather materials and find and
choose selections. She lent her rock-solid judgement to many
important decisions.
My esteemed friend and colleague Will Balliett made it happen and
made it a pleasure. I could not wish for a better collaborator.

Finally, I am grateful to the writers whose work appears in this book.

We gratefully acknowledge all those who gave permission for written material to appear in this book. We have made every effort to trace and contact copyright holders. If an error or omission is brought to our notice we will be pleased to remedy the situation in future editions of this book. For further information, please contact the publisher.

Excerpt from *Mawson's Will* by Lennard Bickel, copyright © 1977 by Lennard Bickel. Reprinted by permission of the author. ❖ "A Bad Time" by Nancy Mitford, excerpted from *The Water Beetle*, reprinted by permission of The Peters Fraser and Dunlop Group Limited on behalf of: The Estate of Nancy Mitford, copyright © 1962. ❖ "A Simple Quest" by Michael J. McRae, from author's collection, *Continental Drifter* (Lyons & Burford, 1993). First published in *Outside* magazine, December 1985. All rights reserved. ❖ Excerpt from *Alone* by Richard E. Byrd, copyright © 1938 by Richard E. Byrd, renewed © copyright 1966 by Marie A. Byrd. Used by permission of Island Press. ❖ Excerpt from *Arctic Dreams* by Barry Holstun Lopez, reprinted by permission of Sterling Lord Literistic, copyright © 1986 by Barry Holstun Lopez. Reprinted by permission of Sterling Lord Literistic. ❖ "The Last Pork Chop" by Edward Abbey, reprinted by permission of Don Congdon Associates. Copyright © 1984 by Edward Abbey. First printed in *Outside* Magazine, March 1984. ❖ Excerpt from *Six Came Back* reprinted by permission of Simon & Schuster, Inc. from *Six Came Back* by David Brainard and Bessie Rowland James. Copyright ⊕ 1940 by The Bobbs-Merrrill Company, Inc.; copyright renewed ©1968 by Bessie Rowland James. ❖ Excerpt from *I May Be Some Time* by Francis Spufford, copyright © 1996 by Francis Spufford. Reprinted by permission of Faber and Faber, London. ❖ Excerpt from *Beyond Cape Horn* by Charles Neider, copyright © 1980 by Charles Neider. Reprinted by permission of Sierra Club Books. ❖ Excerpt from *The Birthday Boys* copyright © Beryl Bainbridge, 1991, Duckworth & Co, UK, 1991 and Carroll & Graf, USA, 1994.

bibliography

The selections used in this anthology were taken from the editions listed below. In some cases, other editions may be easier to find. Hard to find or out-of-print titles often can be acquired through inter-library loan services. Internet sources also may be able to locate these books.

The Best of Outside: *The First 20 Years.* New York: Villard Books, 1997. (For "The Last Pork Chop" by Edward Abbey).

Bainbridge, Beryl. *The Birthday Boys.* Carroll & Graf USA 1991.

Bickel, Lennard. *Mawson's Will.* New York: Stein and Day, 1977.

Brainard, David L. *Six Came Back: The Arctic Adventure of David L. Brainard.* New York: 1940.

Byrd, Richard E. *Alone.* New York: G.P. Putnam's Sons, 1938.

Cherry-Garrard, Apsley. *The Worst Journey in the World.* New York: Carroll & Graf Publishers, Inc. 1992.

DeLong, George W. (edited by Emma DeLong). *The Voyage of the* Jeannette. New York: Houghton, Mifflin and Company, 1884.

Lopez, Barry. *Arctic Dreams.* New York: Bantam Books, 1986.

Out of the Noösphere: The Best of Outside *Magazine.* New York: Simon & Schuster, 1992. (For "A Simple Quest" by Michael McRae).

Mitford, Nancy. *The Water Beetle.* New York: Harper & Row, 1962. (For "A Bad Time").

Neider, Charles. *Beyond Cape Horn: Travels in the Antarctic.* San Francisco: Sierra Club Books, 1980.

Scott, Robert Falcon. *Scott's Last Expedition: The Journals.* New York: Carroll & Graf Publishers, Inc., 1996.

Shackleton, Ernest. *South: A Memoir of the* Endurance *Voyage.* New York: Carroll & Graf Publishers, Inc., 1998.

Spufford, Francis. *I May Be Some Time.* New York: St. Martin's Press, 1997.